FABULAE ROMANAE
STORIES OF
FAMOUS ROMANS

FABULAE ROMANAE

STORIES OF

FAMOUS ROMANS

Edited by
Gilbert Lawall
David Perry

Longman

Fabulae Romanae

Longman, 10 Bank Street, White Plains, N.Y. 10606

Associated companies:
Longman Group Ltd., London
Longman Cheshire Pty., Melbourne
Longman Paul Pty., Auckland
Copp Clark Pitman, Toronto

Credits appear on page 228.

Executive Editor: Lyn McLean

ISBN: 0-8013-0992-1

5 6 7 8 9 10-MA-95

Contents

List of Maps and Charts

Preface for Students

This book contains a series of stories that outline the history of Rome from its founding in the middle of the eighth century B.C. down to the death of Cicero in 43 B.C. The stories have been collected from a variety of ancient authors and arranged for students at the intermediate level of Latin. The majority come from Livy, the famous historian of the first century B.C., who wrote a history of Rome from its founding entitled *Ab urbe condita.* In some cases stories have been shortened or simplified somewhat, but the editors have attempted to keep the accounts in this volume as close as possible to the original ancient sources.

The main purpose of this book is to help you become more proficient at reading Latin. You will do this primarily through extensive reading, but you will also need to review and consolidate your knowledge of the grammar you have already learned, to learn a few new grammatical items, and to enlarge your vocabulary. In addition, the stories in this book will provide you with an overview of Roman history, an acquaintance with the outstanding figures in Roman tradition, and some understanding of the process by which Rome grew from a small city-state into a world empire. To help you with these tasks the present edition contains the following features:

1. Running vocabularies for each paragraph of the Latin text, printed on facing pages
2. Grammatical notes incorporated into the running vocabularies
3. Fuller descriptions of selected elements of grammr, illustrated by examples taken from the Latin readings; these are contained in boxes, and are placed at the bottom of the page; these grammar notes are written to help you translate from Latin to English as easily as possible
4. Exercises to reinforce some of the grammatical points
5. Notes on rhetorical figures

At the end of the book you will find:

1. A time line to help you follow the events in Roman history
2. A list of the grammatical topics covered in both the running vocabulary notes and in the boxed grammar notes
3. Charts of Latin grammatical forms

4. A Latin to English vocabulary list with all the information you need about individual words
5. An index of people and a separate index of peoples, places, and maps with references to the first place in the stories where each person, people, and place is mentioned and with references to the maps in this book on which the places mentioned in the stories may be located

The running vocabularies contain all the words you will meet in the stories except for those taught in ECCE ROMANI, Books 1–4. Asterisks in the running vocabularies indicate that the new words so marked should be learned when you first meet them in reading. They will reappear in the stories but will usually not be given again in the facing vocabularies; they are, however, included in the vocabulary or the indexes of proper names at the end of the book. The vocabulary at the end of the book also includes all of the words taught in ECCE ROMANI, Books 1–4, that appear in these stories.

Upon completion of this book, you will be ready to read any of a variety of Latin authors as they are presented in the standard school and college textbooks. You will find that your background in Roman history, as well as the reading skills you have gained from this book, will be a great help in appreciating authors such as Caesar, Cicero, Vergil, Horace, and many others.

At the lower left are Romulus and Remus with the she-wolf. Above them is the Palatine Hill with some animals, including an eagle, symbol of Jupiter. In the upper right are shepherds who have found Romulus and Remus. At the lower right is Father Tiber, the god of the river.

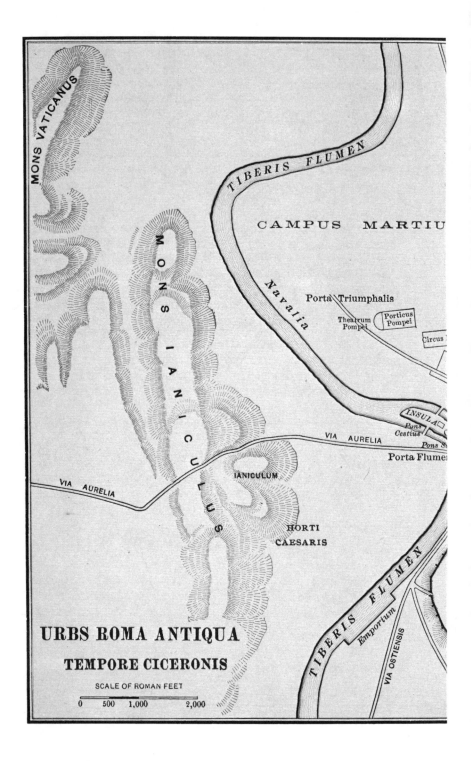

MONS VATICANUS

MONS IANICULUS

TIBERIS FLUMEN

CAMPUS MARTIU

Navalia

Porta Triumphalis

Theatrum
Pompei

Porticus
Pompei

Circus

VIA AURELIA

INSULA

Pons
Cestius

Pons S

Porta Flumen

IANICULUM

VIA AURELIA

HORTI
CAESARIS

TIBERIS FLUMEN

Emporium

VIA OSTIENSIS

URBS ROMA ANTIQUA

TEMPORE CICERONIS

SCALE OF ROMAN FEET

0   500   1,000   2,000

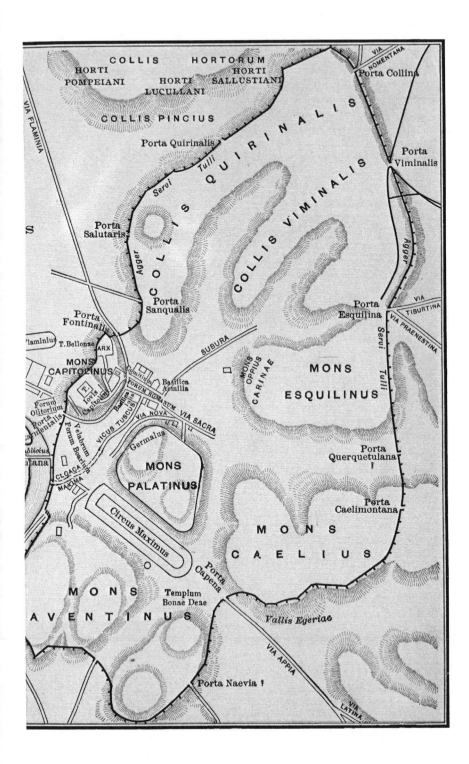

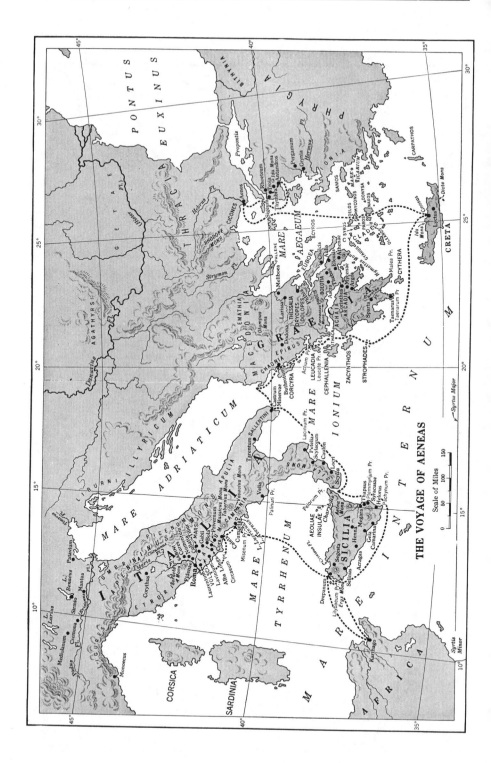

THE VOYAGE OF AENEAS

PART I

The Kings of Rome

The first section of this book will be concerned with the founding of the city of Rome and with the first 240 years of its existence, when it was ruled by kings. The Romans told many stories about this period, most of which can be described more accurately as legends than as historical facts. One of these legends concerned Aeneas, son of the goddess Venus and the mortal Anchises, who lived in Troy on the western coast of Asia Minor. This legend is particularly famous because the great Roman poet Publius Vergilius Maro (Vergil) used it as the basis of his epic poem, the *Aeneid*.

Troy was attacked by the Greeks and besieged for ten years; it finally fell when Greek soldiers entered the city through the famous trick of the wooden horse. As Troy began to burn, Aeneas was ordered by the gods to flee with his family; he obeyed, although he would have preferred to stay and die in his homeland. Aeneas escaped carrying his crippled father Anchises and accompanied by his son Ascanius, but his wife Creusa became separated from the group and was killed by Greek soldiers. Jupiter then told Aeneas that it was his destiny to found a new city in the "Western Land," and he promised that Aeneas' descendants would someday rule the world. Aeneas collected other survivors of Troy and set sail. He did not know exactly where this "Western Land" was, and he and his followers sailed the Mediterranean for several years. They tried to set up their new home in several places, but the gods continually urged them westward until finally they reached Italy. The Romans regarded Aeneas as their most distant ancestor, and so we begin this book with the story of his arrival in Italy.

1

1   **Asia, -ae** (*f.*), Asia Minor (what is now Turkey).
     ***appellō** (1), to call, name.
3   **Priamus, -ī** (*m.*), Priam (king of Troy).
     ***interficiō, interficere** (3), **interfēcī, interfectum**, to kill.
4   **Aenēās, -ae** (*m.*), Aeneas (son of Venus and Anchises).
     ***clārus, -a, -um**, clear, distinguished, famous.
     dēfēnsor, dēfēnsōris (*m.*), defender.
5   **cum profugōs**: "when. . . . " (see below).
     ***profugus, -ī** (*m.*), refugee.
6   **coēgisset**: *pluperfect subjunctive*, "had . . . ," indicating time before the
       action of the main verb.
     ***migrō** (1), to move, migrate.

9   **Laurentum, -ī** (*m.*), Laurentum (a coastal town in Latium).
     cum: "because. . . . " (see below).
     ***praeda, -ae** (*f.*), booty, loot; (*here*) cattle (taken in foraging raids).
     agerent: *imperfect subjunctive*, "were . . . ," indicating time contempora-
       neous with the action of the main verb.
10   **Latīnus, -ī** (*m.*), Latinus (king of the Aborigines in Latium).
     Aborīginēs, Aborīginum (*m. pl.*), the Aborigines (a people living in
       Latium and ruled by Latinus).
11   ***colloquium, -ī** (*n.*), conversation, conference, parley.
12   **orīgō, orīginis** (*f.*), origin.
     ***dux, ducis** (*m.*), leader.
13   **Lāvīnia, -ae** (*f.*), Lavinia (daughter of Latinus and wife of Aeneas).
15   **Lāvīnium, -ī** (*n.*), Lavinium (a town in Latium founded by Aeneas).

Cum Circumstantial Clauses, Cum Causal Clauses, and Cum as a Preposition

The word **cum** may function as a *subordinating conjunction* and may introduce a clause with its verb in the *subjunctive mood*. When the context suggests that **cum** means "when" or "after," we say that it introduces a *circumstantial clause*; when the context suggests that it means "since" or "because," we say that it introduces a *causal clause*, e.g.:

> **cum** profugōs . . . **coēgisset**, . . . (opposite: 5–6)
> *when he had collected refugees, . . .*

> **cum** Troiānī praedam . . . **agerent**, . . . (opposite: 9–10)
> *because the Trojans were driving cattle, . . .*

Only by considering the context of the sentence as a whole can you determine whether a **cum**-clause is circumstantial or causal.

     When **cum** is followed immediately by a word in the *ablative case*, it is likely to be a *preposition*, e.g.:

> Aenēās . . . **cum paucīs comitibus** ex urbe effūgit. (opposite: 4–5)
> *Aeneas . . . fled from the city with a few companions.*

1. Aeneas Arrives In Italy

Ōlim in Asiā erat urbs antīqua, quae Troia appellāta est.   1
Eam urbem Graecī decem annōs obsēdērunt tandemque   2
cēpērunt. Priamō rēge fīliīsque interfectīs, urbem dēlē-   3   1184 B.C.
vērunt. Sed Aenēās, quī inter clārissimōs dēfēnsōrēs urbis   4
fuerat, cum paucīs comitibus ex urbe effūgit; cum profugōs   5
ex omnibus partibus coēgisset, in Italiam migrāre cōnsti-   6
tuit.   7

Post septem annōs vēnit in eam partem Italiae ubi erat   8
urbs Laurentum. Ibi cum Troiānī praedam ex agrīs age-   9
rent, Latīnus rēx Aborīginēsque, quī ea loca tenēbant, agrōs   10
dēfendere parāvērunt. Sed Latīnus, postquam in colloquiō   11
orīginem multitūdinis ducisque cognōvit, pācem cum Aenēā   12
fēcit atque posteā eī Lāvīniam fīliam in mātrimōnium dedit.   13
Troiānī urbem condidērunt, quam Aenēās ab nōmine uxōris   14
Lāvīnium appellāvit.   15

Accusative of Duration of Time

A word or phrase in the *accusative case* may tell how long an action lasts; this is called the *accusative of duration of time*. No preposition is used in the Latin, but a preposition is often used in the English translation, e.g.:

Eam urbem Graecī **decem annōs** obsēdērunt. (above: 2)
*The Greeks besieged this city **for ten years**.*

Ablative Absolutes

You will often meet nouns or pronouns and participles in the *ablative case* forming constructions of their own set off from the rest of the sentence, e.g.:

Priamō rēge fīliīsque <u>interfectīs</u>, urbem dēlēvērunt. (above: 3–4)
After king Priam and his sons <u>had been killed</u>, they (i.e., the Greeks) destroyed the city.

These constructions are called *ablative absolutes*, and they usually indicate time or describe circumstances. The *perfect passive participle* in an ablative absolute denotes an action that was completed *before* the action of the main verb in the sentence, thus **interfectīs** above is translated "had been killed."

16   **Turnus, -ī** (*m.*), Turnus (king of the Rutuli).

      Rutulī, -ōrum (*m. pl.*), the Rutuli (a people living in Latium with their capital at Ardea).

      ***adventus, -ūs** (*m.*), arrival.

17   **bellō**: *ablative* with **aggressus est**, literally, "attacked with war," better English, "went to war with." Always try to think of the best way to translate ablatives into English. Other ablatives in this paragraph (**famā**, 20, **multitūdine opibusque**, 21, and **moenibus**, 25) may be translated with "with," "in," or "by means of."

      ***aggredior, aggredī** (3), **aggressus sum**, to attack.

19   ***āmittō, āmittere** (3), **āmīsī, āmissum**, to lose.

      Etrūscus, -a, -um, Etruscan; (*m. pl.*), the Etruscans (the people who controlled Italy north of the Tiber River).

20   ***fāma, -ae** (*f.*), fame, reputation, story.

      ***impleō, implēre** (2), **implēvī, implētum**, to fill.

      ***metuō, metuere** (3), **metuī**, to fear, be afraid of.

21   ***ops, opis** (*f.*), wealth; (*pl.*) resources, power.

      ***crēscō, crēscere** (3), **crēvī, crētum**, to grow, prosper, thrive.

22   ***discrīmen, discrīminis** (*n.*), crisis.

      ut: "so that," introducing a *purpose clause* (see the grammar note on page 12).

23   ***iūs, iūris** (*n.*), law, jurisdiction, justice.

      Latīnī, -ōrum (*m. pl.*), Latins (the name given by Aeneas to the Aborigines and Trojans united as one people).

24   **Cum**: "Although. . . . ," introducing a *concessive clause* (see the grammar note on page 5).

      ***adversus** (*prep. + acc.*), contrary to, opposite, against.

25   ***moenia, moenium** (*n. pl.*), walls, fortifications.

      ***aciēs, -ēī** (*f.*), line of battle, battle formation, battle.

      ***cōpia, -ae** (*f.*), supply, abundance; (*pl.*) troops.

27   ***reperiō, reperīre** (4), **repperī, repertum**, to find.

28   ***trānseō, trānsīre** (*irreg.*), **trānsiī, trānsitum**, to go across, cross over.

      eum ad deōs trānsīsse: i.e., that he had been taken up into heaven and become a god.

Deinde Turnus, rēx Rutulōrum, cui Lāvīnia ante adven- 16
tum Aenēae dēspōnsa erat, bellō Latīnum Troiānōsque ag- 17
gressus est. Victī sunt Rutulī, sed victōrēs ducem Latīnum 18
āmīsērunt. Inde Turnus auxilium petiit ab Etrūscīs, quī tō- 19
tam Italiam fāmā nōminis suī implēverant; illī metuentēs 20
novam urbem multitūdine opibusque crēscentem laetī aux- 21
ilium tulērunt. Aenēās in tantō discrīmine, ut Aborīginēs 22
Troiānōsque sub eōdem iūre atque nōmine habēret, Latīnōs 23
utramque gentem appellāvit. Cum adversus Etrūscōs sē 24
moenibus dēfendere posset, tamen in aciem cōpiās ēdūxit. 25
Etrūscī victī sunt; victōrēs tamen ducem ut anteā āmī- 26
sērunt; post pugnam enim Aenēam reperīre nōn potuērunt; 27
multī igitur eum ad deōs trānsīsse crēdidērunt. 28

Cum Concessive Clauses

Sometimes the context of a sentence as a whole will suggest that the conjunction **cum** may best be translated "although." The clause that it introduces is then called a *concessive clause*. The word **tamen** "nevertheless" often appears in the main clause and gives a clue that **cum** means "although," e.g.:

Cum adversus Etrūscōs sē moenibus dēfendere **posset, tamen** in aciem cōpiās ēdūxit. (above: 24–25)
Although he was able to defend himself against the Etruscans with his walls, *nevertheless* he led his troops out into battle.

The concessive use of the conjunction **cum** is less common than the circumstantial or causal uses discussed on page 2.

1   ***rēgnō** (1), to reign, rule.
    *quoad (*adv.*), as long as, until.
    Ascānius, -ī (*m.*), Ascanius (son of Aeneas and Creusa; founder of Alba Longa).
2   ***adolēscō, adolēscere** (3), **adolēvī, adultum,** to mature, grow up.
    *abundō (1), to overflow, be in flood.
4   **Albānus, -a, -um,** Alban.
    Alba Longa, -ae (*f.*), Alba Longa (mother city of Rome; founded by Ascanius).
5   ***imperium, -ī** (*n.*), power, empire, dominion, rule.
      imperium gerere, to hold power.
6   **cui:** "whose," *dative of possession* (see the grammar note on page 7).
    Proca, -ae (*m.*), Proca (king of Alba Longa and father of Numitor and Amulius).
    Numitor, Numitōris (*m.*), Numitor (rightful king of Alba Longa and grandfather of Romulus and Remus).
7   **Amūlius, -ī** (*m.*), Amulius (king of Alba Longa, brother of Numitor).
    maior: short for **maior nātū,** "greater in age" = "older."
8   ***pellō, pellere** (3), **pepulī, pulsum,** to drive, drive out, repulse, defeat.
9   **Rhēa Silvia, -ae** (*f.*), Rhea Silvia (daughter of Numitor and mother of Romulus and Remus).
    *speciēs, -ēī (*f.*), appearance, pretext.
    per speciem: "on the pretext (of)" (+ *gen.*).
10 ***sacerdōs, sacerdōtis** (*m.* or *f.*), priest *or* priestess.
    Vesta, -ae (*f.*), Vesta (Roman goddess of the hearth and home).
    Vesta's priestesses could not marry during their thirty years of service; hence Amulius thought that Rhea Silvia would not have any children who could contest his claim to the throne.
    *legō, legere (3), **lēgī, lēctum,** to read, gather, choose.
    Note the *double accusative* here: **filiam . . . sacerdōtem . . . lēgit,** "chose his daughter (to be *or* as) the priestess."

The Line of Aeneas

AENEAS (founds Lavinium)
|
ASCANIUS (founds Alba Longa)
|
[several kings of Alba Longa]
|
PROCA
|
NUMITOR   AMULIUS
|
Mars = Rhea Silvia
|
ROMULUS   REMUS

2. The Founding of Alba Longa

Lāvīnia inde rēgnāvit, quoad Ascānius, Aenēae fīlius, 1
adolēvit. Tum ille propter abundantem Lāvīniī multi- 2
tūdinem mātrī urbem relīquit; ipse novam aliam urbem sub 3
Albānō monte condidit, quae Alba Longa appellāta est. 4   1152 B.C.
Multī rēgēs post Ascānium imperium Albānum gessērunt. 5
Quīdam ex hīs, cui nōmen Proca erat, duōs fīliōs, Nu- 6
mitōrem atque Amūlium, habuit. Numitōrī, quī maior erat, 7
rēgnum relīquit. Pulsō tamen frātre, Amūlius rēgnāvit. 8   ca. 775 B.C.
Fīlium frātris necāvit; fīliam Rhēam Silviam per speciem 9
honōris sacerdōtem Vestae lēgit. 10

Dative of Possession

You will sometimes find the *dative case* used in a clause with some form of the verb **esse**, e.g.:

Quīdam ex hīs, **cui** nōmen Proca **erat**, . . . (above: 6)
*A certain one of them, **to whom there was** the name Proca (better English) **whose** name **was** Proca, . . .*

This use of the dative is called the *dative of possession*. The word in the dative case indicates the owner, and the thing owned is the subject of the verb **esse**.

Here is another example:

Rhēae Silviae fuērunt duo fīliī.
*Two sons **were to Rhea Silvia**.*
(Better English) Rhea Silvia had two sons.

Here are two more examples for you to translate:

Nōbīs erat pecūnia.
Sunt Aenēae plūrēs nāvēs.

1 Rōmulus, -ī (*m.*), Romulus (son of Rhea Silvia and founder and first king of Rome).
  Remus, -ī (*m.*), Remus (brother of Romulus).
2 Mārs, Mārtis (*m.*), Mars (god of war and father of Romulus and Remus).
3 *rēgius, -a, -um, royal, king's.
4 *custōdia, -ae (*f.*), watch, custody, prison.
  Tiberis, Tiberis, (*acc.*) Tiberim (*m.*), Tiber (river that flows past Rome).
  iniciō, inicere (3), iniēcī, iniectum, to throw into.
7 *alveus, -ī (*m.*), basket.
  tenuis, -is, -e, thin, shallow.
8 siccum, -ī (*n.*), dry land.
  sedeō, sedēre (2), sēdī, sessum, to sit; (*here*) to settle, come to rest.
  lupa, -ae (*f.*), she-wolf.
  sitiō, sitīre (4), sitīvī, to be thirsty.
  est trāditum: "it has been related," *impersonal passive.*
9 *circā (*adv.*), around, nearby.
  vāgītus, -ūs (*m.*), crying, wailing.
10 *cursus, -ūs (*m.*), running, course, path.
  *flectō, flectere (3), flexī, flexum, to turn, go, change.
  Faustulus, -ī (*m.*), Faustulus (shepherd who found Romulus and Remus).
  *pāstor, pāstōris (*m.*), shepherd.
11 nūtriō, nūtrīre (4), nūtrīvī, nūtrītum, to nurse, care for.
  Lārentia, -ae (*f.*), Larentia (wife of Faustulus).
  *ēducō (1), to bring up, educate.
12 vēnor, vēnārī (1), vēnātus sum, to hunt.
  *latrō, latrōnis (*m.*), robber.
13 onustus, -a, -um, laden, burdened.
14 *dīvidō, dīvidere (3), dīvīsī, dīvīsum, to force apart, divide, distribute.

15 Dum . . . celebrantur, . . . fēcērunt: the *present tense* with dum is to be translated into English as a past progressive when the verb of the main clause is in the *perfect tense,* "While . . . were being celebrated, (they) made" (see the grammar note on page 24).
  celebrō (1), to frequent, celebrate.
  *ob (*prep. + acc.*), on account of, because of.
16 in: + *acc.* of person's name = "against."
18 *incūsō (1), to reproach, accuse, complain (+ *acc.* and *infin.*).
  ad: + *acc.,* here expressing *purpose* = "for."
  *supplicium, -ī (*n.*), punishment.
19 *dēdō, dēdere (3), dēdidī, dēditum, to hand over, surrender, give up.

Iubeō + Accusative and Infinitive

An accusative and an infinitive are regularly found with the verb iubeō, e.g.:

Puerōs rēx in Tiberim inicī iussit. (opposite: 4–5)
*The king **ordered the boys to be thrown** into the Tiber.*

3. Romulus and Remus

Ex hāc fīliā nātī sunt duo fīliī, Rōmulus et Remus. Pater 1
eōrum, ut fāma est, Mārs deus erat. Sed nec deī nec hom- 2
inēs mātrem et puerōs ā crūdēlitāte rēgiā dēfendērunt. 3
Sacerdōs in custōdiam data est; puerōs rēx in Tiberim inicī 4
iussit. Forte Tiberis abundāverat, neque eī quī puerōs ferē- 5
bant adīre ad altam aquam poterant. Itaque puerōs in 6
alveō posuērunt atque in tenuī aquā relīquērunt. Sed 7
alveus in siccō sēdit. Deinde lupa sitiēns—sīc enim est 8
trāditum—ex montibus quī circā sunt ad puerōrum vāgītum 9
cursum flexit. Faustulus, pāstor rēgius, eam invēnit puerōs 10
nūtrientem. Ab eō atque Lārentiā uxōre puerī ēducātī sunt. 11
Cum prīmum adolēvērunt, vēnārī coepērunt et in latrōnēs 12
praedā onustōs impetūs facere pāstōribusque praedam 13
dīvidere. 14

Dum quīdam lūdī celebrantur, latrōnēs īrātī ob praedam 15
āmissam impetum in Rōmulum et Remum fēcērunt; captum 16
Remum rēgī Amūliō trādidērunt. Puerōs praedam ex agrīs 17
Numitōris ēgisse incūsābant. Sīc ad supplicium Numitōrī 18
Remus dēditur. 19

Present Passive Infinitives

The infinitive in the example in the grammar note on page 8 (**inicī**) is a *present passive* infinitive. Present passive infinitives may be recognized by the presence of -**ī** instead of the final -**e** of the present active infinitive, e.g.:

	Present Active	*Present Passive*
1st	**amāre**, to like	**amārī**, to be liked
2nd	**tenēre**, to hold	**tenērī**, to be held
3rd	**pellere**, to drive	**pellī**, to be driven
3rd-iō	**iacere**, to throw	**iacī**, to be thrown
4th	**impedīre**, to hinder	**impedīrī**, to be hindered

Note that in the 3rd conjugation -**ī** replaces the whole -**ere** ending of the active infinitive.

20   **initium, -ī** (*n.*), beginning.
    *iussū (+ *gen.*), by the order (of).
    *expōnō, expōnere (3), **exposuī, expositum**, to set out, expose, explain.
23   ***geminus, -a, -um**, twin, double.
    *comparō (1), to compare, couple, match.
        Note that this is a different verb from **comparō** (1), to buy, obtain, get
          ready.
    *aetās, aetātis (*f.*), age, time of life.
24   **animum**: this word can mean "spirit" or "character" as well as "mind."
    *nepōs, nepōtis (*m.*), grandson.
    manū: this word can mean "band (of men)" as well as "hand."
27   **avus, -ī** (*m.*), grandfather.
    *restituō, restituere (3), **restituī, restitūtum**, to bring back, restore.

2   ***dēcernō, dēcernere** (3), **dēcrēvī, dēcrētum**, to determine, decide, settle.
3   ***augurium, -ī** (*n.*), a sign of divine will, augury (the science of interpreting
        the will of the gods from the flight of birds and other events in nature).
    *ūtor, ūtī (3), **ūsus sum** (+ *abl.*), to use, practice.
    vultur, vulturis (*m.*), vulture.
4   **sēsē** (*an alternate form of* **sē**), themselves.
5   ***postulō** (1), to demand.
6   **Ex**: "According to."
7   **illūdō, illūdere** (3), **illūsī, illūsum**, to make fun of, mock.
    *trānsiliō, trānsilīre (4), **trānsiluī**, to jump over.
9   ***pereō, perīre** (*irreg.*), **periī, peritum**, to perish, die.
    pereat quīcumque alius . . . : "let him perish, whoever else . . . !"
        The present subjunctive, when used as the main verb in a sentence,
          may express a *command* and can be translated with "let . . . !" (see
          the grammar note on page 28).
    quīcumque, quaecumque, quodcumque, whoever, whatever.
10   **potior, potīrī** (4), **potītus sum** (+ *abl.*), to get control of, get possession of.

Deponent Verbs

Some verbs appear in passive forms but are to be translated actively.
These are called *deponent* verbs. Compare the following sentences:

    Turnus . . . Troiānōs **aggressus est**. *Turnus . . .* ***attacked*** *the
    Trojans.* (*deponent verb*) (1:16–18)
    Victī **sunt** Rutulī. *The Rutulians **were defeated**.* (*regular verb, pas-
    sive voice*) (1:18)

If a verb that appears to be passive has a direct object (as in the first
example above), it is a deponent verb, since true passive verbs never
have direct objects.

Ab initiō Faustulus crēdiderat puerōs iussū rēgis ex- 20
positōs apud sē ēducārī. Tum perīculō Remī mōtus rem 21
Rōmulō aperit. Forte Numitor quoque audīverat frātrēs 22
geminōs esse; tum comparāns et aetātem eōrum et nōbilem 23
animum Remī nepōtem agnōvit. Rōmulus cum manū 24
pāstōrum in rēgem Amūlium impetum facit; Remus aliā 25
parātā manū adiuvat. Ita rēx interfectus est. Imperium 26
Albānum Numitōrī avō ab iuvenibus restitūtum est. 27
Deinde Rōmulus et Remus in eīs locīs ubi expositī ubique 28
ēducātī erant urbem condere cōnstituērunt. 29

4. The Founding of Rome

*According to tradition, Rome was founded on April 21, 753 B.C.
While we cannot accept this as an accurate date, studies by modern archaeologists have confirmed that people began living on the Palatine
hill during the eighth century B.C. Romulus, as you will see, became
the first king; six other kings ruled after him during the period of the
Monarchy (753–509 B.C.)*

Uterque iuvenis nōmen novae urbī dare eamque regere 1   753 B.C.
cupiēbat. Sed quod geminī erant nec rēs aetāte dēcernī 2
poterat, auguriīs ūsī sunt. Ā Remō prius vīsī sunt sex vul- 3
turēs. Rōmulō posteā duodecim sēsē ostendērunt. Uterque 4
ab amīcīs rēx appellātus est atque rēgnum postulābat. 5
Cum īrātī arma rapuissent, in pugnā Remus cecidit. Ex 6
aliā fāmā Remus illūdēns frātrem novōs mūrōs urbis trān- 7
siluit, inde interfectus est ab īrātō Rōmulō, quī haec verba 8
quoque addidit: "Sīc deinde pereat quīcumque alius trān- 9
siliet moenia mea." Ita sōlus potītus est imperiō Rōmulus; 10
conditam urbem ā suō nōmine Rōmam appellāvit. 11

Deponent Verbs *(continued)*

You can also tell if a verb is deponent by looking at its principal
parts. Deponent verbs have only three principal parts, e.g.:

cōnor, cōnārī (1), **cōnātus sum,** to try
aggredior, aggredī (3), **aggressus sum,** to attack

You will find a few deponent verbs that are used with the *ablative
case.* You met **ūtor** and **potior** in lines 3 and 10 of the paragraph above;
the verb **vēscor, vēscī** (3), "to feed upon," "to eat," is also used with the
ablative.

12   Palātium, -ī (n.), Palatine Hill (one of the seven hills of Rome).
      *mūniō (4), to build, fortify, protect.
13   concilium, -ī (n.), council.
      *īnsigne, īnsignis (n.), insignia, mark, token.
14   curūlis, -is, -e, curule, official.
          The sella curūlis was a special chair used by consuls, praetors, and pa-
          trician aediles. It was made of ivory with carved decoration and
          could be folded and moved easily.
15   asȳlum, -ī (n.), refuge.
16   Capitōlīnus, -a, -um, Capitoline.
      quō (adv.), to where.
      *fīnitimus, -a, -um, neighboring.
      *profugiō, profugere (3), profūgī, to flee, flee to.

1   *firmus, -a, -um, firm, stable, strong.
      *cīvitās, cīvitātis (f.), citizenship, state.
      *pār, paris, equal.
3   *cōnūbium, -ī (n.), marriage, right of marriage.
          iūs cōnūbiī: in order for a marriage between two partners from differ-
          ent communities to be legal and for children to be considered legiti-
          mate, there had to exist a formal right of intermarriage between the
          two states.
4   quī . . . peterent: "to seek," a relative clause of purpose (see the grammar
          note on page 13).
      *societās, societātis (f.), alliance.
5   *benignus, -a, -um, kind.
6   *spernō, spernere (3), sprēvī, sprētum, to scorn, reject.
8   *statuō, statuere (3), statuī, statūtum, to set up, determine, decide.

11   Sabīnus, -a, -um, Sabine; (m. pl.) the Sabines (a people to the northeast of
          Rome).
12   *coniūnx, coniugis (m. or f.), spouse, husband, wife.
15   *hospitium, -ī (n.), hospitality, rules of hospitality.
          Rōmānōs hospitium violāvisse: "that the Romans had. . . .," indirect
          statement (see the grammar note on pages 18–19).
16   *spēs, speī (f.), hope.
      *indignātiō, indignātiōnis (f.), anger, indignation, sense of injury.

19   *superbia, -ae (f.), pride, arrogance.

Purpose Clauses

A subordinate clause, introduced by ut (affirmative) or nē (negative),
and with its verb in the *subjunctive*, can tell why the subject of the
main clause does or did something and is called a *purpose clause*, e.g.:

> Multī convēnērunt ut lūdōs spectārent et novam urbem vidērent.
>   (5:10–11)
> *Many assembled **so that they might watch/to watch** the games and
> **so that they might see/to see** the new city.*

Palātium prīmum, in quō ipse erat ēducātus, mūnīvit. 12
Vocātā ad concilium multitūdine, iūra dedit. Īnsignia 13
quoque imperiī, sellam curūlem togamque praetextam, et 14
duodecim līctōrēs sūmpsit. Asȳlum aperuit in monte 15
Capitōlīnō, quō multī ex fīnitimīs populīs profūgērunt. 16
Creāvit etiam centum senātōrēs, quī honōris causā patrēs 17
appellātī sunt. 18

5. The Sabine Women

Iam rēs Rōmāna firma et fīnitimīs cīvitātibus bellō pār 1
erat. Sed Rōmānī neque uxōrēs neque cum fīnitimīs iūs 2
cōnūbiī habēbant. Tum Rōmulus quōsdam ex patribus 3
lēgātōs in vīcīnās gentēs mīsit quī societātem cōnūbiumque 4
novō populō peterent. Nusquam benignē lēgātī audītī sunt; 5
nam fīnitimī nōn sōlum Rōmānōs spernēbant, sed etiam 6
tantam in mediō crēscentem urbem metuēbant. Itaque 7
īrātī Rōmānī vī ūtī statuērunt. 8

Ad eam rem Rōmulus, lūdīs parātīs, fīnitimōs ad spec- 9
tāculum invītāvit. Multī convēnērunt ut lūdōs spectārent 10
et novam urbem vidērent. Sabīnōrum omnis multitūdō cum 11
līberīs ac coniugibus vēnit. Ubi spectāculī tempus vēnit 12
omnēsque intentī in lūdōs erant, tum, signō datō, Rōmānī 13
rapere virginēs coepērunt. Parentēs virginum profūgērunt 14
clāmantēs Rōmānōs hospitium violāvisse. Nec raptae vir- 15
ginēs aut spem dē sē meliōrem aut indignātiōnem minōrem 16
habēbant. 17

Sed ipse Rōmulus circumībat ostendēbatque id patrum 18
virginum superbiā factum esse. "Quamquam vī captae es- 19
tis," inquit, "omnia iūra Rōmānōrum habēbitis." 20

Relative Clauses of Purpose

A clause introduced by a *relative pronoun* and with its verb in the *sub-junctive* may express *purpose* and be called a *relative clause of purpose*, e.g.:

Rōmulus quōsdam ex patribus . . . mīsit **quī** societātem cōnūbiumque . . . **peterent.** (5:3–5)
*Romulus sent some of the senators who . . . should seek/to seek al-
liance and the right of intermarriage. . . .*

22 *iniūria, -ae (f.), wrongdoing, injustice, insult, injury.
23   pertineō, pertinēre (2), pertinuī, to reach, concern.
     *concitō (1), to stir up, rouse.
24   novissimum: the *superlative* of **novus** means "most recent" or "last."
25 *arx, arcis (f.), citadel, fortress.
26 *dolus, -ī (m.), trick.

28   tēlum, -ī (n.), weapon, spear.
     volō (1), to fly.
        Do not confuse this 1st conjugation verb with the verb **volō, velle**
           (*irreg.*), **voluī**, to want, wish, be willing.
29 *īnferō, īnferre (*irreg.*), intulī, illātum, to bring in, carry in.
     sē īnferre, to rush in.
     virīs: this word can mean "husband" as well as "man."
     implōrō (1), to beg for.
31   rēgnum: (*here*) "kingship."
     cōnsociō (1), to associate, unite.
32 *sēdēs, sēdis (f.), seat, home.
33   Quirītēs, Quirītium (m. pl.), Quirites (the name given by Romulus to the
        Romans and Sabines united as one people).
           Multitūdō . . . Quirītēs appellāta est: "The multitude was called
              Quirites" (see the grammar note on page 15).
        Curēs, Curium (m. pl.), Cures (capital city of the Sabines).
        caput: this word can mean "capital" as well as "head."
34 *cūria, -ae (f.), curia (a political unit).
     *trīgintā, thirty.

Semi-deponent Verbs

You already know about *deponent verbs* (review the grammar note on
pages 10 and 11, if necessary). The form **ausae sunt**, "they dared," that
you met in line 28 on page 15 is deponent, but look at the principal
parts of this verb:

   audeō, audēre (2, *semi-deponent*), **ausus sum**

In the present, imperfect, and future tenses (those formed from the present infinitive stem), such *semi-deponent* verbs have normal active
forms. In the perfect, pluperfect, and future perfect, they are deponent.
There are not many semi-deponent verbs; you can identify them by
looking at their principal parts. Here are two other semi-deponents
that you may know:

   gaudeō, gaudēre (2, *semi-deponent*), **gavīsus sum,** to be happy, re-
      joice
   soleō, solēre (2, *semi-deponent*), **solitus sum** (+ *infinitive*), to be ac-
      customed (to doing), be in the habit (of doing), usually (do)

Iam multō minus perturbātī animī raptārum erant. At 21
parentēs eārum cīvitātēs fīnitimās, ad quās eius iniūriae 22
pars pertinēbat, ad arma concitābant. Hae cīvitātēs omnēs 23
ā Rōmulō victae sunt. Novissimum bellum ab Sabīnīs or- 24
tum est, quod multō maximum fuit. Sabīnī arcem Rōmā- 25
nam in monte Capitōlīnō dolō cēpērunt. Rōmānī posterō diē 26
arcem recipere cōnātī sunt. 27

Tum Sabīnae mulierēs ausae sunt sē inter tēla volantia 28
īnferre, ut pācem ā patribus virīsque implōrārent. Ducēs eā 29
rē mōtī nōn modo pācem sed etiam cīvitātem ūnam ex 30
duābus faciunt; rēgnum quoque cōnsociant atque Rōmam 31
faciunt sēdem imperiī. Multitūdō ita aucta novō nōmine 32
Quirītēs appellāta est ex Curibus, quae urbs caput Sa- 33
bīnōrum erat. Deinde Rōmulus, populō in cūriās trīgintā 34
dīvīsō, nōmina mulierum raptārum cūriīs dedit. 35

Predicate Nominative with Verbs of Calling

You will find that with verbs meaning "to call" or "to name" a *predicate
nominative* is used, not a direct object in the accusative, e.g.:

Multitūdō . . . **Quirītēs appellāta est.** (above: 32–33)
The multitude . . . **was called Quirites**.

. . . quae **Troia appellāta est.** (1:1)
. . . *which* **was called Troy**.

Archaeologists have found on the Palatine Hill the remains of simple
huts, one of which is shown reconstructed above. The very first inhabitants of Rome lived in shelters such as these.

36 *exercitus, -ūs (*m.*), army.
Campus Mārtius, -ī (*m.*), Campus Martius or Field of Mars (a flat open
area, which was used for military training, to the northwest of the
original city of Rome).
37 recēnseō, recēnsēre (2), recēnsuī, recēnsum, to count, survey, hold a review of.
nimbus, -ī (*m.*), cloud.
38 *proximus, -a, -um, nearest, closest.
sublīmis, -is, -e, high, lofty, in the sky.
39 ūniversus, -a, -um, all.
deus: note that with this noun the *vocative* is the same as the *nominative.*
40 deō: "from a god," *ablative of source* with nāte, perfect participle of
nāscor.
41 *alloquor, alloquī (3), allocūtus sum, to speak to.
*nūntiō (1), to announce, report.
42 *orbis, orbis (*m.*), circle, globe.
*orbis terrārum, the world, universe.
*proinde (*adv.*), consequently, accordingly, therefore.
*rēs mīlitāris, reī mīlitāris (*f.*), the art of war, military science.
43 colenda est: "must be cultivated," *passive periphrastic* (see the grammar
note on page 60).
44 Quirīnus, -ī (*m.*), Quirinus (epithet applied to Romulus after his deifica-
tion; also the name of a god resembling Mars worshiped on the
Quirinal Hill in Rome).

Dative Case with Special Intransitive Verbs

In your reading you met this sentence (opposite: 43–44):

> . . . nūllae opēs hūmānae **armīs Rōmānīs resistere** possunt.
> . . . no human power can **resist Roman arms**.

Notice that the meaning of **resistere** is completed by an *indirect object
in the dative case* and not by a *direct object in the accusative.* There
are a number of *special intransitive* verbs in Latin, such as **resistere**
above, that take the dative case, while in English we often translate
them as if they had accusative direct objects. These verbs are identified
in vocabulary lists by "(+ *dat.*)." Here are some other intransitive verbs
that you will find used with dative indirect objects:

crēdō, crēdere (3), crēdidī, crēditum (+ *dat.*), to believe in, trust
faveō, favēre (2), fāvī, fautum (+ *dat.*), to give favor to, support
parcō, parcere (3), pepercī (+ *dat.*), to spare
permittō, permittere (3), permīsī, permissum (+ *dat.*), to permit
persuādeō, persuādēre (2), persuāsī, persuāsum (+ *dat.*), to persuade (*literally*, to make sweet or pleasant to)

For a few years Romulus and Titus Tatius, king of the Sabines, ruled jointly. After Tatius' death, Romulus ruled alone until—

Dum Rōmulus quōdam tempore exercitum in Campō   36   716 B.C.
Mārtiō recēnset, tempestās subitō coorta eum nimbō ope-   37
ruit. Patrēs quī proximī steterant dīxērunt rēgem sub-   38
līmem raptum esse. Deinde ūniversī clāmant: "Salvē, deus   39
deō nāte." Rōmulus dīcitur posteā cuidam cīvī sē ostendisse   40
et eum hīs verbīs allocūtus esse: "Nūntiā Rōmānīs deōs   41
velle meam Rōmam caput orbis terrārum esse; proinde rēs   42
mīlitāris colenda est; nam nūllae opēs hūmānae armīs   43
Rōmānīs resistere possunt." Posteā nōmen Quirīnus   44
Rōmulō additum est. Rēgnāvit septem et trīgintā annōs.   45

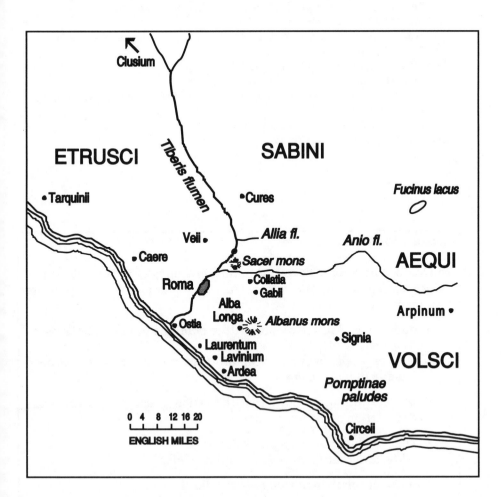

Rome and neighboring states of central Italy

1 *certāmen, certāminis (n.), contest, struggle, strife.
   *factiō, factiōnis (f.), doing, (political) faction.
3 *peregrīnus, -a, -um, foreign.
   *recūsō (1), to object, protest, refuse, reject.
   *interrēgnum, -ī (n.), interregnum (period between one king's death and
      the election of his successor).
4 *plēbs, plēbis (f.), common people, plebeians, plebs.
5 *prō (prep. + abl.), in place of.
   vīsum est: "it seemed/appeared" (see the grammar note on page 22).
6 *mora, -ae (f.), delay.

7 Curibus: "at Cures" (the old capital of the Sabines), locative case (see the
      grammar note on pages 52–53).
   Numa Pompilius, Numae Pompiliī (m.), Numa Pompilius (second king
      of Rome).
8 *iūstus, -a, -um, just, fair.
   *perītus, -a, -um (+ gen.), skilled in, experienced, expert.
   dīvīnus, -a, -um, divine.
9 *dēferō, dēferre (irreg.), dētulī, dēlātum, to carry, bring, grant, award.
10 *lēx, lēgis (f.), law.
11 *firmō (1), to strengthen, consolidate.
   īnstrūctus, -a, -um (+ abl.), fitted out with.
   Iānus, -ī (m.), Janus (god of boundaries and transitions, depicted with
      two faces).
12 index, indicis (m.), indicator, sign.
14 *foedus, foederis (n.), treaty.

Indirect Statement

You know that verbs of saying, thinking, or feeling are often followed by
an *accusative and infinitive construction*. This is known as *indirect
statement*, e.g.:

Deinde plēbs clāmāre coepit **multōs dominōs** prō ūnō **factōs esse**.
   (opposite: 4–5)
*Then the people began to complain **that many masters had been
   made** in place of one.*

A *present infinitive* shows that the action takes place at the *same
time* as the action of the main verb, e.g.:

Crēdō populum novum rēgem **velle**.
   *I believe that the people **want** a new king.*

Crēdēbam populum novum rēgem **velle**.
   *I believed that the people **wanted** a new king.*

The rest of Part I will relate some of the stories that were handed down in Roman tradition concerning the six kings who followed Romulus.

6. Numa Pompilius

Certāmen inde dē rēgnō inter factiōnēs ortum est.   1
Sabīnī rēgem suae factiōnis creārī cupiēbant. Rōmānī vet-   2
erēs peregrīnum rēgem recūsābant. Interrēgnō secūtō,   3
senātus imperium gessit. Deinde plēbs clāmāre coepit   4
multōs dominōs prō ūnō factōs esse. Optimum igitur vīsum   5
est sine morā rēgem creāre.   6

Habitābat eō tempore Curibus Numa Pompilius, vir   7
iūstissimus perītusque omnis dīvīnī atque hūmānī iūris.   8
Rēgnum eī omnium cōnsēnsū dēlātum est. Is urbem no-   9   715 B.C.
vam, quae ā Rōmulō armīs condita erat, iūre lēgibusque   10
firmāvit. Arcum portīs īnstrūctum fēcit, quī arcus Iānī ap-   11
pellātus est; apertus bellī index erat, clausus pācis. Per   12
omne rēgnum Numae clausus fuit. Pāx cum cīvitātibus   13
fīnitimīs societāte ac foederibus facta est.   14

Indirect Statement (continued)

A *perfect infinitive* shows that the action took place *prior to* the action of the main verb, e.g.:

Patrēs dīcunt rēgem sublīmem **raptum esse.**
*The senators say that the king **was taken up** into heaven.*

Patrēs . . . dīxērunt rēgem sublīmem **raptum esse.** (5:38–39)
*The senators . . . said that the king **had been taken up** into heaven.*

A *future infinitive* shows that the action will take place *after* the action of the main verb, e.g.:

Crēdimus Numam rēgem **futūrum esse.**
*We believe that Numa **will be** king.*

Crēdēbāmus Numam rēgem **futūrum esse.**
*We believed that Numa **would be** king.*

In the examples above, notice how the translation of the infinitive in indirect statment changes as the tense of the main verb changes.

15   *mōs, mōris (m.), custom; (pl.) habits, character.
     *cultus, -ūs (m.), cultivation, worship, training, education.
16   *conciliō (1), to bring together, win over, bring about, acquire.
17   Ēgeria, -ae (f.), Egeria (nymph whom King Numa visited for advice).
     *congressus, -ūs (m.), meeting.
     monitus, -ūs (m.), advising, command.
     sacra: "sacred things," "religious rites."
18   ad: "according to."
     *lūna, -ae (f.), moon.
19   *discrībō, discrībere (3), discrīpsī, discrīptum, to divide.
     nefāstus, -a, -um, forbidden, unlawful, unlucky.
20   comitia, -ōrum (n. pl.), assembly, election.
     Vestālis, -is -e, Vestal, of Vesta.
       The Vestal Virgins were chosen from the most aristocratic families and
         served for thirty years, keeping the sacred fire lighted and perform-
         ing other duties on behalf of the state.
21   *caerimōnia, -ae (f.), ceremony.
     sānctus, -a, -um, holy, sacred.

22   rītus, -ūs (m.), rite.
23   sacerdōtium, -ī (n.), priesthood.
24   *imitor, imitārī (1), imitātus sum, to imitate.
25   *vertō, vertere (3), vertī, versum, to turn.
26   deinceps (adv.), in succession, one after the other.
27   *quadrāgintā, forty.

Sē in Indirect Statement

The *reflexive pronoun* sē as the subject of an indirect statement refers
to the subject of the *main verb*. Compare these two sentences:

Numa simulāvit sē cum deā Ēgeriā congressūs habēre. (opposite:
  16–17)
*Numa pretended that **he (Numa himself)** had meetings with the
  goddess Egeria.*

Numa simulāvit **eum** cum deā Ēgeriā congressūs habēre.
*Numa pretended that **he (someone else)** had meetings with the goddess Egeria.*

Rēx inde ad mōrēs populī cultumque deōrum animum 15
convertit. Ut populī fidem conciliāret, simulāvit sē cum deā 16
Ēgeriā congressūs habēre et monitū eius sacra īnstituere 17
sacerdōtēsque legere. Annum ad cursum lūnae in duodecim 18
mēnsēs discrīpsit. Quōsdam diēs nefāstōs fēcit, per quōs 19
diēs comitia nōn habēbantur. Virginēs Vestālēs lēgit, quās 20
caerimōniīs quibusdam sānctās fēcit. 21

Multa etiam alia ā rēge īnstitūta sunt, rītūs, caerimō- 22
niae, sacerdōtia. Multitūdō hīs rēbus ā vī et armīs conversa 23
rēgis mōrēs imitābātur. Fīnitimī populī cīvitātem Rōmā- 24
nam tōtam in cultum deōrum versam violāre nōlēbant. Ita 25
duo deinceps rēgēs, Rōmulus bellō, Numa pāce,* cīvitātem 26
auxērunt. Numa annōs trēs et quadrāgintā rēgnāvit. 27 673 B.C.

*Note the *parallel word order* in line 26 above: **Ita duo deinceps rēgēs,
Rōmulus bellō, Numa pāce, cīvitātem auxērunt**.

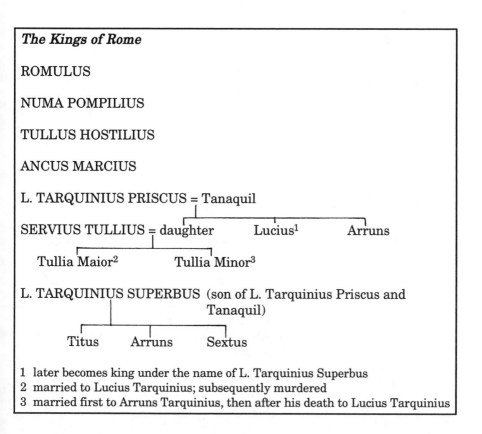

The Kings of Rome

ROMULUS

NUMA POMPILIUS

TULLUS HOSTILIUS

ANCUS MARCIUS

L. TARQUINIUS PRISCUS = Tanaquil

SERVIUS TULLIUS = daughter   Lucius[1]   Arruns

Tullia Maior[2]   Tullia Minor[3]

L. TARQUINIUS SUPERBUS (son of L. Tarquinius Priscus and
                                              Tanaquil)

Titus   Arruns   Sextus

1 later becomes king under the name of L. Tarquinius Superbus
2 married to Lucius Tarquinius; subsequently murdered
3 married first to Arruns Tarquinius, then after his death to Lucius Tarquinius

1   **Numā mortuō**: *ablative absolute* with a *perfect participle* of a *deponent*
    verb, "Numa having died," "After Numa had died."
2   **Tullus Hostīlius, -ī** (*m.*), Tullus Hostilius (third king of Rome).
    rēx: *predicate nominative*, translate after **creātus est**.
3   **torpeō, torpēre** (2), to be stiff, be lazy, be inactive.
    *ōtium, -ī (*n.*), leisure, free time, peace.
4   **Albānī, -ōrum** (*m. pl.*), the Albans (inhabitants of Alba Longa).
6   **Cluilius, -ī** (*m.*), Cluilius (an Alban king).
7   *dictātor, dictātōris (*m.*), dictator (chosen to lead the state for six months
    during a crisis).
    Mettius Fufetius, -ī (*m.*), Mettius Fufetius (elected dictator of Alba
    Longa).
    Note the *double accusative* in this sentence, and note that the more
    important of the two accusative objects is placed first in the Latin
    although we must place it second in English: "The Albans make
    Mettius Fufetius dictator."
10 **cupīdō, cupīdinis** (*m.* or *f.*), desire, greed, passion.
    cognātus, -a, -um, related.
11 *potius (*adv.*), rather.
12 **cum . . . erimus, . . . aggredientur**: the *future tense* in the subordinate
    clause is to be translated with a present tense in English, "when we
    are. . . ." This is similar to the translation of the future tense in **sī-**
    clauses (see the grammar note on page 104).
    cōnfectī: the *perfect passive participle* of **cōnficiō** is here used as a simple
    adjective meaning "worn out," "exhausted."
14 *proelium, -ī (*n.*), battle.
    dēcernāmus: "let us decide," *present subjunctive* expressing an *exhorta-*
    tion (see the grammar note on page 28).
15 *probō (1), to approve.

Videō in the Passive

The verb **vidēre** is often found in the *passive voice* with the special
meaning "to seem" or "to appear," e.g.:

Optimum igitur **vīsum est** sine morā rēgem creāre. (6:5–6)
*Therefore, **it seemed/appeared** best to choose a king without delay.*

Quod cīvitās torpēre ōtiō **vidēbātur, . . .** (opposite: 3)
*Because the citizens (literally, the state) **seemed/appeared** to be get-*
ting lazy because of peace, . . .

The principal parts of this verb in the passive are:

videor, vidērī (2), **vīsus sum**, to seem, appear

7.   Tullus Hostilius

Numā mortuō, interrēgnum ut anteā secūtum est. Inde 1   673 B.C.
Tullus Hostīlius rēx creātus est. Hic ferōcior etiam quam 2
Rōmulus fuit. Quod cīvitās torpēre ōtiō vidēbātur, causās 3
undique bellī quaerēbat. Bellum cum Albānīs prīmum or- 4
tum est.   Albānī priōrēs magnō exercitū in agrum 5
Rōmānum impetum fēcērunt. Ibi Cluilius, Albānus rēx, 6
moritur. Albānī dictātōrem Mettium Fufetium creant. Ubi 7
is ab Tullō colloquium petiit, rēx Rōmānus nōn recūsāvit. 8
Mettius sīc locūtus est: "Uterque populus sē bellum gerere 9
propter iniūriās dīcit. Rē vērā cupīdō imperiī duōs cognātōs 10
vīcīnōsque populōs ad arma concitat. Sed potius metuere 11
dēbēmus Etrūscōs, quī, cum dēfessī cōnfectīque erimus, 12
simul victōrem ac victum aggredientur. Certāmen igitur dē 13
imperiō paucōrum proeliō potius dēcernāmus." Tullus cōn- 14
silium probāvit, quamquam magnam spem victōriae habē- 15
bat. 16

Comparative Adjectives

The letters **-ior** (masculine and feminine) or **-ius** (neuter) added to the
stem of adjectives express the *comparative degree*, e.g.:

ignāvus, -a, -um	**ignāvior, ignāvius**
	lazier, quite lazy, rather lazy, too lazy
aeger, aegra, aegrum	**aegrior, aegrius**
	sicker, quite sick, rather sick, too sick
ferōx, ferōcis	**ferōcior, ferōcius**
	more savage, quite savage, etc.

Comparative adjectives have 3rd declension endings. Use the chart on
page 181 to review their forms.

When two items are being compared, the adverb **quam**, "than," may
be found, e.g.:

Hic **ferōcior** etiam **quam** Rōmulus fuit. (above: 2–3)
*This man was even **more savage than** Romulus.*

Instead of **quam**, you will often find the second item of the comparison in the ablative case (*ablative of comparison*), e.g.:

Hic ferōcior etiam **Rōmulō** fuit.

17   *trigeminus, -a, -um, threefold, triple, triplet.
18   vīribus: *ablative plural* of the noun vīs (*f.*), which in the singular means "violence," "power," or "force" and in the plural "strength."
     *dispār, disparis, unequal, different.
       Note the force of the *ablatives* **aetāte** and **vīribus** used with this adjective, "*with respect to* neither age nor strength."
     Horātiī, -ōrum (*m. pl.*), Horatii (triplet Roman brothers).
     Cūriātiī, -ōrum (*m. pl.*), Curiatii (triplet Alban brothers).
     Hī: "these," i.e., "the latter"; illī: "those, i.e., "the former."
19   *dēligō, dēligere (3), dēlēgī, dēlēctum, to choose, pick out.
21   *ērēctus, -a, -um, attentive, alert.
     *ānxius, -a, -um, nervous, anxious.
     intendō, intendere (3), intendī, intentum, to stretch out, aim at.
22   ternī, -ae, -a, three each, three at once.

24   *integer, integra, integrum, unharmed, complete, whole.
     circumsistō, circumsistere (3), to surround.
25   Cum iam: "As soon as."
26   intervāllum, -ī (*n.*), space, interval.
31   *properō (1), to hurry.
32   *priusquam (*conj.*), before.
33   *singulī, -ae, -a, one at a time, one each.
     *supersum, superesse (*irreg.*), superfuī, to survive, be left over.
34   *superior, superius, *gen.* superiōris, higher, previous.
36   *sustineō, sustinēre (2), sustinuī, sustentum, to hold up, sustain, withstand, endure.
37   *caedō, caedere (3), cecīdī, caesum, to strike, cut down, kill.
     *spoliō (1), to strip.
       It was customary for a victorious soldier to take his enemy's armor and weapons as plunder.

Dum = "*while*"

The *conjunction* **dum** often introduces subordinate clauses with their verbs in the *present tense*; when the verb of the main clause is in the *perfect tense*, the present tense with **dum** is to be translated with a past progressive in English, e.g.:

     . . . **dum** exercitus Albānus Cūriātiōs **obsecrant** ut frātrī auxilium ferant, Horātius eum interfēcit. . . . (opposite: 28–29)
     . . . *while* the Alban army *was begging* the Curiatii to help their brother, Horātius killed him. . . .

Other examples may be found in 3:15–16 and 5:36–38.

In this construction, the present tense with **dum** indicates an action that was continuing over a period of time but was then interrupted by the action of the verb of the main clause.

Forte in utrōque exercitū erant trigeminī frātrēs, nec 17
aetāte nec vīribus disparēs, Horātiī et Cūriātiī. Hī Albānī 18
erant, illī Rōmānī. Trigeminī ad hanc pugnam dēlēctī arma 19
capiunt et in medium inter duās aciēs prōcēdunt. Duo ex- 20
ercitūs, ērēctī ānxiīque, in spectāculum animōs intendunt. 21
Signō datō, ternī iuvenēs concurrunt.   22

Prīmō congressū duo Rōmānī interfectī sunt et trēs Al- 23
bānī vulnerātī. Eum quī integer fuit trēs Cūriātiī circum- 24
sistere cōnātī sunt. Cum iam Rōmānus paulum fūgisset, 25
respexit atque vīdit trēs Cūriātiōs magnīs intervāllīs se- 26
quentēs. Subitō cōnstitit et in proximum Cūriātium impe- 27
tum facit; dum exercitus Albānus Cūriātiōs obsecrant ut 28
frātrī auxilium ferant, Horātius eum interfēcit; deinde vic- 29
tor secundum frātrem petit. Tum magnō clāmōre Rōmānī 30
adiuvant mīlitem suum et ille cōnficere proelium properat. 31
Priusquam cōnsecūtus est tertius, Horātius alterum 32
Cūriātium cōnficit. Iamque singulī supererant, sed nec spē 33
nec vīribus parēs;* alter integer et ferōx superiōribus vic- 34
tōriīs erat; alter dēfessus vulnere, animō fractus** in certā- 35
men vēnit. Nec illud proelium fuit. Cūriātium vix susti- 36
nentem arma Horātius caedit et iacentem spoliat.   37

*nec spē nec vīribus parēs: note the echo of nec aetāte nec vīribus dis-
parēs (17–18). Explain the significance of the echo.
**dēfessus vulnere, animō fractus: note the *chiastic word order* (ABBA
pattern). Compare the *parallel word order* noted on page 21. What
is the effect of the chiastic arrangement of words here?

Indirect Commands

Verbs meaning "to beg," "to ask," "to order," "to encourage," or something similar often introduce subordinate clauses with **ut** (negative **nē**)
and the *subjunctive*, e.g.:

   ... dum exercitus Albānus Cūriātiōs obsecrant **ut frātrī auxilium
     ferant**, Horātius eum interfēcit.... (above: 28–29)
   ... *while the Alban army was begging the Curiatii **to help their
     brother**, Horatius killed him....*

The clause **ut frātrī auxilium ferant** is called an *indirect command*
because it tells what the bystanders were encouraging the Curiatii to
do.

The best translation for a Latin indirect command is usually an
English infinitive ("to help").

38   **sepultūra, -ae** (*f.*), burial.
     suōrum: "of their men," i.e., of their dead. This use of a *possessive adjective*, with a noun understood, is particularly common in military language.
39   **nēquāquam** (*adv.*), by no means, not at all.
     nēquāquam paribus animīs: "with spirits not at all equal," *ablative of manner*.
     vertuntur: translate actively in English.
     alterī . . . alterī: "the ones . . . the others."
40   **domōs**: "to their homes," "home" (see the grammar note on pages 52–53).
     ***abdūcō, abdūcere** (3), **abdūxī, abductum**, to lead away, take away.
41   **ūnī**: *dative singular* of **ūnus**.
     spolium, -ī (*n.*), booty, spoils, loot.
     palūdāmentum, -ī (*n.*), cloak worn by soldiers.
42   ***solvō, solvere** (3), **solvī, solūtum**, to release, untie, loosen, free.
     For a woman to wear her long hair untied was a sign of mourning.
43   **multīs cum lacrimīs**: "with many tears," *ablative of manner*. Note that **cum** is optional in this construction when the noun is modified by an adjective (compare **nēquāquam paribus animīs** above).
44   **maeror, maerōris** (*m.*), grief.
46   **relāta est**: "was referred" (for trial).
     ***iūdicium, -ī** (*n.*), judgment, decision, trial.
47   **Pūblius Horātius, -ī** (*m.*), Publius Horatius.
     iūre: "in accordance with the law," "justifiably," "rightly," *ablative of manner* (without **cum**).
48   **admīrātiōne . . . iūre**: "because of. . . .," *ablative of cause*.
     ***virtūs, virtūtis** (*f.*), virtue, courage.
     causae: as a legal term this means "case."
     absolvō, absolvere (3), **absolvī, absolūtum**, to release, acquit.

50   ***pestilentia, -ae** (*f.*), disease, plague.
51   ***afficiō, afficere** (3), **affēcī, affectum**, to affect, afflict, strike.
     ***calamitās, calamitātis** (*f.*), disaster, calamity.
     ***frangō, frangere** (3), **frēgī, frāctum**, to break, overcome, crush.
52   ***quia** (*conj.*), because.
53   **fulmen, fulminis** (*n.*), lightning bolt (weapon of Jupiter).
54   **cōnflagrō** (1), to be burned up.

Relative Pronouns

The following sentences contain *relative clauses*:

Horātiī soror, **quae** ūnī ex Cūriātiīs dēspōnsa erat, . . . (opposite: 40–41)

*Horatius' sister, **who** had been betrothed to one of the Curiatii, . . .*

. . . palūdāmentum spōnsī, **quod** ipsa cōnfēcerat. (opposite: 41–42)
*. . . her fiancé's cloak, **which** she had made herself.*

Ad sepultūram inde suōrum Rōmānī atque Albānī 38
nēquāquam paribus animīs vertuntur, alterī victōrēs alterī 39
victī. Exercitūs domōs abductī sunt. Horātiī soror, quae 40
ūnī ex Cūriātiīs dēspōnsa erat, agnōvit inter spolia palū- 41
dāmentum spōnsī, quod ipsa cōnfēcerat. Solvit crīnēs et 42
multīs cum lacrimīs spōnsum mortuum appellat. Frāter, 43
īrātus propter maerōrem sorōris in victōriā suā tantōque 44
pūblicō gaudiō, gladiō eam interfēcit. Rēs ad populum 45
relāta est. Hominēs vehementer mōtī sunt in eō iūdiciō, 46
Pūbliō Horātiō patre clāmante fīliam iūre caesam esse. Sed 47
magis admīrātiōne virtūtis quam iūre causae iuvenem ab- 48
solvērunt. 49

Posteā pestilentia gravis in urbem incidit, quā rēx 50
quoque affectus est. Hāc calamitāte frāctus sacrīs posteā 51
animum dedit. Postrēmō, quia sacrum quoddam nōn rīte 52
fēcerat—ita fāma est—Tullus fulmine percussus cum domō 53
cōnflagrāvit. Rēgnāvit annōs duōs et trīgintā. 54   642 B.C.

Relative Pronouns (continued)

Posteā pestilentia . . . **quā** rēx quoque affectus est. (above: 50–51)
Later on a plague . . . by which the king also was stricken.

Use the chart on page 184 to review the forms of the *relative pronoun*. The relative pronoun agrees with its *antecedent* (the word that it modifies in the main clause) in *gender* and *number*; it takes its *case* from its use in its own clause. In the first example on the opposite page, **quae** is feminine singular because its antecedent, **soror**, is feminine singular; it is nominative because it is the subject of the verb in its own clause, **erat**. Perform a similar analysis for the other two examples.

Ablative Absolutes

The *ablative absolutes* you have met so far in these stories have used *perfect participles* (see the grammar note on page 3). The *present participle* may also be used, e.g.:

Hominēs vehementer mōtī sunt in eō iūdiciō, **Pūbliō Horātiō patre clāmante** fīliam iūre caesam esse. (above: 46–47)
*Men were very upset in this trial, **when Publius Horatius the father was shouting** that his daughter had been justly slain.*

(continued on next page)

Ablative Absolutes (continued)

The present participle denotes an action going on *at the same time* as that of the main verb in the sentence, thus **clāmante** in the example in the box on page 27 is translated "was shouting" because the main verb (**mōtī sunt**) is in the past tense.

Subjunctive in Main Clauses (= Independent Subjunctive)

You have often seen the *subjunctive* used in clauses introduced by the conjunction **cum** and in purpose clauses introduced by **ut**, e.g.:

Multī convēnērunt **ut lūdōs spectārent et novam urbem vidērent**. (5:10–11)
*Many assembled **so that they might watch/to watch** the games and **so that they might see/to see** the new city.*

In such sentences the subjunctive verb is not in the *main clause* in the sentence; rather, it is in a *subordinate clause* that depends on the main clause. The subjunctive can, however, be used in the main clause of a sentence and is then said to be an *independent subjunctive*. In such cases it may express a *command*, an *exhortation*, a *wish*, a *deliberative question*, or a *possibility*, e.g.:

Command (Jussive Subjunctive):

Pereat quīcumque alius trānsiliet moenia mea. (4:9–10)
***Let him perish**, whoever else jumps over my walls!*

Exhortation (Hortatory Subjunctive):

Certāmen dē imperiō paucōrum proeliō **dēcernāmus**. (7:13–14)
***Let us decide** the contest for power by the battle of a few.*

Wish (Optative Subjunctive):

Nē Remus rēx **sit**!
***May** Remus not **be** king!*

Wishes may be introduced with the word **utinam**, with no difference in translation, e.g.:

Utinam nē Remus rēx **sit**!
***May** Remus not **be** king!*

Nē is used for the negative in commands, exhortations, and wishes, as in the examples above.

Subjunctive in Main Clauses *(continued)*

Deliberative Question *(Deliberative Subjunctive):*

Quid **agāmus**? Quid nōn **agāmus**?
*What **are we to do**? What **are we** not **to do**?*

Possibility *(Potential Subjunctive):*

Velim hoc faciās. Nōn **ausim** hoc facere.
*I **would like** you to do this. I **would** not **dare** to do this.*

Nōn is used for the negative in deliberative questions and expressions of possibility, as in the examples above.

Exercise 1

Read aloud and translate. In each sentence identify the use of the subjunctive as expressing a command, an exhortation, a wish, a deliberative question, or a possibility. Some of these sentences may be translated more than one way. Be ready to explain your translation of each sentence.

1. Vincant Rōmānī Albānōs!
2. Spectēmus pugnam inter trigeminōs frātrēs!
3. Mettius, "Dēligāmus," inquit, "paucōs virōs. Nē pereant multī!"
4. Sī Rōmulus et Remus Albae habitāre nōlunt, condant novam urbem!
5. Nē Amulius puerōs in Tiberim iaciat! Nē Rheam Silviam in custōdiam det!
6. Rōmulus Remō, "Albā," inquit, "ēgrediāmur et cīvitātem nostram īnstituāmus."
7. Rōmulus et Remus auguriīs ūtantur. Is quī augurium maius videt, det nōmen urbī!
8. Utinam bonus rēx sit Rōmulus!
9. Rōmulus cīvibus suīs, "Obtineāmus," inquit, "uxōrēs dē populō Sabīnō."
10. Romulō mortuō, patrēs, "Fīat rēx," inquiunt, "Numa Pompilius."
11. Tullus Hostīlius, cum rēx factus esset, sēcum dīxit: "Quid nunc agam? Bellum cum Albānīs aut cum Etrūscīs geram? Impetumne in agrum Albānum faciam?"
12. Dīcam ego Horātiōs fortius quam Cūriātiōs pugnāvisse; dīcās autem tū fortūnam Horātiīs fāvisse.
13. Nōlīmus contrā exercitum Rōmānam pugnāre; pācem igitur cum eīs faciāmus.
14. Horātius pater sē rogat, "Condemnem fīlium meum, quod sorōrem suam necāvit? Ignōscam eī, quod magnam victōriam Rōmānīs obtinuit?"

1   **religiō, religiōnis** (*f.*), reverence, awe; (*pl.*) religious observances.
     Ancus, -ī (*m.*), Ancus Marcius (grandson of Numa and fourth king of
        Rome).
2   **indīcō, indīcere** (3), **indīxī, indictum**, to proclaim, announce.
     bellum indīcere, to declare war.
3   ***negōtium, -ī** (*n.*), business, task.
     ***mandō** (1), to order, command, commit, entrust.
     fētiālis, fētiālis (*m.*), fetial (one of the priests who represented the
        Romans in their dealings with other peoples and who performed the
        rituals for declaring war).
        Note the *double accusative* with the verb of naming.

5   **Iāniculum, -ī** (*n.*), Janiculum (a hill across the Tiber from the original city
        of Rome).
6   ***sublicius, -a, -um**, resting on piles.
     ponte sublicio: this bridge came to be called the Pons Sublicius.
     coniungō, coniungere (3), **coniūnxī, coniūnctum**, to join together.
     ***carcer, carceris** (*m.*), cell, jail.
     ***exstō** (1), to stand out, be visible, exist.
7   ***usque ad** (+ *acc.*), as far as, up to, all the way to.
8   **Ōstia, -ae** (*f.*), Ostia (a town that eventually became the major seaport for
        Rome).
     condita: note that **est** does not need to be repeated with this second per-
        fect passive participle.

Relative Pronouns

Review the rules about *relative pronouns* given above on pages 26–27.
Then identify the form of the following relative pronouns in the para-
graphs on page 31 and explain why each pronoun is in the gender,
number, and case that it is:

> **quibus** (line 2)
> **quibus** (line 3)
> **quī** (line 5)
> **quī** (line 6)

Note that in line 5 the antecedent (**collis**) of the relative pronoun
(**quī**) appears within the relative clause itself. Instead of **Iāniculum,
collis quī. . . .** , in which **collis** is in apposition to **Iāniculum**, we have
Iāniculum, quī collis. . . . , with the appositional noun incorporated into
the relative clause and still serving as the antecedent of the relative
pronoun. You will often find this arrangement in your Latin readings.

8.   Ancus Marcius

Numa in pāce religiōnēs īnstituerat, sīc Ancus caeri- 1 642 B.C.
mōniās īnstituit, quibus bella posteā indicta sunt. Sacer- 2
dōtēs, quibus id negōtium mandātum est, fētiālēs appel- 3
lāvit. 4

Iāniculum, quī collis trāns Tiberim est, cum urbe ponte 5
subliciō coniūnxit. Carcer, quī etiam nunc exstat, sub 6
monte Capitōlīnō aedificātus est. Imperium usque ad mare 7
prōlātum est, et in ōre Tiberis Ōstia urbs condita. 8

Superlative Adjectives

The letters **-issimus, -a, -um** added to the stem of most adjectives express the *superlative degree*, e.g.:

cupidus, -a, -um	**cupidissimus, -a, -um**
	greediest, very greedy
fortis, -is, -e	**fortissimus, -a, -um**
	bravest, very brave
prūdēns, prūdentis	**prūdentissimus, -a, -um**
	wisest, very wise

The letters **-errimus, -a, -um** are found to mark the superlative with
adjectives of which the masculine nominative singular ends in **-er**, e.g.:

miser, misera, miserum	**miserrimus, -a, -um**
	most wretched, very wretched
pulcher, pulchra, pulchrum	**pulcherrimus, -a, -um**
	most beautiful, very beautiful

The letters **-illimus, -a, -um** are found to mark the superlative with
a few (but not all) adjectives that end in **-lis**, e.g.:

similis, -is, -e	**simillimus, -a, -um**
	most similar, very similar

Other adjectives that follow this same pattern are:

difficilis, -is, -e, difficult
dissimilis, -is, -e, unlike
facilis, -is, -e, easy
gracilis, -is, -e, slender
humilis, -is, -e, low, humble

9 Lucumō, Lucumōnis (m.), Lucumo (an Etruscan prince).
10 Tarquiniī, -ōrum (m. pl.), Tarquinii (an important Etruscan city).
     Tarquiniīs: "at Tarquinii," *locative case* (see the grammar note on
       pages 52–53).
     Dēmarātus, -ī (m.), Demaratus (father of Lucumo).
11 Corinthius, -a, -um, Corinthian, from Corinth (a city in Greece).
12 Tanaquil, Tanaquīlis (f.), Tanaquil (wife of Tarquinius Priscus).
13 *exul, exulis (m.), an exile.
     *indignitās, indignitātis (f.), insult, disgrace.
14 cōnsilium migrandī: "a plan of moving" (for the *gerund*, see the grammar
       note on page 58).
     Rōmam: "to Rome" (see the grammar note on pages 52–53).
15 aquila, -ae (f.), eagle (symbol of Jupiter).
16 pilleus, -ī (m.), cap (worn by Romans at festivals, especially at the Sat-
       urnalia).
     *repōnō, repōnere (3), reposuī, repositum, to replace, put back.
17 *potentia, -ae (f.), power.
18 caelestis, -is, -e, heavenly.
     *prōdigium, -ī (n.), miraculous event, sign, portent.

19 L. Tarquinius Prīscus, -ī (m.), Lucius Tarquinius Priscus (who was to be-
       come the fifth king of Rome; husband of Tanaquil).
20 īnsignis, -is -e, famous, well-known.
     factus est: "he became" (see the grammar note on page 33).
21 dīvitiae, -ārum (f. pl.), riches, wealth.
     dīvitiīs aliīsque rēbus: *ablatives* with īnsignis, "famous *because of
       his* . . ."
     *amīcitia, -ae (f.), friendship.
22 *tūtor, tūtōris (m.), guardian.
     testāmentum, -ī (n.), will.

Perfect Active and Passive Infinitives

The forms **abstulisse** and **reposuisse** in lines 16 and 17 on page 33 are
perfect active infinitives. They are formed by adding the suffix **-isse** to
the perfect stem, and they are translated "to have taken away" and "to
have replaced."

The sentence in which these infinitives appear may be rewritten as
follows:

> Dum iter faciunt, pilleus dīcitur ab capite Lucumōnis ab aquilā
> **ablātus esse** et rūrsus **repositus** (**esse**).

The forms in boldface are *perfect passive infinitives*, formed by
combining the *perfect passive participle* with **esse**. These forms are
translated "to have been taken away" and "to have been replaced."

See the chart on page 197 for an overview of all infinitive forms.

Ancō rēgnante, vir quīdam, nōmine Lucumō, habitābat 9
Tarquiniīs, quae urbs Etrūsca erat. Pater eius erat Dē- 10
marātus, profugus Corinthius. Lucumō in mātrimōnium 11
Tanaquīlem, mulierem nōbilem, dūxerat. Etrūscī sper- 12
nēbant Lucomōnem, exulis fīlium. Tanaquil, quae ferre in- 13
dignitātem nōn poterat, cōnsilium migrandī Rōmam cēpit. 14
Facile coniugī persuādet. Dum iter faciunt, aquila dīcitur 15
pilleum ab capite Lucumōnis abstulisse et rūrsus reposu- 16
isse. Laeta Tanaquil accēpit id augurium potentiae 17
futūrae. Etrūscī enim caelestium prōdigiōrum perītī erant. 18

Postquam Rōmam vēnērunt, Lucumō nōmen L. Tar- 19
quinium Prīscum sibi sūmpsit. Ibi paulātim īnsignis factus 20
est dīvitiīs aliīsque rēbus. Postrēmō in amīcitiam rēgis re- 21
ceptus tūtor līberōrum rēgis testāmentō īnstitūtus est. An- 22
cus annōs quattuor et vīgintī rēgnāvit. 23 617 B.C.

Fīō: An Irregular Verb

The verb **fīō, fierī** (*irreg.*), **factus sum** has several meanings: "to be
made," "to be done," "to become," and "to happen." It serves as the passive of the verb **faciō, facere** (3), **fēcī, factum**, "to make," "to do." Latin
does not use passive forms of **faciō** in the present, imperfect, or future
tenses (the tenses formed from the present stem), but uses forms of **fīō**
instead, as in the following sentence:

Labor ā servīs **fit.**
*The work **is being done** by the slaves.*

The verb **fīō** can also mean "to happen," as in the following:

Quid **fīet?**
*What **will happen**?*

In the perfect passive, pluperfect passive, and future perfect passive, the forms of **fīō** and **faciō** are identical, and they can mean "to be
made," "to be done," "to become," or "to happen," e.g.:

Ibi paulātim īnsignis **factus est.** . . . . (above: 20–21)
*There he gradually **became** well-known. . . .*

Use the charts on pages 194 and 196 to review the forms of **fīō**.

1   *adultus, -a, -um, grown, mature, adult.
2   rēx: *predicate nominative*; translate after creārī.
    Is prīmus palam: "He was the first openly to . . . . " (literally, "He, the
      first, openly. . . ."). Such uses of prīmus are best translated by "X was
      the first to Y."
    *palam (*adv.*), openly.
    *memorō (1), to remind, mention, bring up.
3   *officium, -ī (*n.*), favor, service, duty, obligation.
    *prīvātus, -a, -um, private, personal.
    *benignitās, benignitātis (*f.*), kindness, good deeds.
    in: "toward."

6   circus, -ī (*m.*), circle, racetrack, circus (stadium for chariot racing).
    The Circus Maximus was the oldest racetrack in Rome, allegedly built
      by Tarquinius Priscus.
    dēsignō (1), to mark out, choose, designate.
7   sollemnis, -is, -e, annual, religious, solemn.

9   *opus, operis (*n.*), work, deed; (*pl.*) public works.
10 *quiētus, -a, -um, quiet, at rest, idle, inactive.
    lapideus, -a, -um, made of stone.
11 cingō, cingere (3), cīnxī, cīnctum, to surround.
    *circā (*prep. + acc.*), around, near.
    forum: i.e., the original forum at the foot of the Capitoline and Palatine
      hills, later referred to as the Forum Romanum. The earliest settle-
      ments in Rome were on the Palatine and Capitoline hills, which offered
      some protection from attack; the lower ground was used for such pur-
      poses as markets and cemeteries.
    convallis, convallis (*f.*), valley.
12 *cloāca, -ae (*f.*), sewer, drain.
    *siccō (1), to dry out, drain.
    fundāmentum, -ī (*n.*), foundation.
    aedēs, aedis (*f.*), temple.
    Iuppiter, Iovis (*m.*), Jupiter (king of the gods).
    Capitōlium, -ī (*n.*), Capitol (one of the two peaks on the Capitoline Hill;
      the other is called the arx or Citadel).
    iēcit: "laid."

9. Tarquinius Priscus

Iam fīliī Ancī prope adultī erant. Sed Tarquinius ipse 1 616 B.C.
rēx creārī cupiēbat. Is prīmus palam rēgnum petiit, memo- 2
rāns officia prīvāta ac pūblica et benignitātem in omnēs. 3
Magnō cōnsēnsū populus Rōmānus eum rēgnāre iussit. 4

Tarquinius, Latīnīs bellō victīs, lūdōs magnificōs fēcit. 5
Tum prīmum locus circō, quī Maximus dīcitur, dēsignātus 6
est. Lūdī sollemnēs mānsērunt, Rōmānī aut Magnī appel- 7
lātī. 8

Magna quoque opera ā rēge incepta sunt, ut populus nōn 9
quiētior* in pāce quam in bellō esset. Mūrō lapideō urbem 10
cingere parāvit, et loca circā forum aliāsque convallēs 11
cloācīs siccāvit. Fundāmenta aedis Iovis in Capitōliō iēcit. 12

*nōn quiētior: *litotes*, a rhetorical figure by which an affirmative is expressed by the negation of its opposite: "not more idle" = "as energetic."

Perfect Passive Participles

The fourth principal part of the verb (the *supine*) is frequently met as
an adjective with 1st and 2nd declension endings. When so used it is
called a *perfect passive participle* and may be translated in a variety of
ways, e.g.:

Lūdī solemnēs mānsērunt, Rōmānī aut Magnī **appellātī**. (above: 7–8)
The annual games continued, **called** *the "Roman" or "Great"*
(games).
. . . , **which were called** *the "Roman" or "Great" (games).*

Tarquinius Prīscus, ā populō **iussus**, rēgnāre incēpit.
Tarquinius Priscus began to rule **after/when/because he had been**
ordered *by the people.*
Tarquinius Priscus, **who had been ordered** *by the people, began to*
rule.

Notice that the action shown by the perfect passive participle is thought
of as having been completed *prior to* the action of the main verb in the
sentence. Thus, in the second example above Tarquinius was ordered
by the people *before* he began to rule.

13   *rēgia, -ae (*f.*), royal palace.
14   Servius Tullius, -ī (*m.*), Servius Tullius (the sixth king of Rome).
15   *cōnspectus, -ūs (*m.*), sight, view.
     restinguō, restinguere (3), restīnxī, restīnctum, to extinguish.
       ad restinguendam flammam: "to exstinguish the flames," *gerundive*
         (see the grammar note on page 59).
18   sēcrētum, -ī (*n.*), secret, isolation.
     in sēcrētum: "aside," "apart."
19   *humilis, -is, -e, humble, low.
     lūmen, lūminis (*n.*), light, torch.
     profectō (*adv.*), in fact, indeed.
     *portendō, portendere (3), portendī, portentum, to predict, portend,
       foretell.
20   *aliquandō (*adv.*), sometime, someday.
     *praesidium, -ī (*n.*), protection, defense, assistance, help.
       eum . . . nōbīs praesidiō futūrum esse: "that he will be our defense,"
         (literally) "that he will be a means of defense with reference to us."
         This use of two datives, often with the verb esse, is called the *double*
         dative (see the grammar notes on pages 77 and 110–111).
            futūrum esse: "is about to be/will be," *future active infinitive* (see
             the grammar note on page 37).
21   *līberālis, -is, -e, worthy of a free man, liberal.
     artibus līberālibus: "in the skills suitable for a free man," *ablative* with
       ērudiendus est.
     ērudiō, ērudīre (4), ērudīvī, ērudītum, to educate, teach.
       ērudiendus est: "he must be educated," *passive periphrastic* (see the
        grammar note on page 60).
22   vērē (*adv.*), really, truly.

Present Active Participles

The letters **-nt-** added to the present stem of a verb and followed by 3rd declension case endings make the *present active participle*, e.g., **dormientis** (*gen. sing.*). The nominative singular has **-ns** added to the verb stem, e.g., **dormiēns**. Like perfect passive participles, present active participles can be translated in several ways, e.g.:

> Caput puerī **dormientis** ārsit. (opposite: 13–15)
> *The head of a **sleeping** boy burst into flames.*
> *The head of a boy **who was sleeping** burst into flames.*
> *The boy's head burst into flames **while/as he was sleeping**.*

Use the charts on pages 182 and 197 to review the formation of present active participles. Notice that the present participle shows an action that is going on *at the same time* as the action of the main verb (not necessarily in present time).

Eō ferē tempore in rēgiā prōdigium mīrābile fuit. Caput 13
puerī dormientis, cui Servius Tullius fuit nōmen, multōrum 14
in cōnspectū ārsit. Servī, quī aquam ad restinguendam 15
flammam ferēbant, ab rēgīnā retentī sunt. Mox cum puer ē 16
somnō excitātus esset, flamma abiit. Tum, abductō in 17
sēcrētum virō, Tanaquil, "Vidēsne tū hunc puerum," inquit, 18
"quem tam humilī cultū ēducāmus? Lūmen profectō por- 19
tendit eum aliquandō nōbīs praesidiō futūrum esse. 20
Proinde artibus līberālibus ērudiendus est." Ingenium iu- 21
venis vērē rēgium erat. Tarquinius igitur eī fīliam suam 22
dēspondit. 23

Future Active Participles

The letters **-ūrus, -a, -um** added to the supine stem of a verb make the
future active participle. Future participles show an action that takes
place *after* the action of the main verb. The future active participle can
often be translated "about to . . . ," "going to . . . ," or "intending to . . . ,"
and the translation may be introduced by words such as *since* or *who,*
e.g.:

Tarquinius, rēgnum sibi **obtentūrus**, officia et benignitātem in omnēs memorābat. (based on 9:1–3)
*Tarquinius, **who intended to obtain** the kingship for himself, kept
pointing out his services and kindness toward everyone.*

The following example shows the future active participle used with
esse to form the *future active infinitive* (here in indirect statement):

Lūmen profectō portendit eum aliquandō nōbīs praesidiō **futūrum
esse.** (above: 19–20)
*. . . that he **is about to be/will be**. . . .*

24 *etsī (conj.), although.
    peregrīnus, -ī (m.), foreigner.
25 Rōmae: "at Rome," locative case (see the grammar note on pages 52–53).
    servō: some thought that the boy (9:14) was the son of a slave-woman.
26 *pateō, patēre (2), patuī, to be open, be available, be attainable.
28 *facinus, facinoris (n.), deed, act, crime, evil deed.
    speciē: = per speciem (see 2:9), "on the pretext," "under a false appear-
      ance" (+ gen.).
29 *appāritor, appāritōris (m.), attendant, servant.
30 in vicem: "in turn."
31 ēlātam: from efferō, to lift, raise.
    secūris, secūris (f.), axe.
32 *dēiciō, dēicere (3), dēiēcī, dēiectum, to throw down, bring down.
    forās (adv.), outside, out of doors.
33 moribundus, -a, -um, dying.
34 *comprehendo, comprehendere (3), comprehendī, comprehēnsum, to catch,
      seize, arrest.

38 *aliēnus, -a, -um, belonging to another, alien, foreign.
39 ērigō, ērigere (3), ērēxī, ērēctum, to raise.
    sē ērigere, to arise, stand up.
    sequere: imperative of sequor (see the grammar note below).
    dīvīnus, -a, -um, divine.
40 *perturbō (1), to disturb, upset, confuse.
42 subitus, -a, -um, sudden.
    fingō, fingere (3), fīnxī, fictum, to shape, conceive, invent.

Imperative

The imperative mood indicates a command, e.g.:

Ērige tē. . . !   Arise . . . ! (opposite: 39)

The singular imperative is formed by dropping the final -re from the
2nd principal part (the infinitive) of a verb. The plural imperative is
formed by adding -te to the singular form, except in the 3rd conjugation,
where the final -e of the singular imperative changes to -i- before the
letters -te are added, e.g.:

	Infinitive	Sing. Imperative	Pl. Imperative
1st	rēgnāre	rēgnā	rēgnāte
2nd	iubēre	iubē	iubēte
3rd	relinquere	relinque	relinquite
3rd -iō	excipere	excipe	excipite
4th	dormīre	dormī	dormīte

You will meet forms of deponent verbs that look exactly like present
active infinitives, e.g., sequere (opposite: 43). These are singular im-
peratives. The plural is sequiminī.

Etsī Ancī fīliī duo anteā īrātī fuerant quod peregrīnus 24
Rōmae rēgnābat, tum maior erat indignātiō, quoniam servō 25
iam rēgnum patēre vidēbātur. Rēgem igitur interficere 26
rēgnumque occupāre cōnstituērunt. Ex pāstōribus duo ferō- 27
cissimī ad facinus dēlēctī in vestibulō rēgiae speciē rixae in 28
sē omnēs appāritōrēs rēgiōs convertērunt. Inde vocātī ad 29
rēgem dīcere in vicem iussī sunt. Ūnus rem expōnit. Dum 30
intentus in eum sē rēx tōtus āvertit, alter ēlātam secūrim in 31
caput rēgis dēiēcit; relictō in vulnere tēlō, ambō forās 32
fugiunt. Tarquinium moribundum appāritōrēs excipiunt; il- 33
lōs fugientēs līctōrēs comprehendunt. 34   579 B.C.

Magnus sequitur populī tumultus, inter quem Tanaquil 35
claudī rēgiam iubet. Serviō inde celeriter ad sē vocātō, aux- 36
ilium ōrāvit. "Tuum est rēgnum," inquit, "Servī, sī vir es, 37
nōn eōrum quī aliēnīs manibus pessimum facinus fēcērunt. 38
Ērige tē deōsque ducēs sequere, quī dīvinā flammā hoc ca- 39
put clārum futūrum esse portendērunt. Nōlī perturbārī 40
quod peregrīnus es. Etiam nōs peregrīnī rēgnāvimus. Sī 41
propter subitam rem cōnsilia fingere nōn potes, mea tamen 42
cōnsilia sequere." 43

Negative Commands

A *negative command* or *prohibition* may be expressed with **nōlī** (sing.)
or **nōlīte** (pl.) plus an infinitive:

    Nōlī perturbārī . . . !   *Don't be upset . . . !* (above: 40)

Vocative Case

The *vocative case* will be found when someone addresses a person di-
rectly. For most nouns, the vocative is the same as the nominative. In
the 2nd declension, however, there are special forms. A noun ending in
-us has its vocative singular in **-e**, and one ending in **-ius** has its vocative singular in **-ī**, e.g.:

Nominative	*Vocative*
servus	**serve**
Ancus	**Ance**
fīlius	**fīlī**
Servius	**Servī** (above: 37)

The word **meus** also has its vocative in **-ī**, e.g.: **mī fīlī**, "my son."

47 *interim (*adv.*), meanwhile.
48 *rēs pūblica, reī pūblicae (*f.*), state, government.
    *administrō (1), to manage, direct, administer.
49 *aliquot (*indeclinable adj.*), several, some, a few.
50 dēmum (*adv.*), finally.
51 prīmus: see note on 9:2 **Is prīmus palam.**
    *iniussū (+ *gen.*), without an order (from).
        iniussū populī: i.e., without being elected by the people.
    *voluntās, voluntātis (*f.*), wish, desire, goodwill.

Cum Clauses

The paragraph on page 41 contains three clauses introduced by **cum.**
Review the grammar notes on pages 2 and 5, and then reread the paragraph, paying particular attention to the **cum** clauses. What type is each one?

Etruscan bronze figurine
of a running girl

Cum iam clāmor multitūdinis vix sustinērī posset, 44
Tanaquil ex superiōre parte rēgiae populum ita allocūta est: 45
"Cum vulnus rēgis grave sit, iam tamen ad sē redit; brevī 46
tempore rēgem ipsum vidēbitis.   Interim vult Servium 47
Tullium rem pūblicam administrāre." Itaque Servius per 48
aliquot diēs, cum Tarquinius iam mortuus esset, suās opēs 49
firmāvit. Tum dēmum mors rēgis nūntiāta est. Servius, 50
praesidiō firmō mūnītus, prīmus iniussū populī voluntāte 51
patrum* rēgnāvit. 52

*iniussū populī voluntāte patrum: an example of *asyndeton* or lack of a
     connective such as **sed**: "without an order from the people (but) with
     the goodwill of the senate." What is the effect of the use of this
     rhetorical device here?

Ablative of Time When or within Which

A word or phrase in the *ablative case* may tell the *time when* or *within which* something happens, e.g.:

> . . . **brevī tempore** rēgem ipsum vidēbitis. (above: 46–47)
> . . . *in a short time you will see the king himself.*

Contrast the accusative case, which may tell how long something lasts (*accusative of duration of time*; see the grammar note on page 3).

1 *cēnsus, -ūs (*m.*), census (register of citizens according to wealth).
 *classis, classis (*f.*), fleet, army; (*here*) class.
2 prō: "on the basis of."
3 *tribuō, tribuere (3), tribuī, tribūtum, to assign, distribute.
  The wealthiest citizens were required to serve in the cavalry, those of
   moderate means in the heavily-armed infantry, and the very poorest
   were exempt from military service.
  ad: "for (the purpose of accommodating) . . . " (cf. ad supplicium, 3:18).
4 Quirīnālis, -is, -e, Quirinal (Hill, located to the north of the Forum).
  Viminālis, -is, -e, Viminal (Hill, located to the northeast of the Forum).
5 *fānum, -ī (*n.*), shrine, temple.
  Diāna, -ae (*f.*), Diana (goddess of the moon, hunting, childbirth, and
   virginity).
6 Ephesius, -a, -um, of Ephesus (a city in southwest Asia Minor).
  commūniter (*adv.*), in common.
8 Asiāticus, -a, -um, Asian, of Asia.
10 cōnfessiō, cōnfessiōnis (*f.*), acknowledgment.
11 totiēns (*adv.*), so many times.
  *certō (1), to contend, compete, fight, struggle.
   certātum erat: "it had been struggled," "there had been a struggle," *im-
    personal passive* (see the grammar note on pages 76–77).

12 Lūcius Tarquiniuis, -ī (*m.*), Lucius Tarquinius (son of Tarquinius Priscus;
   to become the sixth king of Rome with the cognōmen Superbus).
  interdum (*adv.*), occasionally, sometimes.
  *queror, querī (3), questus sum, to complain.
14 *virītim (*adv.*), separately, to individuals.

17 Arrūns, Arruntis (*m.*), Arruns Tarquinius (brother of Lucius Tarquinius).
20 *cupidus, -a, -um (+ *gen.*), desirous of, eager for.
  Tullia, -ae (*f.*), Tullia (daughter of Servius Tullius; he had two daughters
   with the same name).
  *item (*adv.*), likewise, in the same way.
21 similitūdō, similitūdinis (*f.*), likeness, similarity.
22 Tulliam: this refers to the younger daughter, wife of Arruns Tarquinius
   and then wife of Lucius Tarquinius; see the charts on pages 21 and 57.
  *contrahō, contrahere (3), contrāxī, contractum, to draw together.
23 *continuus, -a, -um, continuous, successive.
  *caedēs, caedis (*f.*), slaughter, murder.
  vacuus, -a, -um, empty.
   vacuās . . . fēcissent: i.e., Lucius Tarquinius and the ambitious Tullia
    both killed their spouses, in quick succession.
24 nūptiae, -ārum (*f. pl.*), marriage.

Ablative of Means

A word or phrase in the *ablative case* is often used with *active* or *passive* verbs to tell *by what means* the action is carried out, e.g.:
   . . . gladiō eam interfēcit. (7:45)
   . . . *killed her* **with his sword**.

10. Servius Tullius

Servius prīmum cēnsum īnstituit et populum in classēs   1   578 B.C.
prō opibus discrīpsit. Ex cēnsū posteā officia bellī pācisque   2
tribūta sunt. Ad multitūdinem crēscentem duo collēs,   3
Quirīnālis Vīminālisque, ad urbem additī sunt. Imperium   4
quoque hōc cōnsiliō auctum est. Fānum erat nōbile Diānae   5
Ephesiae, quod commūniter ā cīvitātibus Asiae factum esse   6
dīcēbātur. Servius per prīncipēs Latīnōrum, eō cōnsēnsū   7
cīvitātum Asiāticārum vehementer laudātō, tandem populīs   8
Latīnīs persuāsit ut Rōmae cum populō Rōmānō fānum   9
Diānae facerent. Ea erat cōnfessiō caput rērum Rōmam   10
esse, dē quō totiēns certātum erat.   11

Lūcius Tarquinius, Prīscī fīlius, interdum querēbātur   12
quod Servius iniussū populī rēgnāret. Servius igitur agrum   13
prius captum ex hostibus virītim dīvīsit; hōc modō volun-   14
tātem plēbis conciliāvit. Populus deinde maximō cōnsēnsū   15
eum rēgnāre iussit.   16

Rēx duās fīliās Lūciō atque Arruntī Tarquiniīs, Prīscī   17
fīliīs, in mātrimōnium dederat. Mōrēs hōrum disparēs er-   18
ant. Nam Arrūns Tarquinius mītis erat, L. Tarquinius   19
ferōx et cupidus rēgnī. Duae Tulliae item disparēs erant.   20
Forte Arrūns ferōcem in mātrimōnium dūxerat. Similitūdō   21
celeriter L. Tarquinium et ferōcem Tulliam contrahit. Cum   22
prope continuīs caedibus domōs vacuās fēcissent, iunguntur   23
nūptiīs. Paulātim inde mulier coniugem ad caedem Servī   24
excitat. Itaque Tarquinius prius omnibus rēbus cīvēs et   25
maximē patrēs conciliāvit.   26

Ablative of Personal Agent

Ā or **ab** with a word or phrase in the *ablative case* is often used with
passive verbs to tell *by whom* the action is carried out, e.g.:

Fānum erat . . . quod commūniter **ā cīvitātibus** Asiae factum esse
    dīcēbātur. (above: 5–7)
*There was a shrine . . . which was said to have been built in com-
mon* **by (the people of) the city-states** *of Asia Minor.*

27   **tempus agendī**: "the time for action," literally "the time of acting," *gerund*
        (see the grammar note on page 58).
      stīpō (1), to crowd, crowd around, accompany.
28   **armātī, -ōrum** (*m. pl.*), armed men.
29   **praecō, praecōnis** (*m.*), herald, crier.
30   **quod . . . occupāvisset**: in **quod** *causal clauses* the *subjunctive* is used, as
        here, when the reason given is being quoted, as if in indirect state-
        ment, as that of someone other than the narrator (here as that of
        Lucius Tarquinius).
31   *****muliebris, -is, -e**, of a woman, womanly.
32   *****populāris, -is, -e**, popular, pleasing to the people.
      dē agrō plēbī dīvīsō, dē cēnsū īnstitūtō: "about the division of land to the
        plebs, about the . . ."; Latin uses the *perfect passive participle in
        agreement with a noun* where in English we would use an abstract
        noun followed by a prepositional phrase. Compare the title of Livy's
        history, *Ab urbe condita* (literally, *From the City Having Been
        Founded*, better English, *From the Foundation of the City*).
33   **interveniō, intervenīre** (4), **intervēnī, interventum**, to come along,
        intrude.
34   **tibi vīs**: **velle** + *reflexive pronoun* = to want for oneself, have as one's
        purpose, aim at.
      Tarquinī: the accent in this vocative form falls on the next to the last
        syllable.
      *****audācia, -ae** (*f.*), boldness, audacity.
35   *****vīvus, -a, -um**, alive, living.
      mē vīvō: "with me (being) alive," *ablative absolute* (without a participle
        since there is no present participle of the verb **esse**).

37   *****hērēs, hērēdis** (*m.*), heir.
      medium . . . Servium: "the middle of Servius," i.e., by the waist.
38   **gradus, -ūs** (*m.*), step, stair.
40   *****carpentum, -ī** (*n.*), two-wheeled carriage.
      *****invehō, invehere** (3), **invexī, invectum**, to carry into; (*passive*) to ride into.
41   **ēvocō** (1), to call out, summon.
      domum: "to home," "home" (see the grammar note on pages 52–53).
42   **dīcitur . . . invēnisse**: "she is said to have found."
43   **scelerātus, -a, -um**, wicked.

Historical Present

Notice that the verbs in three sentences of the second paragraph on
page 45 are in the present tense (**arripit, dēicit, redit, fugiunt,** and **interficitur**). The verbs in the first paragraph, and in the rest of the second, are in the past tense. In order to make the action more vivid for
the reader, the writer switched to the present tense at the crucial mo-
ment when Tarquinius made his move against Servius. This is called
the *historical present*. The present tense may be kept in English translation.

Postrēmō, ubi iam tempus agendī vīsum est, stīpātus 27
armātīs in forum irrūpit. Inde in rēgiā sēde prō Cūriā 28
sedēns patrēs in Cūriam per praecōnem ad rēgem Tar- 29
quinium vocārī iussit. Ibi incūsābat rēgem, quod rēgnum 30
muliebrī dōnō occupāvisset; querēbātur item dē cōnsiliīs 31
populāribus, dē agrō plēbī dīvīsō, dē cēnsū īnstitūtō. Dum 32
loquitur, Servius intervēnit et ā vestibulō Cūriae magnā 33
vōce, "Quid tibi vīs," inquit, "Tarquinī? Quā audāciā tū, mē 34
vīvō, vocāre patrēs aut in sēde meā cōnsīdere ausus es?" 35

Tarquinius ferōciter respondit sē sēdem patris suī 36
tenēre, sē rēgnī hērēdem esse. Tum medium arripit 37
Servium, ēlātumque ē Cūriā per gradūs dēicit; inde in 38
Cūriam redit. Appāritōrēs rēgis fugiunt. Rēx ipse ā servīs 39
Tarquiniī interficitur. Tullia carpentō in forum invecta con- 40
iugem ēvocāvit rēgemque prīma appellāvit. Dum domum 41
redit, dīcitur patrem in viā iacentem invēnisse et per corpus 42
carpentum ēgisse. Hic locus posteā "scelerātus" vocātus est. 43
Servius Tullius rēgnāvit annōs quattuor et quadrāgintā. 44   535 B.C.

Adverbs

Words formed from adjectives and ending in **-ē** or **-iter** are *adverbs*. The
ending **-ē** is found on 1st and 2nd declension adjectives, and the ending
-iter on 3rd, e.g.:

Adjectives	*Adverbs*
1st and 2nd Declension:	
vērus, -a, -um, *true*	**vērē**, *truly*
pulcher, pulchra,	
pulchrum, *beautiful*	**pulchrē**, *beautifully*
3rd Declension:	
fortis, -is, -e, *brave*	**fortiter**, *bravely*
ferōx, ferōcis, *savage*	**ferōciter**, *savagely*

Third declension adjectives ending in **-ns**, such as **prūdēns, prūdentis**, "wise," add **-er** to the stem, e.g., **prūdenter**, *wisely*.

1 *factum, -ī (*n.*), deed.
2 Superbus, -ī (*m.*), the Proud.
3 circumsaepiō, circumsaepīre (4), circumsaepsī, circumsaeptum, to fence in, surround.
4 capitālis, -is, -e, capital (involving the death sentence).
5 *exilium, -ī (*n.*), exile.
6 *bona, bonōrum (*n. pl.*), goods, possessions.
 *spoliō (1), to strip, rob, deprive someone (*acc.*) of something (*abl.*).
8 domesticus, -a, -um, of one's own household, individual, private.
10 Octāvius Mamilius Tusculānus, -ī (*m.*), Octavius Mamilius Tusculanus (from Tusculum) (Tarquin's son-in-law).

13 iniūstus, -a, -um, unjust.
14 prāvus, -a, -um, bad, incompetent.
15 Volscī, -ōrum (*m. pl.*), the Volscians (a people to the south of Rome).
16 Gabiī, -ōrum (*m. pl.*), Gabii (a town to the south of Rome in Latium).
17 *fraus, fraudis (*f.*), deception, trickery.
 Sex. Tarquinius, -ī (*m.*), Sextus Tarquinius (the youngest son of Tarquinius Superbus).

> Sextus, the king's youngest son, went to Gabii and said that he could not endure his father's cruelty any longer and would help the people of Gabii in their war against Rome. After winning the people's trust, he executed their leaders on trumped-up charges and then handed the city over to his father.

Comparative and Superlative Adverbs

Adverbs form their *comparative degree* by adding **-ius** to the stem, e.g.:

 superbius *more arrogantly, quite arrogantly, rather arrogantly*
 ferōcius *more savagely, quite savagely, rather savagely*

This is identical to the *neuter singular nominative or accusative comparative adjective.* For the forms, review the grammar note on page 23.

 The *superlative adverb* may be recognized by the ending -ē attached to the stem of the superlative adjective (review the grammar note on page 31), e.g.:

 fortissimē *very bravely, most bravely*
 miserrimē *very wretchedly, most wretchedly*
 facillimē *very easily, most easily*

11. Tarquinius Superbus

Inde L. Tarquinius rēgnāre coepit, cui propter facta 1   534 B.C.
cognōmen Superbus datum est. Prīncipēs patrum, quī 2
Servium dīlēxerant, interfēcit. Suum corpus armātīs cir- 3
cumsaepsit. Iūdicia capitālium rērum sine cōnsiliīs per sē 4
sōlus exercēbat. Ita poterat occīdere, in exilium agere, 5
bonīs spoliāre omnēs quōs cupiēbat. Etsī rēgēs superiōrēs 6
senātum dē omnibus rēbus cōnsulere solitī erant, Tar- 7
quinius domesticīs cōnsiliīs rem pūblicam administrāvit. 8
Bellum, pācem, foedera, societātēs* per sē ipse fēcit. La- 9
tīnōrum gentem sibi maximē conciliābat. Octāviō Mamiliō 10
Tusculānō—is longē nōbilissimus Latīnōrum erat—fīliam in 11
mātrimōnium dat. 12

Tarquinius, quamquam iniūstus in pāce rēx fuit, ducem 13
bellī tamen nōn prāvum** sē praebuit. Is prīmus cum 14
Volscīs bellum gessit, et magnam praedam cēpit. In aliō 15
bellō, cum Gabiōs, vīcīnam urbem, vī capere nōn posset, 16
fraude ac dolō per fīlium suum Sex. Tarquinium aggressus 17
est. 18

*Notice the four nouns **Bellum, pācem, foedera, societātēs** strung together without any conjunctions such as **et** (*asyndeton*; see note on
   page 41).
The phrase **nōn prāvum is an example of *litotes* (see note on page 35):
   "not incompetent" = "competent."

Reconstruction of the temple on the Capitoline Hill as it was built by
Tarquinius Superbus, who completed a plan drawn up by his father
Tarquinius Priscus (see 9:12 and 11:20). The temple was dedicated to
Jupiter Optimus Maximus, Juno, and Minerva.

19 *recipiō, recipere (3), recēpī, receptum, to receive, accept, seize.
20 Tarpeius, -a, -um, Tarpeian (adjective derived from the name of a young
woman, Tarpeia, who was executed by being hurled from the
Capitoline Hill, which as a result was also called the Tarpeian Hill).
21 dēdicō (1), to dedicate, consecrate.
22 voveō, vovēre (2), vōvī, vōtum, to vow, pledge (to a god).
faber, fabrī (m.), craftsman.
operārius, -ī (m.), workman, laborer.
24 *trādūcō, trādūcere (3), trādūxī, trāductum, to bring across, transfer.
forus, -ī (m.), block of seats, bleachers.
26 colōnus, -ī (m.), settler, farmer.
colōnī: "as settlers."
Signia, -ae (f.), Signia (a city in Latium).
Circeiī, -ōrum (m. pl.), Circeii (a city at the southern edge of Latium).
quī . . . essent: "to serve as protection for the city," relative clause of purpose (see the grammar note on page 13).
The early Romans, in an attempt to secure their borders against hostile neighbors, often founded new towns or planted colonies of
Roman citizens in cities they conquered. Both Signia and Circeii
were intended to block any northern expansion by the Volscians.

28 portentum, -ī (n.), portent, sign from the gods.
anguis, anguis (m.), snake.
29 columna, -ae (f.), column, pillar.
ligneus, -a, -um, wooden.
*ēlābor, ēlābī (3), ēlāpsus sum, to slip down, slide down, escape.
fuga, -ae (f.), flight.
31 Titus, -ī (m.), Titus Tarquinius (son of Tarquinius Superbus).
Arrūns, Arruntis (m.), Arruns Tarquinius (second son of Tarquinius
Superbus).
Delphī, -ōrum (m. pl.), Delphi (a city in central Greece, site of a famous
oracle of Apollo).
32 *ōrāculum, -ī (n.), oracle (a prediction of future events given by a god; the
place where such predictions are given).
33 L. Iūnius Brūtus, -ī (m.), Lucius Junius Brutus (nephew of Tarquinius
Superbus).
Tarquinia, -ae (f.), Tarquinia (mother of L. Junius Brutus).
35 in quibus: "among whom."
36 cōnsultō (adv.), deliberately.
37 stultitia, -ae (f.), stupidity.
*patior, patī (3), passus sum, to suffer, endure, allow.
38 cognōmen Brūtī: note that brutus, -a, -um means both "brutish" (i.e., like
animals) and "lacking intelligence."
Tarquiniī: i.e., the sons of Tarquinius, namely Titus and Arruns.
39 lūdibrium, -ī (n.), derision, laughing-stock, object of scorn, plaything.
40 Apollō, Apollinis (m.), Apollo (god whose oracle was at Delphi).
inclūdō, inclūdere (3), inclūsī, inclūsum, to enclose.
41 corneus, -a, -um, made of cornel wood.
*tamquam (conj.), as, just as, like.
effigiēs, -ēī (f.), representation, likeness, image.

Gabiīs receptīs, Tarquinius ad negōtia urbāna animum 19
convertit. Prīmum templum in monte Tarpeiō aedificāre tō- 20
tumque montem Iovī dēdicāre cōnstituit. Hoc templum pa- 21
ter iam anteā vōverat. Ad hoc opus fabrīs Etrūscīs et ope- 22
rāriīs ex plēbe Rōmānā ūsus est. Plēbs etiam ad alia opera 23
trāducta forōs in Circō fēcit cloācamque maximam sub ter- 24
ram ēgit, quam etiam nunc vidēmus. Multī quoque ex plēbe 25
colōnī Signiam Circeiōsque missī sunt quī praesidia urbī es- 26
sent. 27

Dum haec aguntur, portentum terribile vīsum est; an- 28
guis ex columnā ligneā ēlāpsus terrōrem fugamque in rēgiā 29
fēcit atque ipsīus rēgis pectus ānxiīs cūrīs implēvit. Itaque 30
Tarquinius fīliōs, Titum et Arruntem, Delphōs ad clārissi- 31
mum in terrīs ōrāculum mittere statuit. Comes eīs additus 32
est L. Iūnius Brūtus, ex Tarquiniā, sorōre rēgis, nātus. 33
Cognōmen eius hōc modō parātum erat; rēx eōs prīncipēs 34
cīvitātis quōs timēbat interficere solēbat, in quibus frātrem 35
Brūtī interfēcit. Hic, ut crūdēlitātem rēgis vītāret, cōnsultō 36
stultitiam imitātus bona sua rēgem spoliāre passus est 37
neque cognōmen Brūtī recūsāvit. Is tum igitur ab Tar- 38
quiniīs ductus est Delphōs, lūdibrium vērius quam comes. 39
Tulit tamen dōnum Apollinī aureum baculum inclūsum in 40
baculō corneō, tamquam effigiem ingeniī suī. 41

Perfect Participles of Deponent Verbs

Perfect participles of deponent verbs are *active* in meaning, unlike perfect participles of regular verbs, which are passive. Compare the following:

Anguis ex columnā ligneā **ēlāpsus** terrōrem fugamque in rēgiā
fēcit. . . . (above: 28–30)
A snake, **having slid** *down a wooden column, caused terror and
flight in the palace.* . . . (deponent verb)

Servius igitur agrum prius **captum** ex hostibus virītim dīvīsit.
(10:13–14)
Servius therefore divided the land **that had been** *previously* **captured** *from the enemy among individuals.* (regular verb)

In the second paragraph above, find and translate another sentence with a perfect participle of a deponent verb.

44   **esset ventūrum**: the *future active participle* used with a form of the verb **esse** makes an *active periphrastic* (compare the *passive periphrastic*, described in the grammar note on page 60); an *active periphrastic subjunctive* is often found in *indirect questions*, as here, where a *future indicative* would have occurred in the *direct question.*

45   **vestrum**: *genitive plural* of **vōs**; *partitive genitive* with the implied antecedent of **quī**, "(the one) of you who . . ."

46   *****ōsculor, ōsculārī** (1), **ōsculātus sum**, to kiss.
       contemnō, contemnere (3), **contempsī, contemptum**, to scorn.

47   **iūs mātris ōsculandae**: "the right of kissing their mother," *gerundive* (see the grammar note on page 59).
       Rōmae: "in/at Rome," *locative case* (see the grammar note on pages 52–53).
       *****sors, sortis** (f.), fate, chance, lot.
       *****permittō, permittere** (3), **permīsī, permissum** (+ *dat.*), to let go, permit, entrust something (*acc.*) to someone or something (*dat.*).
          iūs mātris ōsculandae . . . sortī permittunt: "entrust to lot the right o‌f kissing their mother"; the sons "drew straws" to see who would kiss their mother first.

48   **interpretor, interpretārī** (1), **interpretātus sum**, to interpret.

49   **scīlicet** (*particle*), as is apparent, evidently.
       commūnis, -is, -e, universal, common.

50   **mortālis, mortālis** (*m.*), mortal, human being.

Postquam iuvenēs Delphōs vēnērunt patrisque mandāta 42
cōnfēcērunt, statuērunt quaerere ex ōrāculō ad quem eōrum 43
rēgnum esset ventūrum. Vōx reddita est: "Imperium sum- 44
mum Rōmae habēbit quī vestrum prīmus, ō iuvenēs, 45
mātrem ōsculābitur." Tarquiniī, Brūtum contemnentēs, 46
ipsī inter sē iūs mātris ōsculandae Rōmae sortī permittunt. 47
Brūtus, quī aliō modō ōrāculum interpretātus erat, cecidit 48
terramque ōsculātus est, scīlicet quod ea commūnis māter 49
est omnium mortālium. Rediērunt inde iuvenēs Rōmam. 50

Delphi, with the ruins of the Temple of Apollo

1   **iam dūdum**: "for a long time already."
2   **aegrē ferre**, to take badly, resent.
     Sex. Tarquiniī: the youngest son of Tarquinius Superbus; see 11:17 and
     the note there.
3   **ut . . . statuerent**: "that they decided," *result clause* (see the grammar
     note on page 56).

5   **Tarquinius Collātīnus, -ī** (*m.*), Lucius Tarquinius Collatinus (nephew of
     Tarquinius Superbus and husband of Lucretia).
     sorōre . . . nātus: "born from the sister," *ablative of source* with **nātus**,
     perfect participle of the verb **nāscor**.
6   **contubernium, -ī** (*n.*), the sharing of a tent in the army, the status of be-
     ing messmates.
         in contuberniō iuvenum rēgiōrum . . . erat: "was a messmate of . . ."
     Ardea, -ae (*f.*), Ardea (a town to the south of Rome).
7   *****līber, lībera, līberum**, free, outspoken, unrestricted, unrestrained.
     ūnusquisque, ūnaquaeque, ūnumquodque, each one.
8   *****nurus, -ūs** (*f.*), daughter-in-law.
9   *****lūxus, -ūs** (*m.*), luxury, luxurious living, extravagance.
     *****dēprehendō, dēprehendere** (3), **dēprehendī, dēprehēnsum**, to get hold of,
     surprise, catch in the act.
     Collātia, -ae (*f.*), Collatia (a town in Latium).
10   **Lucrētia, -ae** (*f.*), Lucretia (wife of Collatinus).
     lanificium, -ī (*n.*), wool-spinning, weaving (a traditional occupation of a
     Roman housewife).
11   **offendō, offendere** (3), **offendī, offēnsum**, to strike against, find, en-
     counter.
     pudīcus, -a, -um, chase, virtuous.
     *****iūdicō** (1), to judge, proclaim, declare, think.
12   *****corrumpō, corrumpere** (3), **corrūpī, corruptum**, to break, corrupt, seduce.
     Ad quam corrumpendam: "To seduce her," *gerundive* (see the grammar
     note on page 59).
13   **propinquitās, propinquitātis** (*f.*), family relationship.
     Sextus Tarquinius was admitted to the house because he was a rela-
     tive.
14   **pudīcitia, -ae** (*f.*), chastity.
     *****expugnō** (1), to assault, storm, conquer.

Place Constructions

The names of cities, towns, and small islands and the words **domus** and
rūs will be found in the *accusative case without a preposition* to show
the *place to which* someone goes:

   Tanaquil . . . cōnsilium migrandī **Rōmam** cēpit. (8:13–14)
   Tanaquil . . . formed a plan of moving to Rome.

   Exercitūs **domōs** abductī sunt. (7:40)
   The armies were taken away to their homes.

12. Sex. Tarquinius and Lucretia

Paulō post Rōmānī, quī iam dūdum superbiam Tarquiniī   1   510 B.C.
rēgis atque fīliōrum aegrē ferēbant, ita scelere quōdam Sex.   2
Tarquiniī concitātī sunt ut rēgiam familiam in exilium   3
pellere statuerent.   4

Tarquinius Collātīnus, sorōre Tarquiniī Superbī nātus,   5
in contuberniō iuvenum rēgiōrum Ardeae erat; cum forte in   6
līberiōre convīviō coniugem suam ūnusquisque laudāret,   7
placuit experīrī. Itaque equīs Rōmam petunt. Rēgiās nurūs   8
in convīviō vel lūxū dēprehendunt. Et inde Collātiam   9
petunt. Lucrētiam, uxōrem Collātīnī, inter ancillās in lani-   10
ficiō offendunt; itaque ea pudīcissima iūdicātur. Ad quam   11
corrumpendam Sex. Tarquinius nocte Collātiam rediit et   12
iūre propinquitātis in domum Collātīnī vēnit et in cubicu-   13
lum Lucrētiae irrūpit, pudīcitiam expugnāvit.   14

Place Constructions (continued)

These words will be found in the *ablative case without a preposition* to show the *place from which* someone comes:

Rōmā ēgressus. . . . .
Having departed from Rome. . . . .

Domō exiēns. . . . .
Leaving home. . . . .

These words will be found in the *locative case without a preposition* to show the *place where* someone is:

Habitābat eō tempore **Curibus** Numa Pompilius. (6:7)
There lived at this time in Cures Numa Pompilius.

Domī manēns. . . . .
Remaining at home. . . . .

The *locative case* has the same endings as the genitive in the 1st and 2nd declensions in the singular. In the 3rd declension and in all plural words, it has the same endings as the dative or ablative.

When other words are used in place constructions, prepositions (**ad**, **ab**, **ex**, and **in**) are regularly used with the *accusative* and *ablative* cases.

15   **advocō** (1), to call, sumon, consult.
17   **cēterum** (*adv.*), for the rest, yet.
      īnsōns, īnsontis, innocent.
18   **testis, testis** (*m.*), witness.
      impūne (*adv.*), without punishment.
          impūne esse, to go unpunished.
      adulter, adulterī (*m.*), adulterer.
19   **fore**: = **futūrum esse**.
          haud . . . fore: *impersonal*, "that it will not go unpunished for the adul-
          terer" = "that the adulterer will be punished."
20   **pestifer, pestifera, pestiferum**, destructive, pernicious.
          pestiferum: take the *datives* **mihi sibique** with this adjective,
          "destructive for me and for himself."
21   **hinc** (*adv.*), from here.

22   **ōrdine**: "in turn."
      cōnsolor, cōnsolārī (1), **cōnsolātus sum**, to console.
      aegram animī: "the (woman who was) sick at heart."
23   **āvertendō**: "by diverting," *gerund* in the *ablative* (see the grammar note
          on page 58).
      noxa, -ae (*f.*), blame.
      ab coāctā: "from her who was forced."
      *****auctor, auctōris** (*m.*), originator, author, person responsible.
      dēlictum, -ī (*n.*), crime.
      *****mēns, mentis** (*f.*), mind.
          mentem . . . abesse: *indirect statement*, depending on the idea of saying
          implied in **cōnsolantur** (see the grammar note on page 98).
24   **peccō** (1), to sin.
25   **vīderitis**: *perfect subjunctive*, used to give a command (*jussive subjunc-
          tive*), "consider!" See the grammar note on page 28; the *perfect sub-
          junctive* may be used in the *second person* to express commands.
26   **peccātum, -ī** (*n.*), sin.
      absolvō, absolvere (3), **absolvī, absolūtum**, to absolve, release from (+
          abl.).
      peccātō . . . suppliciō: "from wrongdoing . . . from punishment," *ablative of*
          separation (see the grammar note on page 55).
      *****ūllus, -a, -um**, any.
27   **impudīcus, -a, -um**, unchaste, unfaithful.
      *****exemplum, -ī** (*n.*), example, precedent.
      culter, cultrī (*m.*), knife.
28   *****tegō, tegere** (3), **tēxī, tēctum**, to cover, hide.
      in: (*here*) "for."
      exitium, -ī (*n.*), destruction.
      *****coniūrō** (1), to take an oath together, plot.
          coniūrārunt: = **coniūrāvērunt**.
29   *****nex, necis** (*f.*), killing, murder, death.
      *****vindicō** (1), to get revenge, avenge.

Illa posterō diē advocātīs patre et coniuge rem hīs verbīs 15
exposuit: "Vēstīgia virī aliēnī, Collātīne, in lectō sunt tuō; 16
cēterum corpus est tantum violātum, animus īnsōns; mors 17
testis erit. Sed date dexterās fidemque haud impūne* adul- 18
terō fore. Sex. est Tarquinius, quī hostis prō hospite priōre 19
nocte vī armātus mihi sibique, sī vōs virī estis, pestiferum 20
hinc abstulit gaudium." 21

Dant ōrdine omnēs fidem; cōnsolantur aegram animī 22
āvertendō noxam ab coāctā in auctōrem dēlictī; mentem 23
peccāre, nōn corpus, et unde cōnsilium āfuerit, culpam 24
abesse. "Vōs," inquit, "vīderitis, quid illī dēbētur. Ego mē 25
etsī peccātō absolvō, suppliciō nōn līberō; nec ūlla deinde 26
impudīca Lucrētiae exemplō vīvet." Sē cultrō, quem veste 27
tēxerat, occīdit. Illī in exitium rēgum coniūrārunt eōrum- 28
que exiliō necem Lucrētiae vindicāvērunt. 29

*haud impūne: *litotes*: "not unpunished" = "punished."

Ablative of Separation

The *ablative case* (often without a preposition) is used with certain
verbs that mean "to rob of," "to deprive," and "to set free." This is called
the *ablative of separation*, e.g.:

Ita poterat . . . **bonīs** spoliāre omnēs quōs cupiēbat. (11:5–6)
*So he was able to deprive **of their property** all whom he wished.*

Ego mē etsī **peccātō** absolvō, **suppliciō** nōn līberō. (above: 25–26)
*I, although I absolve myself **of wrongdoing**, do not free myself **from**
punishment."*

2   *iūrō (1), to swear.
3   *quisquam, quicquam (quidquam), anyone, anything.
4   *castra, -ōrum (n. pl.), military camp.
6   execror, execrārī (1), execrātus sum, to curse.

7   nūntius, -ī (m.), messenger, message.
8   pergō, pergere (3), perrēxī, perrēctum, to go straight on to, proceed to.
9   *dīversus, -a, -um, different.
11 līberātor, līberātōris (m.), liberator.
12 exigō, exigere (3), exēgī, exāctum, to drive out.
13 Caere (indeclinable) (n.), Caere (a city in Etruria).
      Caere, quae urbs: for the antecedent contained within the relative
         clause, see the grammar note on page 30.
14 Gabiōs: see 11:16–18.
      ultor, ultōris (m.), avenger.

17 *ducentī, -ae, -a, two hundred.
      *dūrō (1), to last, endure.

Result Clauses

You have seen that subordinate clauses introduced by **ut** and having
their verbs in the subjunctive can express *purpose* (see the grammar
note on page 12) or *indirect commands* (see the grammar note on page
25). They can also express *result*, e.g.:

> Rōmānī . . . **ita** scelere quōdam Sex. Tarquiniī concitātī sunt **ut** rē-
>   giam familiam in exilium pellere **statuerent**. (12:1–4)
> *The Romans . . . were so aroused by a certain crime of Sextus Tar-*
>   *quinius **that they decided** to drive the royal family into exile.*

Result clauses are introduced by **ut** (affirmative) and **ut nōn**
(negative); compare purpose clauses and indirect commands that use **ut**
and **nē**.
   Result clauses are easy to identify since the presence of words such
as **ita**, **sīc**, "in such a way," "so," **tot**, "so many," **tālis**, "such," **tantus**, "so
great," or **adeō**, "so," in the main clause provides a clue that a result
clause may follow. Note the use of **ita** in the example above.

13. The Banishment of Tarquinius Superbus

Tum prīmum vērum ingenium Brūtī apertum est. Eō 1 510–
enim duce populus iūrāvit sē nec Tarquinium nec alium 2 509 B.C.
quemquam rēgnāre Rōmae passūrum esse. Brūtus inde in 3
castra profectus est, ubi exercitus Rōmānus Ardeam, caput 4
Rutulōrum, obsidēbat. Tulliam rēgīnam domō profugien- 5
tem omnēs virī mulierēsque execrātī sunt. 6

Ubi nūntiī hārum rērum in castra perlātī sunt, rēx Rō- 7
mam perrēxit. Brūtus adventum rēgis sēnsit flexitque 8
viam. Ita eōdem ferē tempore dīversīs itineribus Brūtus 9
Ardeam, Tarquinius Rōmam vēnērunt. Hic portās clausās 10
invēnit; Brūtum līberātōrem urbis laeta castra accēpērunt 11
exāctīque sunt līberī rēgis; duo patrem secūtī exulēs ad- 12
vēnērunt Caere, quae urbs Etrūsca erat; Sextus Tarquinius 13
Gabiōs, tamquam in suum rēgnum, profectus ab ultōribus 14
veterum iniūriārum quās ipse intulerat interfectus est. 15

L. Tarquinius Superbus rēgnāvit annōs quīnque et 16
vīgintī. Rēgnum Rōmae annōs ducentōs quadrāgintā dūrā- 17
verat. Duo cōnsulēs inde creātī sunt, L. Iūnius Brūtus et L. 18
Tarquinius Collātīnus. 19 509 B.C.

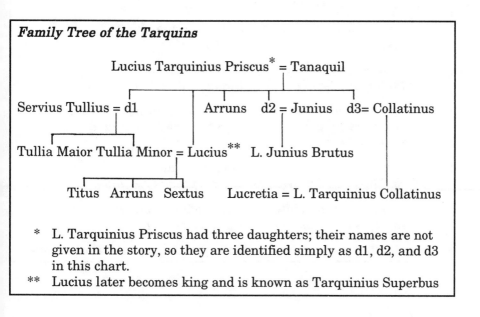

Family Tree of the Tarquins

Lucius Tarquinius Priscus* = Tanaquil

Servius Tullius = d1   Arruns   d2 = Junius   d3= Collatinus

Tullia Maior Tullia Minor = Lucius**   L. Junius Brutus

Titus Arruns Sextus   Lucretia = L. Tarquinius Collatinus

* L. Tarquinius Priscus had three daughters; their names are not given in the story, so they are identified simply as d1, d2, and d3 in this chart.
** Lucius later becomes king and is known as Tarquinius Superbus

Gerunds

A *gerund* is a *verbal noun*—that is, a noun formed from a verb. In the following sentences "swimming" and "running" are gerunds:

He likes swimming. He escaped by running.

The Latin gerund may be recognized by the letters **-nd-**, e.g.:

	Infinitive	*Gerund*
1	creāre	crea<u>nd</u>um
2	habēre	habe<u>nd</u>um
3	vincere	vince<u>nd</u>um
3 -iō	capere	capie<u>nd</u>um
4	impedīre	impedie<u>nd</u>um

Notice the **-ie-** before the **-ndum** ending in the 3rd -iō and 4th conjugations. Gerunds of deponent verbs are formed in the same way as those of regular verbs.

The gerund is declined as a 2nd declension neuter noun. It is used only in the singular. Gerunds will be found in various cases, like other nouns:

Tullus erat cupidus **pugnandī**. (genitive)
*Tullus was desirous **of fighting**.*

Hic locus est idōneus **pugnandō**. (dative)
*This place is suitable **for fighting**.*

Tarquinius in sēde rēgālī **cōnsīdendō** tumultum fēcit. (ablative)
*Tarquinius caused an uproar **by sitting** in the king's chair.*

Gerunds are not used in the nominative case. Instead, the infinitive is used as a verbal noun in the nominative, e.g.:

Expellere familiam Tarquiniōrum erat difficile.
***Expelling** the family of the Tarquinii was difficult.*

Gerunds are often used to express purpose, with the prepositions **ad** (+ *acc.*), "for the purpose of," and **causā** or **grātiā** (+ *a preceding gen.*), "for the sake of," e.g.:

Tarquinius Servium interfēcit **ad rēgnandum**.
*Tarquinius killed Servius **for the purpose of reigning**.*

Tarquinius Servium interfēcit **rēgnandī causā/grātiā**.
*Tarquinius killed Servius **for the sake of reigning**.*

Notice that the prepositions **causā** and **grātiā** come *after* the gerunds.

Gerundives

The *gerundive* may also be recognized by the letters **-nd-**, but it is a 1st and 2nd declension *adjective* rather than a 2nd declension noun, e.g.:

1	**creandus, -a, -um**	3 -iō	**capiendus, -a, -um**
2	**habendus, -a, -um**	4	**impediendus, -a, -um**
3	**vincendus, -a, -um**		

The gerundive is a *future passive verbal adjective* or *participle*, and you will always find it modifying a noun or pronoun. Latin usually uses a gerundive rather than a gerund when the gerund would have a direct object. For example, instead of the following:

Brutus rēgem expulit **ad iuvandum cīvitātem**.
[**iuvandum**, "helping": gerund used as the accusative object of the preposition **ad**, with **cīvitātem** its direct object]
Brutus drove out the king to help the city.

Latin usually uses a gerundive, e.g.:

Brūtus rēgem expulit **ad cīvitātem iuvandam**.
[**cīvitātem**: accusative object of the preposition **ad**, modified by the gerundive **iuvandam**]
Brutus drove out the king for the purpose of the city about to be helped.
Brutus drove out the king for the purpose of helping the city.
Brutus drove out the king to help the city.

Notice how the gerundive agrees with the noun that it modifies in gender, number, and case. The underlined endings highlight this.

Exercise 2

Read aloud and translate each sentence; then decide whether you are dealing with a gerund or a gerundive. If there is a gerundive, tell what noun it agrees with.

1. Tullus Hostilius pugnandō multum agrum cīvitātī addidit.
2. Fīliī Ancī Marcī pāstōrēs in rēgiam dūxērunt ad Tarquinium Priscum interficiendum.
3. Tanaquil Serviī adiuvandī grātiā dīxit rēgem vulnus habēre.
4. Servius erat cupidus rēgnandī.
5. Servius Tullius agrum captum dīvīsit ad plēbem conciliandam.
6. Tarquinius Superbus in forum irrūpit ad rēgem occīdendum.
7. Occīdit Tarquinius Servium Tullium rēgnī occupandī causā.
8. Tullia, carpentum per patris corpus agendō, ostendit sē esse cupidam rēgnandī.

9. Tarquinius Superbus fīliōs Delphōs mīsit ad portentum interpretandum.
10. Brūtus ad castra īvit rēgis expellendī grātiā.

Exercise 3
Form a gerund (genitive case) and gerundive from each verb:

	Gerund	**Gerundive**
Model: occupō, occupāre	occupandī	occupandus, -a, -um

1. flectō, flectere
2. aperiō, aperīre
3. dēligō, dēligere
4. vereor, verērī
5. profugiō, profugere
6. coniūrō, coniūrāre
7. pateō, patēre
8. rēgnō, rēgnāre
9. queror, querī

Passive Periphrastic

The *passive periphrastic* is a construction that combines a *gerundive* with forms of the verb **esse** to express *obligation* or *necessity*, e.g.:

Rōma nōbīs **servanda est**.
Rome **is to be saved** by us.
Rome **must be saved** by us.
We **must save** Rome.

Intransitive verbs are used *impersonally* in this construction, with an implied "it" as grammatical subject, e.g.:

Nōbīs ad urbem **redeundum erat**.
It had to be returned by us to the city.
We **had to return** to the city.

The *dative case*, such as **nōbīs** in the examples above, not the ablative with **ā/ab**, is usually used for the *agent* (the person by whom the thing must be done).

The verb **īre** and its compounds have an irregular gerund, **eundī** (compare the present participle of this verb, **iēns, euntis**).

Exercise 4
Read aloud and translate each sentence, first literally and then in better English:

1. Tarquiniō Prīscō ex Etrūriā Rōmam migrandum erat.
2. Tarquiniō Prīscō mortuō, Tanaquīl rēgia erat claudenda et cōnsilium Serviō Tulliō dandum.
3. Eundem est Delphōs fīliīs Tarquinī Superbī.
4. Duae fīliae Servī Tulliī in mātrimōniō dandae sunt Lūciō atque Arruntī Tarquiniīs.
5. Mandāta patris iuvenibus cōnficienda sunt.

PART II

The Early Republic

The form of government established after the expulsion of the Tarquin kings was known as the Republic (509–31 B.C.). It should be clearly understood, however, that this was not a democracy; rather, it was an oligarchy (rule by a small group). Although the people could vote on certain laws and elect some officials, the government as a whole was firmly under the control of the senators, and only those of noble birth were usually elected to high office.

Two themes run through the stories that Livy and other Roman historians tell about this period. The first is Rome's struggle for survival against external enemies, beginning with the attempt by Tarquinius Superbus to regain his throne and continuing with events such as the Gallic invasion of Italy, as well as many lesser wars between Rome and her neighbors. The second theme is the struggle of the plebeians for fairer treatment from the senators and for a greater share in the powers of government. The stories in Part II clearly illustrate both of these aspects of the early Republic (509–264 B.C.).

Many of the stories, such as those of Horatius Cocles and Gaius Fabricius, have an additional function. They are what the Romans termed **exempla**, that is, they provide models of how good Romans should behave. As you read the stories, think about what they tell us about the ideals and values of Roman culture during this period.

1   **Lars Porsena, Lartis Porsenae** (*m.*), Lars Porsena (king of the Etruscan city of Clusium).

The name is also spelled Porsenna and Porsina.

2   **Clūsīnus, -a, -um**, of Clusium (the most important Etruscan city).

Eī persuāsit nē . . . paterētur: *dative* and *indirect command* with **persuāsit**.

3   ***prīvō** (1) (+ *abl.*), to deprive of.

*īnfestus, -a, -um, dangerous, hostile.

īnfestō exercitū: "with . . ."; the *ablative of accompaniment* is often found without **cum** in military phrases like this.

8   **obiciō, obicere** (3), **obiēcī, obiectum**, to throw toward, place in between.

*tūtus, -a, -um, safe.

mūrīs . . . Tiberī obiectō: translate these ablatives with **tūta**, "because of . . ."

9   **nī**: = **nisi**, if not, unless.

nī . . . fuisset: "if there hadn't been . . . ," "if it hadn't been for . . . ," *pluperfect subjunctive* in a *past contrary to fact condition* (see the grammar note on pages 104–105).

Horātius Cocles, Horātiī Coclitis (*m.*), Horatius Cocles (the **cognōmen** Cocles means "one-eyed").

10   **positus erat**: i.e., he had been stationed as a guard at the bridge.

Clūsīnī, -ōrum (*m. pl.*), the Clusians.

repentīnus, -a, -um, sudden.

11   **vēlōx, vēlōcis**, swift, fast.

*flūmen, flūminis (*n.*), river.

*dēcurrō, dēcurrere (3), **dēcurrī, dēcursum**, to run down.

12   **suōs**: "his men."

13   ***rescindō, rescindere** (3), **rescidī, rescissum**, to cut down.

sē . . . exceptūrum esse: *indirect statement* with *future active infinitive*, depending on the idea of saying implied in **ōrāvit** (see the grammar note on page 98).

14   **quantum** (*adv.*), so far as.

posset id facere: "could do it," subjunctive in a *future more vivid construction in indirect statement* (see the grammar note on pages 99–100; Cocles' original words would have been **impetum hostium excipiam quantum ūnus poterit id facere**).

15   **aditus, -ūs** (*m.*), entrance, approach.

*turbō (1), to disturb, upset, throw into confusion.

The fresco by G. F. Romanelli on page 61 shows Gaius Mucius, the heroic young Roman who saved Rome from Porsena (see the introduction to section 15, page 69, for the story). (Paris, Louvre)

14.   Horatius Cocles

*After the establishment of the Republic in 509 B.C., government
was in the hands of the Senate and of the elected officials. The new
government's first task was to fight for its survival against the Tarquin
family and their Etruscan allies.*

Tarquinius, ut rēgnum reciperet, ad Lartem Porsenam,   1   508 B.C.
Clūsīnum rēgem, fūgit. Eī persuāsit nē rēgem Etrūscae   2
sanguinis rēgnō prīvārī paterētur. Porsena Rōmam īnfestō   3
exercitū vēnit. Magnus terror senātum occupāvit; adeō   4
firma rēs Clūsīna tum erat magnumque Porsenae nōmen.   5

Cum hostēs adessent, omnēs in urbem ex agrīs veniunt   6
urbemque ipsam mūniunt praesidiīs. Alia loca mūrīs, alia   7
Tiberī obiectō vidēbantur tūta. Pōns sublicius tamen iter   8
paene hostibus dedit, nī ūnus vir fuisset, Horātius Cocles,   9
quī forte ad pontem positus erat. Clūsīnī repentīnō impetū   10
Iāniculum cēpērunt atque inde vēlōciter ad flūmen dēcur-   11
rēbant. Cocles, cum suōs fugere vīdisset, ōrāvit eōs ut   12
manērent et pontem rescinderent; sē impetum hostium,   13
quantum ūnus posset id facere, exceptūrum esse. Prōcessit   14
inde in prīmum aditum pontis ipsāque audāciā turbāvit   15
hostēs.   16

17   *pudor, pudōris (m.), sense of honor, sense of shame.
     Sp. Larcius, -ī (m.), Spurius Larcius.
     T. Herminius, -ī (m.), Titus Herminius.
20   in tūtum: "to safety."
21   sublātō: *perfect passive participle* of tollō.
22   *dēnique (adv.), finally.
23   *trānō (1), to swim across.
     grātus, -a, -um, pleasing, dear to, thankful.
24   *comitium, -ī (n.), comitium (an open area in the Forum, in front of the
     Senate House, used for assemblies).
25   agrī quantum: "as much (of) land as," *partitive genitive* (see the grammar
     note on page 82).
     circumarō (1), to plow around.

Sequence of Tenses

Simple rules determine what tense of the *subjunctive* will appear in a
subordinate clause. The tense of the subjunctive verb depends upon the
tense of the main verb; this relationship of the verb in the subordinate
clause to the verb in the main clause is called *sequence of tenses*. The
usual relationships are shown in the chart below.

Sequence of Tenses with the Subjunctive		
	Main Clause Indicative or Imperative or Independent Subjunctive	**Subordinate Clause** Tense of Subjunctive *Relation of Action to That of Main Clause* *Type of Action*
Primary Sequence	Present Future Future Perfect	Present = *Simultaneous or subsequent* *Incomplete* Perfect = *Prior* *Completed*
Secondary Sequence	Imperfect Perfect Pluperfect	Imperfect = *Simultaneous or subsequent* *Incomplete* Pluperfect = *Prior* *Completed*

Duōs tamen cum eō pudor tenuit, Sp. Larcium et T. Her-   17
minium, ambōs clārōs genere factīsque. Cum hīs prīmam   18
pugnam paulīsper sustinuit. Deinde eōs, parvā parte pontis   19
relictā, cēdere in tūtum iussit. Pudor inde commōvit   20
Etrūscōs, et, clāmōre sublātō, undique in ūnum hostem tēla   21
coniciunt. Dēnique, ponte paene rescissō, Cocles armātus   22
in Tiberim dēsiluit incolumisque ad suōs trānāvit. Grāta   23
ergā tantam virtūtem cīvitās fuit; statua eius in comitiō   24
posita est, et agrī quantum ūnō diē circumarāvit datum.   25

Sequence of Tenses *(continued)*

The following examples illustrate some of the rules for sequence of
tenses given on page 64:

Tarquinius, ut rēgnum **reciperet**, ad Lartem Porsenam . . . **fūgit**.
    (14:1–2)
[imperfect subjunctive, secondary sequence]
*Tarquinius, **in order to regain** his throne, **fled** to Lars Porsena.*

In this example, the action of recovering the kingdom was *incomplete* at
the time when Tarquin decided to flee to Lars Porsena for help; it is
thought of as taking place *subsequent to* the action of the main clause.

Cocles, cum suōs fugere **vīdisset**, ōrāvit eōs. . . . (14:12)
[pluperfect subjunctive, secondary sequence]
*Cocles, when he **had seen** his men fleeing, **begged** them. . . .*

Here the action of Horatius seeing his men fleeing took place *prior* to
his begging them to stay and cut down the bridge; it had already been
completed when he began to speak.

Lays of Ancient Rome

Thomas Babington Macaulay (1800–1859) published his Lays of
Ancient Rome *in 1842, and the poems immediately became widely
popular. In this work Macaulay assumed the persona of an ancient
bard, reciting to a Roman audience tales about the heroic past of their
nation. The stories, drawn mainly from Livy, emphasize such tradi-
tional Roman virtues as courage, devotion to duty, and self-sacrifice in
the service of the state. Macaulay, writing in a thoroughly Romantic
style, delighted in painting vivid pictures of the heroes and villains of
early Rome, as the following stanzas, taken from his poem about
Horatius, show. The bridge has been broken down, and Horatius is
about to leap into the Tiber.*

LVIII.

But he saw on Palatinus
    The white porch of his home;
And he spake to the noble river
    That rolls by the towers of Rome.

LIX.

"Oh, Tiber! father Tiber!
    To whom the Romans pray,
A Roman's life, a Roman's arms,
    Take thou in charge this day!"
So he spake, and speaking sheathed
    The good sword by his side,
And with his harness° on his back,   °armor
    Plunged headlong in the tide.

LX.

No sound of joy or sorrow
    Was heard from either bank;
But friends and foes in dumb surprise,
With parted lips and straining eyes,
    Stood gazing where he sank;
And when above the surges
    They saw his crest appear,
All Rome sent forth a rapturous cry,
And even the ranks of Tuscany°   °homeland of the
    Could scarce forbear to cheer.   Etruscans

LXI.

But fiercely ran the current,
    Swollen high by months of rain:

And fast his blood was flowing;
    And he was sore in pain,
And heavy with his armour,
    And spent with changing blows:
And oft they thought him sinking,
    But still again he rose.

LXII.

Never, I ween,° did swimmer,   °believe
    In such an evil case,
Struggle through such a raging flood
    Safe to the landing place:
But his limbs were borne up bravely
    By the brave heart within,
And our good father Tiber
    Bare° bravely up his chin.   °bore

LXIV.

And now he feels the bottom;
    Now on dry earth he stands;
Now round him throng the Fathers
    To press his gory hands;
And now, with shouts and clapping,
    And noise of weeping loud,
He enters through the River-Gate,
    Borne by the joyous crowd.

LXV.

They gave him of the corn-land°   °wheat-land
    That was of public right
As much as two strong oxen
    Could plough from morn till night;
And they made a molten image,
    And set it up on high,
And there it stands unto this day
    To witness if I lie.

LXVI.

It stands in the Comitium,
    Plain for all folk to see;
Horatius in his harness,
    Halting upon one knee:
And underneath is written,
    In letters all of gold,
How valiantly he kept the bridge
    In the brave days of old.

1   **Cloelia, -ae** (*f.*), Cloelia.
     ***obses, obsidis** (*m.*), hostage.
2   **rīpa, -ae** (*f.*), bank (of a river).
     rīpā: *ablative* with the *quasi-preposition* **procul**.
     locō (1), to place, locate.
     ***frūstror, frūstrārī** (1), **frūstrātus sum**, to deceive, trick.
          frūstrāta: remember that the *perfect participle* of a *deponent verb* is
          active in meaning (see the grammar note on pages 10–11).
3   **dux**: "as the leader."
     agmen, agminis (*n.*), column, line.
     inter tēla hostium: i.e., the Etruscans threw spears at the girls as they
          swam across the Tiber.
4   **sōspes, sōspitis**, safe, unhurt.
5   **Quod**: "And . . . this," *linking* **quī** (see the grammar note on pages 125–
          126).
6   **dēposcō, dēposcere** (3), **dēpoposcī**, to demand (that someone be handed
          over).
     aliās: = **aliās virginēs**; what gives the clue that a feminine noun must be
          supplied?
7   **magnī facere**, to consider of great (importance), value highly.
     versus: "having turned."
     suprā Coclitēs Mūciōsque: "superior to (those of people such as) Cocles
          and Mucius."
8   **facinus**: this word usually means "bad deed" or "crime," but here it has its
          original meaning of "deed" or "act," with no negative connotation.
9   **prō ruptō**: "as broken."
     habitūrum (esse): habēre here means "to consider."
10   **intāctus, -a, -um**, untouched.
     inviolātus, -a, -um, unharmed.
     ad suōs: "to her own (people)."

11   **utrimque** (*adv.*), on both sides.
13   **redintegrō** (1), to restore.
15   ***equester, equestris, equestre**, equestrian.
     ***dōnō** (1), to give, present; (*here*) to present or honor someone or some-
          thing (*acc.*) with something (*abl.*).
     Sacra via, -ae (*f.*), Sacred Way.
          In summā Sacrā viā: the Sacred Way was one of the main streets of
               Rome, beginning in the heart of the Forum Romanum near the
               Senate House and running east southeast between the Esquiline and
               Caelian hills. The street climbs up a small hill as it leaves the
               Forum, hence the position of Cloelia's statue "at the top of the Sacred
               Way."
16   **īnsidō, īnsidere** (3), **īnsēdī, īnsessum** (+ *dat.*), to sit upon.

15. Cloelia

Porsena's attack on Rome was brought to a conclusion as follows. Gaius Mucius, a young Roman, was eager to save his homeland from danger. He obtained the Senate's permission to cross the Tiber and enter the Etruscan camp in hopes of killing Porsena. He succeeded in approaching the king's dais, but he did not know which of the two men seated there was the king. He killed the king's secretary and was seized by guards as he tried to flee. While being interrogated by the king, Mucius hinted that others might attempt to kill Porsena. The king ordered that Mucius be burned alive unless he revealed all he knew about this "plot." Mucius, to show his contempt for Porsena and to demonstrate the bravery of the Romans, thrust his hand into the fire that was burning on an altar. Amazed at the young man's courage, Porsena ordered him released. Mucius then told him that 300 young nobles like himself had sworn to kill him; they would try, one at a time, until Porsena was dead. The king was so terrified by this idea that he agreed to a diplomatic settlement.

Under the terms of the peace treaty, Porsena withdrew and the Tarquinii were not restored to power in Rome; however, the Romans had to give the Etruscans hostages to guarantee their good behavior in the future. The following story is about one of those hostages, a maiden named Cloelia.

Cloelia virgō, ūna ex obsidibus, cum castra Etrūscōrum   1   508 B.C.
forte haud procul rīpā Tiberis locāta essent, frūstrāta   2
custōdēs, dux agminis virginum inter tēla hostium Tiberim   3
trānāvit sōspitēsque omnēs Rōmam ad propinquōs restituit.   4
Quod ubi rēgī nūntiātum est, prīmō incēnsus īrā ōrātōrēs   5
Rōmam mīsit ad Cloeliam obsidem dēposcendam; aliās   6
haud magnī fēcit. Deinde in admīrātiōnem versus suprā   7
Coclitēs Mūciōsque dīcit id facinus esse; apertē nūntiat sē,   8
nisi dēdātur obses, prō ruptō foedus habitūrum, sed, sī   9
dēdātur, intāctam inviolātamque ad suōs remissūrum.   10

Utrimque cōnstitit fidēs: et Rōmānī obsidem resti-   11
tuērunt, et apud rēgem Etrūscum nōn tūta sōlum sed   12
honōrāta etiam virtūs Cloeliae fuit. Pāce redintegrātā   13
Rōmānī novam in fēminā virtūtem novō genere honōris,   14
statuā equestrī, dōnāvērunt; in summā Sacrā viā posita est   15
virgō īnsidēns equō.   16

1 *dissēnsiō, dissēnsiōnis (f.), disagreement, strife.
2 aes, aeris (n.), bronze, money.
   aes aliēnum, aeris aliēnī (n.), debt.
3 *premō, premere (3), pressī, pressum, to push on, crush, oppress.
   premēbantur: note the *plural verb* with the *collective noun* plēbs.
   crēditor, crēditōris (m.), creditor, lender.
4 dēbitor, dēbitōris (m.), debtor, person who owes.
   reddēbātur: "was interpreted"; Roman law at this time was unwritten.
7 *eques, equitis (m.), horseman, cavalryman.
8 exultō (1), to exult, rejoice.
9 nē nōmina darent: i.e., not to sign up for service in the army (as a means
   of protesting their unfair treatment by the aristocrats).
   ē cōnsulibus: "of the consuls"; note the use of ē/ex + *abl.* instead of the
   partitive genitive with numbers.
10 intermittō, intermittere (3), intermīsī, intermissum, to delay, put off.
11 cōnsulō, cōnsulere (3), cōnsuluī, cōnsultum, to consult (+ *acc.*); to give
   thought to, pay attention to (+ *dat.*).

14 iūs dīcere, to give judgment (in a legal case).
   crēdō, crēdere (3), crēdidī, crēditum (+ *dat.*), to trust, believe, lend.
16 *dēspērō (1), to give up hope, despair of.
17 Sacer mōns, Sacrī montis (m.), Sacred Mount (three miles from Rome,
   across the Anio River).
   *sēcēdō, sēcēdere (3), sēcessī, sēcessum, to withdraw, go away.
18 Aniēn, Aniēnis (= Aniō, Aniōnis) (m.), Anio (a tributary of the Tiber).
   *passus, -ūs (m.), step, pace.
     *mīlle passūs, *pl.* mīlia passuum, a mile.
      tria . . . mīlia: *accusative of extent of space* (see the grammar note on
      page 71).
19 arbitror, arbitrārī (1), arbitrātus sum, to judge, believe, think.
   *concordia, -ae (f.), harmony, agreement.
   *reliquus, -a, -um, left, remaining, other.
20 Menēnius Agrippa, Menēniī Agrippae (m.), Menenius Agrippa (a plebeian
   who served as consul in 503 B.C.).
21 *plēbeius, -a, -um, plebeian.

16. The Secession of the Plebs

The first 200 years and more of the Republic were marked by a struggle on the part of the plebeians to gain fairer treatment under the law as well as some political power. During the Monarchy, the political and judicial systems had been completely dominated by the patricians.

Prīmīs temporibus reī pūblicae līberae magna dissēnsiō   1   495 B.C.
orta est inter patrēs et plēbem propter aes aliēnum, quō   2
paene tōta plēbs premēbantur. Crēditōrī enim licēbat   3
dēbitōrem etiam in servitūtem dūcere. Praetereā iūs red-   4
dēbātur ā cōnsulibus, quī magistrātus tantum patribus   5
patēbat. Cum iam plēbs auxilium ā cōnsulibus postulārent,   6
Latīnī equitēs nūntiāvērunt Volscōs ad urbem oppugnan-   7
dam venīre. Plēbs exultābant gaudiō, atque inter sē   8
hortābantur nē nōmina darent. At ūnus ē cōnsulibus, plēbe   9
convocātā, pollicitus est iūdicia intermittere quoad mīlitēs   10
in castrīs essent; bellō cōnfectō, senātum plēbī cōnsultūrum   11
esse. Eō modō plēbī persuāsit ut nōmina darent. Volscī ali-   12
īque populī fīnitimī victī sunt.   13

Posteā tamen iūs dē crēditīs pecūniīs crūdēliter, ut an-   14   494 B.C.
teā, dictum est. Tandem plēbs, cum exercitus, aliō bellō   15
coōrtō, in armīs esset, dēspērātō cōnsulum senātūsque aux-   16
iliō, in Sacrum montem sēcessērunt. Hic mōns trāns   17
Aniēnem flūmen est, tria ab urbe mīlia passuum. Patrēs   18
arbitrātī nūllam spem nisi in concordiā cīvium reliquam   19
esse, ad plēbem mīsērunt Menēnium Agrippam, ipsum   20
plēbeium et plēbī cārum.   21

Accusative of Extent of Space

A word or phrase in the *accusative case* may tell how far someone travels or how far one thing is from another; this is called the *accusative of extent of space*, e.g.:

Hic mōns . . . est, **tria** ab urbe **mīlia** passuum. (above: 17–18)
This mountain is . . . , three miles from the city.

Here is another example:

Mīlitēs **multa mīlia** passuum ad mare prōgressī sunt.
The soldiers advanced many miles toward the sea.

1 *fertur: "is said."
2 *indignor, indignārī (1), indignātus sum, to be unhappy, complain, be indignant.
3 *ministerium, -ī (n.), service, work.
   *venter, ventris (m.), stomach.
   quaererentur . . . fruerētur: for the use of the *subjunctive in a* **quod**
      causal clause, see the grammar note on page 78.
4 *voluptās, voluptātis (f.), enjoyment, pleasure.
   fruor, fruī (3), frūctus sum (+ abl.), to enjoy.
5 nēve (conj.), and . . . not.
      The conjunction nēve is used to continue the *indirect command* intro-
         duced by nē.
6 dēns, dentis (m.), tooth.
   cōnficiō, cōnficere (3), cōnfēcī, cōnfectum, to finish, finish off; (here), to
      chew.
   *famēs, famis (f.), hunger.
      famē: *ablative.*
   domō (1), to tame, master, dominate.
7 membrum, -ī (n.), part, limb.
8 iners, inertis, useless, idle.
10 similis, -is, -e (+ gen. or dat.), like.

12 *reconciliō (1), to reconcile, restore.
   plēbī permissum est: "it was permitted to the plebs," "the plebs were
      permitted," *impersonal passive of special intransitive verb* (see the
      grammar note below).
13 *tribūnus, -ī (m.), tribune.
      The title tribūnus was given to several different officials in the Roman
         world; the tribūnī plēbeiī, tribunes of the people, had the specific re-
         sponsibility of protecting the interests of the plebs.
   quī auxilium plēbī . . . ferrent: "who would help the plebs," *relative clause
      of characteristic* (see the grammar note on page 116).

Impersonal Passive of Special Intransitive Verbs

You know that the meaning of some intransitive verbs such as **resistere,**
crēdere, favēre, and **persuādēre** is completed by an *indirect object* in the
dative case instead of by a *direct object* in the *accusative* (see the
grammar note on page 16). Another such verb is **permittere,** as seen in
the following sentence:

Patrēs plēbī suōs magistrātūs creāre permīsērunt.
The senators **permitted** **the plebeians** *to elect their own magistrates.*

The English sentence above can be turned into the *passive* as follows:

*The plebeians were permitted by the senators to elect their own
   magistrates.*

17. Menenius Agrippa

Menēnius hoc nārrāvisse fertur: "Ōlim reliquae partēs 1   494 B.C.
corporis hūmānī indignābantur quod suā cūrā, suō labōre 2
ac ministeriō ventrī omnia quaererentur, venter in mediō 3
quiētus datīs voluptātibus fruerētur; coniūrāvērunt inde nē 4
manūs ad ōs cibum ferrent, nēve ōs datum cibum acciperet, 5
nēve dentēs cōnficerent. Sed dum ventrem famē domāre 6
volunt, ipsa membra tōtumque corpus paene periērunt. 7
Inde sēnsērunt ventris quoque ministerium haud iners 8
esse." Ostendit deinde dissēnsiōnem inter partēs corporis 9
similem esse īrae plēbis in patrēs et ita flexit mentēs 10
hominum. 11

Concordiā reconciliātā, plēbī permissum est suōs magi- 12
strātūs creāre tribūnōs plēbeiōs, quī auxilium plēbī adver- 13
sus cōnsulēs ferrent. 14

Impersonal Passive of Special Intransitive Verbs (continued)

Latin, however, does not allow these special intransitive verbs to be used in the passive with personal subjects. Latin cannot say "They were permitted" or "I was permitted." Instead, the *passive* idea with these *special intransitive verbs* is expressed *impersonally*, with an implied "it" as the subject (see the note on impersonal passives on pages 76–77). Thus instead of saying "the plebeians were permitted," Latin says "It was permitted to the plebeians," **plēbī permissum est**, keeping the dative case. In lines 12–13 above, we have:

> ... plēbī **permissum est** suōs magistrātūs creāre. ...
> ... *it was permitted to the plebs to elect their own magistrates.* ...
> ... *the plebs were permitted to elect their own magistrates.* ...

Here are examples with other special intransitive verbs:

> Eīs ācriter resistēbātur.
> *It was fiercely resisted to them.*
> *They were fiercely resisted.*

> Eī nōn crēditum est.
> *It was not believed to him.*
> *He was not believed.*

> Horātiō ā Rōmānīs favēbātur.
> *It was favored to Horatius by the Romans.*
> *Horatius was favored by the Romans.*

1   īnsignis, -is, -e, outstanding, notable, remarkable.
     maestitia, -ae (f.), grief, sadness.
2   Veturia, -ae (f.), Veturia (mother of Coriolanus).
     nurum nepotēsque: i.e., Coriolanus' wife and children.
4   Coriolānus, -ī (m.), Gnaeus Marcius Coriolanus (his cognōmen comes
         from his capture of the Volscian town of Corioli in Latium).
     prope ut āmēns: "almost as a madman."
5   cōnsternō (1), to confound, shock, drive in consternation.
     obvius, -a, -um, in the way, on the way, coming to meet.
     complexus, -ūs (m.), embrace.
6   prex, precis (f.), prayer, request, entreaty.
         in īram ex precibus: Veturia had intended to beg Coriolanus and the
             Volscians not to continue their attack against Rome, but as she ap-
             proaches him and he comes forward to embrace her she is over-
             whelmed with anger.
         Sine . . . (ut) sciam: "Permit that I know," "Allow me to know," "Let me
             know."
8   . . . an . . . , whether . . . or . . .
     -ne, whether . . . or . . .
         an . . . vēnerim . . . -ne . . . sim: indirect questions dependent on sciam
             (7) (see the grammar note on page 90).
9   īnfēlīx, īnfēlīcis, unhappy, unfortunate, unlucky.
     *senectūs, senectūtis (f.), old age.
10   populor, populārī (1), populātus sum, to devastate, lay waste.
11   gignō, gignere (3), genuī, genitum, to give birth, produce.
     alō, alere (3), aluī, to nourish, raise.
     quamvīs (adv.), however much you wish.
12   mināx, minācis, threatening.
         Quamvīs īnfestō animō et minācī: "With however hostile and threaten-
             ing a spirit."
         tibi ingredientī: "from you, as you were . . ."
     *fīnis, fīnis (m.), end, boundary; (pl.) borders, territory.
13   succurrō, succerrere (3), succurrī, succursum, to run up to, occur to, enter
         the mind of.
14   penātēs, penātium (m. pl.), household gods.
15   ergō (particle), therefore.
     pariō, parere (3), peperī, partum, to give birth (to).
         nisi peperissem, Rōma nōn oppugnārētur; nisi . . . habērem, . . . mort꜄
             essem: "If I had not given birth, Rome would not (now) be attacked;
             If I did not have . . . , I would have died. . . ." contrary to fact condi-
             tion (see the grammar note on page 105).
     *oppugnō (1), to attack.
16   *patria, -ae (f.), native land, fatherland, country.
17   *turpis, -is, -e, disgraceful.
18   hīs: Coriolanus' mother points to his children as she says this.
     vīderis: "you should look," "you should consider," perfect subjunctive used
         as a command (jussive subjunctive) (see the grammar note on page 28).
19   pergō, pergere (3), perrēxī, perrēctum, to continue.
     immātūrus, -a, -um, early, too early, untimely.
     *servitūs, servitūtis (f.), slavery.

18. Coriolanus and His Family

Gnaeus Marcius Coriolanus angered the people of Rome by his tyrannical behavior and by his opposition to the distribution of grain to the plebeians during a time of famine. The people's anger was so great that the Senate agreed that Coriolanus should be put on trial. Infuriated at this treatment, he withdrew from Rome to the territory of the Volscians, a people hostile to the Romans. There he conspired with the leading citizens to arrange the downfall of Rome. He led a Volscian army into Roman territory, and the Romans appeared to have no hope of survival. The women of Rome prevailed on Veturia, Coriolanus' mother, and Volumnia, his wife, to go with his children to the Volscian camp, along with a large delegation of other women. At first Coriolanus was not moved by this group, any more than he had been by the official ambassadors who had previously been sent.

Deinde familiārium quīdam quī īnsignem maestitiā in-   1   491 B.C.
ter cēterās cognōverat Veturiam inter nurum nepotēsque   2
stantem, "Nisi mē frūstrantur," inquit, "oculī, māter tibi   3
coniūnxque et līberī adsunt." Coriolānus prope ut āmēns   4
cōnsternātus ab sēde suā cum ferret mātrī obviae com-   5
plexum, mulier in īram ex precibus versa est. "Sine,   6
priusquam complexum accipiō, sciam," inquit, "ad hostem   7
an ad fīlium vēnerim, captīva māterne in castrīs tuīs sim.   8
In hoc mē longa vīta et īnfēlīx senectūs trāxit, ut exulem tē,   9
deinde hostem vidērem? Potuistī populārī hanc terram,   10
quae tē genuit atque aluit? Quamvīs īnfestō animō et   11
mināci pervēnerās, nōn tibi ingredientī fīnēs īra cecidit?   12
Nōn, cum in cōnspectū Rōma fuit, succurrit, 'Intrā illa moe-   13
nia domus ac penātēs meī sunt, māter coniūnx līberīque?'   14
Ergō ego nisi peperissem, Rōma nōn oppugnārētur; nisi   15
fīlium habērem, lībera in līberā patriā mortua essem. Sed   16
ego nihil iam patī nec tibi turpius nec mihi miserius possum   17
nec, ut sum miserrima, diū futūra sum; dē hīs vīderis, quōs,   18
sī pergis, aut immātūra mors aut longa servitūs manet."   19

20   **amplector, amplectī** (3), **amplexus sum**, to clasp.
      amplexī sunt: Coriolanus' wife and children clasp him as suppliants.
      flētus, -ūs (*m.*), weeping.
21   **complōrātiō, complōrātiōnis** (*f.*), lamentation.
      suī: "for themselves."
22   **complector, complectī** (3), **complexus sum**, to embrace.
      suōs: "his own," "his family."
23   **retrō** (*adv.*), back, backwards, away.
24   *__legiō, legiōnis__ (*f.*), legion, army.
      invidia, -ae (*f.*), envy, hatred, resentment.
25   **invideō, invidēre** (2), **invīdī, invīsum**, to envy, be jealous of (+ *dat.*); (*here*)
      to be unwilling to give, to begrudge someone (*dat.*) something (*abl.*).
      *__laus, laudis__ (*f.*), praise.
26   **obtrectātiō, obtrectātiōnis** (*f.*), disparagement, detraction, envy.
27   **vīvēbātur**: "life was lived," "they lived" (literally, "it was lived"), *imper-
      sonal passive* (see the grammar note below).
      monumentō: "as a memorial," *dative of purpose* (see the grammar note on
      page 77)
      quod esset: the *antecedent* of **quod** is **templum**. Here the *relative clause*
      is placed before its *antecedent* and is a *relative clause of characteristic*,
      "which would (be of a type to) serve," "which would serve" (see gram-
      mar note on page 116).
      Fortūna, -ae (*f.*), Fortune (a goddess thought of as directing events and
      symbolizing one's condition or fortune).
28   **dēdicō** (1), to dedicate.

Impersonal Passive

Look at the following sentences:

> Ea erat cōnfessiō caput rērum Rōmam esse, dē quō totiēns **certātum
> erat.** (10:10–11)
> *This was an acknowledgment that Rome was the leader (head of af-
> fairs), about which **it had been struggled** so many times.*
> *. . . **there had been** so many **struggles.***

> . . . adeō sine obtrectātiōne glōriae aliēnae **vīvēbātur** . . .
> (opposite: 26–27)
> *. . . **it was lived (life was lived)** to such an extent without envy of
> others' glory . . .*

Intransitive verbs such as **certāre** and **vīvere** will sometimes be found in
the *passive* (3rd person singular or infinitive) with no expressed personal subject. They are then said to be used *impersonally*, and one may
supply "it" as a subject in a literal translation. You will usually want to
think of a more idiomatic English translation, as in the examples above.

Uxor deinde ac līberī Coriolānum amplexī sunt, flē- 20
tusque ab omnī turbā mulierum ortus et complōrātiō suī 21
patriaeque frēgērunt tandem virum. Complexus inde suōs 22
dīmittit; ipse retrō ab urbe castra mōvit. Abductīs deinde 23
legiōnibus ex agrō Rōmānō, Coriolānum invidiā reī oppres- 24
sum periisse trādunt. Nōn invīdērunt laude suā mulieribus 25
virī Rōmānī—adeō sine obtrectātiōne glōriae aliēnae 26
vīvēbātur—monumentōque quod esset, templum Fortūnae 27
muliebrī aedificātum dēdicātumque est. 28

Impersonal Passive *(continued)*

This use of the *impersonal passive* places emphasis on the action of
the verb rather than the people involved in the action, as in the following example: **Ācriter pugnābātur**, "It was fought fiercely," "There was
fierce fighting."

Dative of Purpose

A noun in the *dative case* will sometimes be found with a form of the
verb **esse** to express the *purpose* that something serves or the *end* that
it accomplishes, e.g.:

Mīlitēs **auxiliō** fuērunt.
*The soldiers were **a source of help** (were **a help**).*

Templum **monumentō** erat. (based on 27 above)
*The temple was **a memorial** (i.e., it served **as a reminder**).*

Here are some other expressions using the dative of purpose that
you may encounter:

admīrātiōnī esse	*to be a source of wonder or surprise*
perīculō esse	*to be a source of danger*
praesidiō esse	*to be a means of defense* (cf. 9:20)
salūtī esse	*to be a source of safety*
subsidiō esse	*to be of help*
ūsuī esse	*to be of use*

1   *cōnsulāris, -is, -e, consular, belonging to a consul.
    dēfīniō (4), to set bounds to, limit.
2   L. Quīnctius Cincinnātus, -ī (m.), Lucius Quinctius Cincinnatus (consul
       in 460 B.C. and dictator in 458 B.C.; the cognōmen Cincinnatus refers to
       artificially curled hair).
    Ut: "When" (see the grammar note on page 79).
3   *ineō, inīre (irreg.), iniī, initum, to enter upon.
4   etiam atque etiam: "again and again."
    turbārent: for the use of the subjunctive in a quod causal clause, see the
       grammar note below.
5   *continuō (1), to extend, continue, renew.
    *contrā (prep. + acc.), contrary to, against, in violation of.
    contrā rem pūblicam: "contrary to the interests of the state."
7   nē quid: see the grammar notes on pages 79 and 80.
    *cēdō, cēdere (3), cessī, cessum, to come, go, withdraw, yield something
       (acc.) to someone (dat.).
9   *auctōritās, auctōritātis (f.), prestige, influence, authority.
    cōnscrībō, cōnscrībere (3), cōnscrīpsī, cōnscrīptum, to enroll, register.
    patrēs cōnscrīptī, enrolled fathers (a title of honor for the senators).
11 senātūs cōnsultum: see lines 5–6.
12 reficiō, reficere (3), refēcī, refectum, to reelect, reappoint.

Quod Causal with the Subjunctive

You know that a clause introduced by the conjunction quod, meaning
"because," is normally completed by a verb in the indicative. Sometimes, however, the subjunctive is used, e.g.:

> Cincinnātus . . . reprehendit et senātum et plēbem, quod . . . tribūnī
> . . . cīvitātem turbārent. (opposite: 2–4)
> Cincinnatus rebuked both the Senate and the plebs, because (on the
> grounds that) the tribunes were disturbing the state.

Quod followed by a verb in the subjunctive indicates that the reason is
being given not on the authority of the writer but on the authority of
someone else. That is, someone else's reason is being given, and the
quod clause with the subjunctive can be thought of as a kind of indirect
statement. In the sentence above, the reason given is that of
Cincinnatus.

19. Lucius Quinctius Cincinnatus

Posteā, dum tribūnī imperium cōnsulāre lēgibus dēfīnīre 1
cōnantur, L. Quīnctius Cincinnātus cōnsul factus est. Ut 2   460 B.C.
magistrātum iniit, reprehendit et senātum et plēbem, quod 3
eīdem tribūnī etiam atque etiam creātī cīvitātem turbārent. 4
Senātus igitur dēcrēvit magistrātūs continuārī contrā rem 5
pūblicam esse. Plēbs tamen eōsdem, quōs anteā, tribūnōs 6
creāvērunt. Patrēs quoque, nē quid cēderent plēbī, Lūcium 7
Quīnctium cōnsulem fēcērunt. At is, "Minimē mīrum est," 8
inquit, "sī nihil auctōritātis, patrēs cōnscrīptī, habētis apud 9
plēbem. Vōs eam minuitis, quī in continuandīs mag- 10
istrātibus plēbem imitāminī. Ego mē contrā senātūs cōn- 11
sultum cōnsulem reficī nōn patiar." Alius igitur cōnsul fac- 12
tus est. 13

Ut with the Indicative

When the conjunction **ut** is followed by a verb in the *indicative*, it is
translated "when," "after," or "as," e.g.:

Ut magistrātum **iniit**, reprehendit et senātum et plēbem . . . (above:
2–3)
When he **entered upon** (his term of) office, he rebuked both the
Senate and the plebs . . .

Rōmānī, ut **scītis**, magnum imperium habēbant.
The Romans, **as** you **know**, had a large empire.

Quis/Quid = "anyone"/"anything"

You know that **quis** normally means "who" and **quid** "what." But if this
word (in any form) comes after **sī**, **nisi**, **num**, or **nē**, the meaning is
"anyone" or "anything," e.g.:

Patrēs quoque, **nē quid** cēderent plēbī, . . . (above: 7)
The sentors also, in order not to yield **anything** to the plebeians, . . .

14   **Aequī, -ōrum** (*m. pl.*), the Aequi (a people of central Italy).
      mūnītiō, mūnītiōnis (*f.*), fortification, rampart.
16   ***dictus est**: "was named."
18   **iūgerum, -ī**, *gen. pl.* **iūgerum** (*n.*), iugerum (a measure of land, about two-
        thirds of an acre).
19   **togātus, -a, -um**, clad in a toga.
20   **admīrātus**: *perfect participles of deponent verbs* may often best be trans-
        lated as *presents*, e.g., "wondering," "in amazement."
      properē (*adv.*), quickly.
      tugurium, -ī (*n.*), hut, cottage.
21   **abstergeō, abstergēre** (2), **abstersī, abstersum**, to wipe off.
      sūdor, sūdōris (*m.*), sweat.
      vēlō (1), to wrap, cover up.
22   **quī . . . sit**: *indirect question* (see the grammar note on page 90).

25   ***iugum, -ī** (*n.*), yoke (collar for hitching two oxen together), arch made by
        planting two spears in the ground and joining them at the top with a
        third spear (a defeated army had to march through the arch as a sign
        of surrender and disgrace).
      *triumphō (1), to celebrate a triumph.
        A victorious general was often granted the right to hold a victory pa-
        rade through the streets of Rome, ending at the temple of Jupiter on
        the Capitoline hill; this was referred to as a **triumphus**.
26   ***dictātūra, -ae** (*f.*), dictatorship.

Negative Purpose Clauses

You remember that affirmative purpose clauses are introduced by **ut**
(see the grammar note on page 12). *Negative* purpose clauses are introduced by **nē**, e.g.:

> Patrēs quoque, **nē** quid **cēderent** plēbī, . . . (19:7)
> *The senators also, **in order not to yield** anything to the plebe-
> ians, . . .*
> *The senators also, **so that they wouldn't yield** anything to the ple-
> beians, . . .*

As with any purpose clause, the verb must be either present or imperfect subjunctive, following the rules for sequence of tenses.

Post paucōs annōs Aequī exercitum Rōmānum mūnī- 14 458 B.C.
tiōnibus clausum obsidēbant. Cum hoc Rōmam nūntiātum 15
esset, L. Quīnctius cōnsēnsū omnium dictātor dictus est. 16
Lēgātī ā senātū missī eum invēnērunt trāns Tiberim agrum 17
quattuor iūgerum colentem atque in opus intentum. 18
Rogāvērunt ut togātus mandāta senātūs audīret. Quīnctius 19
admīrātus iubet uxōrem togam properē ē tuguriō prōferre. 20
Cum, abstersō sūdōre, togā vēlātus prōcessisset, dictātōrem 21
eum lēgātī salūtant atque in urbem vocant; quī terror sit in 22
exercitū expōnunt. 23

Quīnctius exercitum obsessum celeriter līberāvit et 24
hostēs sub iugum mīsit. Triumphāns urbem iniit sextōque 25
decimō diē dictātūram in sex mēnsēs acceptam dēposuit. 26

2   **Senonēs, Senonum** (*m. pl.*), the Senones (a tribe of Gauls that migrated
    into Etruria; led by Brennus).
    Gallicus, -a, -um, of Gaul, Gallic.
3   **Gallus, -a, -um**, of Gaul, Gallic; (*m. pl.*) the Gauls.
5   **iūs gentium**: "law of nations," "international law." The ambassadors
    were not supposed to get involved in the fighting.
7   **prō** (*prep. + abl.*), (*here*) in return for, in compensation for.
8   ***negō** (1), to refuse, deny, say no.

10 **idōneus, -a, -um**, suitable.
11 **Allia, -ae** (*f.*), Allia (a river north of Rome).
12 **Alliēnsis, -is, -e**, Allian (an adjective formed from the name of the river
    Allia).
13 **exercitūs**: *partitive genitive* (see the grammar note below).
    Veiī, -ōrum (*m. pl.*), Veii (an Etruscan city under Roman control at the
    time of the Gallic invasion).
    ***perfugiō, perfugere** (3), **perfūgī, perfugitum**, to flee to.
14 ***nē . . . quidem**, not even (emphasizing the word in between).
15 **arcem**: the Citadel, one of the two peaks on the Capitoline Hill; the other
    is called the **Capitōlium** or Capitol.
    ***cōnferō, cōnferre** (*irreg.*), **contulī, collātum**, to bring together, collect.
    ***sē cōnferre**, to bring oneself, go.

Partitive Genitive

Magna pars **exercitūs** incolumis Veiōs perfūgit. (opposite: 13)
A large part of the army fled safely to Veii.

In this example, the word **exercitūs** is in the genitive case and shows
the larger thing of which a part reached Veii. This is called the *partitive genitive.*
    Here are some other examples:

nēmō **captīvōrum**	none *of the captives*
aliquid **novī**	something *of new,* something *new*
nihil **novī**	nothing *of new,* nothing *new*

Note that with cardinal numbers and **quīdam** a prepositional
phrase with **ex** or **dē** plus the ablative is used instead of a partitive
genitive, e.g.:

ūnus **ē cōnsulibus** (16:9)
one of the consuls

quīdam ē **mīlitibus**
a certain one of the soldiers

20. The Gallic Invasion

*About 400 B.C. a group of Celtic people known as Gauls were
pushed out of their homeland in central Europe. Some moved into what
is now France; another group crossed the Alps and occupied northern
Italy as far south as the Po River. The Gauls settled permanently in
this area, but they were a warlike people and frequently made incur-
sions into the Etruscan and Latin territories to the south.*

Ōlim lēgātī ab Clūsīnīs Rōmam vēnērunt auxilium pe-   1   390 B.C.
tentēs adversus Senonēs, gentem Gallicam. Tum Rōmānī   2
mīsērunt lēgātōs quī monērent Gallōs nē amīcōs populī   3
Rōmānī oppugnārent. Proeliō tamen commissō, lēgātī   4
Rōmānī contrā iūs gentium arma cēpērunt auxiliumque   5
Clūsīnīs tulērunt. Gallī posteā ā senātū Rōmānō pos-   6
tulāvērunt ut prō iūre gentium ita violātō lēgātī Rōmānī   7
dēderentur. Hōc negātō, exercitus Gallicus Rōmam profec-   8
tus est.   9

Rōmānī, quī nihil ad tantum perīculum idōneum   10
parāverant, apud flūmen Alliam superātī sunt. Diem quō   11
hoc proelium factum est Rōmānī posteā Alliēnsem appel-   12
lāvērunt. Magna pars exercitūs incolumis Veiōs perfūgit.   13
Cēterī Rōmam petiērunt et nē clausīs quidem portīs urbis   14
in arcem Capitōliumque cum coniugibus et līberīs sē con-   15
tulērunt.   16

17   nēminī parcunt: for the *dative case with special intransitive verbs*, see
       the grammar note on page 16.
      *dīripiō, dīripere (3), dīripuī, dīreptum, to tear apart, pillage, ravage.
18   tēctum, -ī (*n.*), roof, house.
20   *obsidiō, obsidiōnis (*f.*), siege, blockade.
22   *frūmentum, -ī (*n.*), grain.
23   *fortūna, -ae (*f.*), fate, luck.
      Camillus, -ī (*m.*), Marcus Furius Camillus.
24   *imperātor, imperātōris (*m.*), general, commander.
      Ardeātēs, Ardeātum (*m. pl.*), inhabitants of Ardea.
25   solūtōs somnō: "released by sleep," i.e., sleeping deeply.
      *trucīdō (1), to slay, slaughter, massacre.
28   voluntāriī, -ōrum (*m. pl.*), volunteers.
      Latium, -ī (*n.*), Latium (district in west-central Italy, in which Rome was
      situated).
29   hostibus: *ablative of separation* (see the grammar note on page 55).
      Omnibus placuit: "It seemed good to all," "All were agreed/resolved," here
      followed by an *accusative and infinitive*, "that . . ."
30   arcessī . . . cōnsulī: *present passive infinitives* (see the grammar note on
      page 9 for help with these forms).
31   Pontius Cominius, -ī (*m.*), Pontius Cominius.
31   sublevō (1), to lift up, support.
      cortex, corticis (*m.*), bark of a tree, bark of the cork tree, a piece of cork
      used as a float.
      secundō: this word can mean "favorable" as well as "second." Cominius
      was traveling downstream with the current, hence the river was
      "favorable."
32   Tiberī: *ablative* (not *dative*).
      Take cortice with sublevātus and secundō Tiberī with dēfertur.

Brennus adds his sword to the scales (see 29:48–50).

Gallī ingressī urbem nēminī parcunt, dīripiunt incen- 17
duntque tēcta. Post aliquot diēs, impetum in arcem 18
fēcērunt. At Rōmānī mediō ferē colle restitērunt, atque 19
inde ex locō superiōre, impetū factō, Gallōs pepulērunt. Ob- 20
sidiō inde ā Gallīs parāta est. Pars exercitūs Gallicī 21
dīmissa est ad frūmentum cōnferendum ex agrīs populōrum 22
fīnitimōrum. Hōs fortūna ipsa dūxit Ardeam, ubi Camillus, 23
imperātor clārissimus, in exiliō vīvēbat. Ardeātēs eō duce 24
castra Gallōrum nocte oppugnant et solūtōs somnō trucī- 25
dant. Veiīs interim nōn animī sōlum in diēs sed etiam vīrēs 26
crēscēbant. Nam praeter Rōmānōs, quī ex pugnā Alliēnsī 27
eō perfūgerant, voluntāriī ex Latiō conveniēbant. Hī iam 28
cōnstituērunt Rōmam hostibus līberāre. Omnibus placuit 29
Camillum arcessī, sed anteā senātum cōnsulī. Ad eam rem 30
Pontius Cominius, audāx iuvenis, sublevātus cortice se- 31
cundō Tiberī ad urbem dēfertur. Senātū probante, Camil- 32
lus dictātor dictus est. 33

The sacred geese alert Manlius (see 20:37–41).

35   *praemittō, praemittere (3), praemīsī, praemissum, to send out ahead,
        send in advance.
36   in summum: supply montem, "onto the top (of the) mountain."
        ēvādō, ēvādere (3), ēvāsī, ēvāsum, to escape, climb (to the top).
37   *fallō, fallere (3), fefellī, falsum, to deceive, trick, escape the notice of.
        ānser, ānseris (m.), goose.
38   Iūnō, Iūnōnis (f.), Juno (wife and sister of Jupiter and queen of the gods).
39   M. Mānlius, -ī (m.), Marcus Manlius Capitolinus (consul in 392 B.C.).
        *ēgregius, -a, -um, distinquished, exceptional.
        clangor, clangōris (m.), clang, din, noise.
        āla, -ae (f.), wing (of a bird).
40   crepitus, -ūs (m.), noise, clatter, rustle.
41   saxum, -ī (n.), rock.
        prōpellō, prōpellere (3), prōpulī, prōpulsum, to drive away, repel.
42   praeceps, praecipitis, headfirst, downhill.

45   dictātōre: i.e., Camillus (see lines 23–33).
        mīlle pondō aurī: "with/at the price of a thousand pounds of gold."
        *aurum, -ī (n.), gold.
46   *pacīscor, pacīscī (3), pactus sum, to make an arrangement, arrange.
47   *pondus, ponderis (n.), burden, weight; (here) weight for use in scales.
48   *inīquus, -a, -um, unfair, unfavorable, too great.
49   Brennus, -ī (m.), Brennus (king of the Gauls).
50   *vae (interjection), woe, woe to (+ dat.).
        perficiō, perficere (3), perfēcī, perfectum, to finish, complete.
51   summoveō, summovēre (2), summōvī, summōtum, to remove, expel,
        banish.
52   pactōs esse: from pacīscor above, "that they had come to terms."
        pactiō, pactiōnis (f.), pact, agreement.
53   creātus esset . . . facta esset: pluperfect passive subjunctives (the sub-
        junctive is used here because these are subordinate clauses within in-
        direct statement). See the grammar note below.
54   dēnūntiō (1), to declare, order, warn someone (dat.) to do something (ut +
        subjunctive).

Subjunctive in Subordinate Clauses within Indirect Statement

Consider the following:

> . . . negāvit eam pactiōnem valēre, quae, postquam ipse dictātor
> creātus esset, iniussū suō facta esset. (opposite: 52–54)
> . . . he denied that this agreement was valid, which, after he himself
> had been chosen dictator, was made without his consent.

Interim arx Rōmae Capitōliumque in ingentī perīculō 34
fuērunt. Nocte enim Gallī, praemissō mīlite quī viam temp- 35
tāret, tantō silentiō in summum ēvāsērunt ut nōn sōlum 36
custōdēs fallerent, sed nē canēs quidem excitārent. Ānserēs 37
autem nōn fefellērunt, quī avēs Iūnōnis sacrae erant. Nam 38
M. Mānlius, vir bellō ēgregius, clangōre eōrum ālārumque 39
crepitū excitātus dēiēcit Gallum quī iam in summō cōnstit- 40
erat. Iamque aliī Rōmānī tēlīs saxīsque hostēs prōpellunt, 41
tōtaque aciēs Gallōrum praeceps dēfertur. 42

Sed famēs iam utrumque exercitum urgēbat, Gallōs 43
pestilentia etiam. Diem ex diē Rōmānī frūstrā auxilium ab 44
dictātōre exspectābant. Postrēmō mīlle pondō aurī cum 45
Gallīs pactī sunt ut obsidiōnem relinquerent. Huic reī per 46
sē turpissimae indignitās addita est; nam pondera ab Gallīs 47
allāta sunt inīqua. Rōmānīs recūsantibus gladius ā 48
Brennō, rēge Gallōrum, ponderī additus est cum hīs verbīs, 49
"Vae victīs." Sed priusquam rēs perfecta est, dictātor per- 50
vēnit auferrīque aurum dē mediō et Gallōs summovērī ius- 51
sit. Cum illī dīcerent sē pactōs esse, negāvit eam pactiōnem 52
valēre, quae, postquam ipse dictātor creātus esset, iniussū 53
suō facta esset; tum dēnūntiāvērunt Gallīs ut sē ad proeli- 54
um parārent. 55

**Subjunctive in Subordinate Clauses within Indirect
Statement** *(continued)*

The original, direct statement would have been:

> Ea pactiō nōn **valet**, quae, postquam ipse dictātor **creātus sum**, in-
> iussū meō **facta est**.
> *This agreement is not **valid**, which, after I myself **had been chosen**
> dictator, **was made** without my consent.*

When a sentence is put into indirect statement, the main verb (**valet**)
becomes an *infinitive* (**valēre**), and the verbs in subordinate clauses
(**creātus sum** and **facta est**) usually become *subjunctives*. This accounts
for the forms **creātus esset** and **facta esset** that appear when the above
statement is reported indirectly. The rules for sequence of tenses apply
(see page 64): the *pluperfect* tense of the subjunctive is used because
secondary sequence is established by the head verb **negāvit** "he denied
[that]," and the actions described in the subordinate clauses had been
completed *prior* to Camillus' denial.

56   **Gabīnus, -a, -um**, relating to Gabii (a town to the south of Rome in
         Latium).
              viā Gabīnā: *ablative of place where* without a preposition.
58   **conditor, conditōris** (*m.*), founder.
60   **agitō** (1), to urge.
61   **ōrātiō, ōrātiōnis** (*f.*), speech.
       ***ācer, ācris, ācre**, sharp, pointed, fierce.
62   ***centuriō, centuriōnis** (*m.*), centurion (commander of an infantry com-
         pany).
63   **opportūnē** (*adv.*), opportunely, at the right time.
       ***cohors, cohortis** (*f.*), military cohort.
64   **signifer, -ī** (*m.*), standard-bearer.
65   **ōmen, ōminis** (*n.*), sign, token, omen.
66   **conclāmō** (1), to shout, exclaim.
       circumfundō, circumfundere (3), **circumfūdī, circumfūsum**, to surround.
          circumfūsa: the *perfect passive participle* here has a *present active
          sense*, "surrounding (them)."

Postquam with Perfect Indicative = "had"

In the English translation of the original, direct statement given in the
grammar note on page 87, observe that the verb in the *perfect tense* in
the clause **postquam . . . creātus sum** is translated with a *pluperfect
tense* (using "had") in English: "after I *had* been chosen." This is normal, since the *perfect tense* in the *temporal clause* in Latin expresses
an action that was *completed prior* to the action of the verb in the
clause upon which it depends, **quae . . . facta est**, "which was made."
When **postquam** is used with a perfect tense in Latin, it is usually best
to translate with an English pluperfect.

Review of Place Constructions

Review the grammar note on pages 52–53. Then reread section 20 and
locate and explain all the place constructions.

Gallī et in urbe et alterō proeliō viā Gabīnā superātī 56
sunt. Dictātor triumphāns in urbem rediit; Rōmulus ac 57
parēns patriae conditorque alter urbis appellābātur. 58
Deinde servātam in bellō patriam iterum in pāce servāvit. 59
Cum enim tribūnī plēbem agitārent ut relictīs Rōmae ruīnīs 60
Veiōs migrārent, Camillus ōrātiōne ācrī cīvibus persuāsit ut 61
Rōmam restituerent. Centuriō quoque populum mōvit vōce 62
opportūnē ēmissā, quī cum cohortibus forum trānsiēns 63
clāmāvit: "Signum statue, signifer; hīc manēbimus optimē." 64
Quā vōce audītā, et senātus ē cūriā ēgressus ōmen accipere 65
sē conclāmāvit, et plēbs circumfūsa probāvērunt. 66

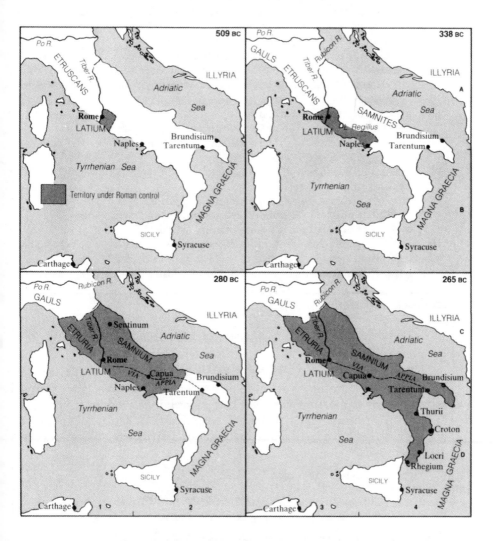

The expansion of Roman power in Italy

1   **Pyrrhus, -ī** (*m.*), Pyrrhus (319–272 B.C.; king of Epirus).
    Ēpīrus, -ī (*m.*), Epirus (a district in northwest Greece).
    superātī: at Heraclea in 280 B.C.
2   **Tarentum, -ī** (*n.*), Tarentum (a town on the southern coast of Italy).
    ***redimō, redimere** (3), **redēmī, redēmptum**, to buy back, rescue, ransom.
3   **C. Fabricius, -ī** (*m.*), Gaius Fabricius Luscinus (a plebeian; consul in 282
       and 278 B.C.).
4   **admodum** (*adv.*), very, quite.
5   ***offerō, offerre** (*irreg.*), **obtulī, oblātum**, to offer.
6   ***suādeō, suādēre** (2), **suāsī, suāsum**, to suggest, propose, recommend.
       sī suādērent: "if they would recommend" (see the grammar note on
          pages 99–100).

9   **dēserō, dēserere** (3), **dēseruī, dēsertum**, to abandon.
       sī dēsereret . . . -que vīveret: "if he would abandon . . . and live" (see the
          grammar note on pages 99–100).
11 **sīn** (*conj.*), if however, if on the other hand, but if.
12 **intericiō, intericere** (3), **interiēcī, interiectum**, to insert.
       Annō interiectō: in 279 B.C. at the battle of Asculum in Apulia Pyrrhus
          defeated the Romans but with great losses of his own men, hence the
          phrase "Pyrrhic victory."
16 **praemium, -ī** (*n.*), reward, bribe.
    ***prōpōnō, prōpōnere** (3), **prōposuī, prōpositum**, to put forth, offer.
       sī . . . prōposuisset: "if he would offer," "if he offered" (see the grammar
          note on pages 93–94).
17 ***venēnum, -ī** (*n.*), poison.
    necātūrum: supply **esse**.
18 **vinciō, vincīre** (4), **vīnxī, vīnctum**, to bind, tie up.
    ***remittō, remittere** (3), **remīsī, remissum**, to send back, return.
    certiōrem facere, to make more certain, inform.
19 **quae . . . pollicitus esset**: *indirect question* (see the grammar note below).
20 **difficilius**: *comparative adverb*, "with greater difficulty."
    honestās, honestātis (*f.*), honorableness, rectitude, integrity.

Indirect Questions

> . . . eum **certiōrem fēcit** quae medicus **pollicitus esset**. (opposite: 18–
> 19)
> . . . *(he)* **informed** him **what** the doctor **had promised**.

This sentence contains a verb of telling and a subordinate clause that is
introduced by a question word and has its verb in the subjunctive. This
kind of subordinate clause is called an *indirect question*. The direct
question would have been **Quae medicus pollicitus est?** "What did the
doctor promise?"

Here is another example of an indirect question:

> . . . **quī terror sit** in exercitū **expōnunt**. (19:22–23)
> . . . *they* **explain** **what** terror *is in the army*.

What would the direct question have been?

21. Gaius Fabricius

Beginning in the late eighth century B.C., the Greeks had founded many colonies in southern Italy—so many that the area was later called by the Romans Magna Graecia. These cities often quarrelled with the Italian tribes that lived nearby. In the late 280s one of these tribes, the Lucani, appealed to Rome for help against the Greeks, who were led by Tarentum, the largest and richest Greek city. The Greeks in turn asked Pyrrhus, king of Epirus (a district in mainland Greece) and a very skillful general, to intervene on their behalf. Pyrrhus crossed to Italy with a large army, including twenty elephants, which had never been seen in Italy before.

Rōmānī ā Pyrrhō, rēge Ēpīrī, proeliō superātī lēgātōs   1   280 B.C.
Tarentum ad eum dē redimendīs captīvīs mīsērunt. Inter   2
lēgātōs Rōmānōs erat C. Fabricius, vir bonus et bellō   3
ēgregius, sed admodum pauper. Pyrrhus, quī cum Rōmānīs   4
pācem facere volēbat, lēgātīs magna dōna obtulit, sī   5
Rōmānīs pācem suādērent. Quamquam haec omnia sprēta   6
sunt, rēx tamen captīvōs dīcitur sine pretiō Rōmam mīsisse.   7

Pyrrhus Fabriciī virtūtem admīrātus illī sēcrētō quār-   8
tam etiam rēgnī suī partem obtulit sī patriam dēsereret   9
sēcumque vīveret; cui Fabricius ita respondit: "Sī mē virum   10
bonum iūdicās, cūr mē vīs corrumpere? Sīn vērō malum,   11
cūr meam amīcitiam cupis?" Annō interiectō, omnī spē pā-   12   279 B.C.
cis inter Pyrrhum et Rōmānōs conciliandae ablātā,   13
Fabricius cōnsul factus contrā eum missus est. Cumque   14   278 B.C.
vīcīna castra ipse et rēx habērent, medicus rēgis nocte ad   15
Fabricium vēnit eīque pollicitus est, sī praemium sibi prō-   16
posuisset, sē Pyrrhum venēnō necātūrum. Hunc Fabricius   17
vīnctum ad Pyrrhum remīsit atque eum certiōrem fēcit   18
quae medicus pollicitus esset. Tum rēx admīrātus eum   19
dīxisse fertur: "Ille est Fabricius, quī difficilius ab honestāte   20
quam sōl ā suō cursū potest āvertī."   21

23   Cīnea, -ae (*m.*), Cinea (an envoy of Pyrrhus).
     sermōnem cōnferre, to engage in conversation.
24   *philosophus, -ī (*m.*), philosopher.
         philosophum: Epicurus (Greek philosopher; 341–270 B.C., founder of
             the Epicurean school of philosophy, which regarded pleasure as the
             highest good).
     quī dīceret . . . facerēmus: *subjunctives in subordinate clauses within in-*
         direct statement (see the grammar note on pages 86–87).
25   exclāmāsse: = exclāmāvisse.
26   Utinam id hostibus nostrīs persuādeāmus: "I wish we could make that
         pleasant to our enemies," "I wish we could persuade our enemies of
         that." For utinam introducing a wish with its verb in the subjunctive
         (*optative subjunctive*), see the grammar note on page 28.
27   *quō: "in order that," "so that"; quō often replaces ut in a *purpose clause*
         that contains a *comparative adjective* or *adverb*; this is a special case of
         a *relative clause of purpose* (see the grammar notes on pages 12 and
         13).
     cum . . . dederint: "when they had given,"*perfect subjunctive*, indicating
         time before the hypothetical future idea expressed in possint.
29   suppellex, suppellectilis (*f.*), furniture, household utensils.
     argenteus, -a, um, made of silver, silver.
     salīnum, -ī (*m.*), salt cellar, salt shaker.
30   *cōnstō, cōnstāre (1), cōnstitī, cōnstātum, to be established, cost, be com-
         posed, consist.
     patella, -ae (*f.*), pan, dish, plate.
     ūsus, -ūs (*m.*), use, practice, occasion.
     corneus, -a, -um, made of horn.
31   pediculus, -ī (*m.*), little foot, base.
     focus, -ī (*m.*), hearth, altar, home.
     rādīx, rādīcis (*f.*), root, radish.
     herba, -ae (*f.*), herb.
32   Samnītēs, Samnītium (*m. pl.*), the Samnites (inhabitants of Samnium, a
         region in the Apennines to the east of Latium and Campania).
33   *quamdiū (*adv.*), as long as.
     *cupiditās, cupiditātis (*f.*), desire, passion, ambition.
34   poterō: *future tense* in a *future more vivid* construction (see the grammar
         note on page 104), to be translated with a present tense in English, "I
         am able."
     *dēsum, dēesse (*irreg.*), dēfuī, dēfutūrus (+ *dat.*), to be lacking, be missing.

36   *glōriōsus, -a, -um, glorious.
     paupertās, paupertātis (*f.*), poverty.
     *exigō, exigere (3), exēgī, exāctum, to pass, spend (time).
37   inops, inopis, poor, needy, destitute.
     *unde (*adv.*), from where, from which.
         unde . . . darētur: "(anything) from which . . . could be given."
     *dōs, dōtis (*f.*), dowry.
38   *pars, partis (*f.*), part, direction; (*pl.*) duty, function.
39   *aerārium, -ī (*n.*), public treasury.
     collocō (1), to place, give in marriage.

Fabricius cum apud Pyrrhum rēgem lēgātus esset, cum 22
Cīneā, lēgātō Pyrrhī, sermōnem contulit. Hic dīxit quen- 23
dam philosophum esse Athēnīs, quī dīceret omnia quae fac- 24
erēmus ad voluptātem esse referenda. Tum Fabricium ex- 25
clāmāsse ferunt: "Utinam id hostibus nostrīs persuādeā- 26
mus, quō facilius vincī possint, cum sē voluptātibus de- 27
derint!" Nihil magis ab eius vītā aliēnum erat quam volup- 28
tās et lūxus. Tōta eius suppellex argentea ex salīnō ūnō 29
cōnstābat et ex patellā ad ūsum sacrōrum, quae corneō 30
pediculō sustinēbātur. Cēnābat ad focum rādīcēs et herbās, 31
cum lēgātī Samnītium ad eum vēnērunt magnamque eī 32
pecūniam obtulērunt; quibus sīc respondit: "Quamdiū cu- 33
piditātibus imperāre poterō, nihil mihi dēerit; vōs autem 34
pecūniam eīs quī eam cupiunt dōnāte." 35

Fabricius omnem vītam in glōriōsā paupertāte* exēgit, 36
adeōque inops dēcessit ut unde dōs fīliārum darētur nōn re- 37
linqueret. Senātus patris sibi partēs sūmpsit et, datīs ex 38
aerāriō dōtibus, fīliās collocāvit. 39

*glōriōsā paupertāte: an *oxymoron*, the use of contradictory words in
the same phrase.

*Pyrrhus inflicted several defeats on the Romans but accomplished
nothing decisive. He then fought for the Greek cities in Sicily in their
wars against Carthage and finally returned to Greece. After his death,
Tarentum and the other Greek cities in Italy came under Roman control; this meant that the entire Italian peninsula was now dominated by
Rome (see the map on page 89).*

Future More Vivid Conditions in Indirect Statement I

For a review of conditional sentences, see pages 104–105. The following
is a *future more vivid condition*, with a *future perfect indicative* in the
sī-clause and a *future indicative* in the main clause:

Sī praemium mihi **prōposueris**, Pyrrhum venēnō **necābō**.
*If **you offer** me a reward, **I will kill** Pyrrhus with poison.*

In indirect statement after a leading verb in the past tense (e.g., **pollicitus est**), this becomes:

Pollicitus est, sī praemium sibi **prōposuisset**, sē Pyrrhum venēnō
    necātūrum [esse]. (21:16–17)
*He promised that, if he **would offer** (if he **offered**) him a reward, he
would kill Pyrrhus with poison.* (continued on next page)

Future More Vivid Conditions in Indirect Statement (continued)

The *future perfect indicative* in the **sī**-clause becomes a *pluperfect subjunctive*, and the *future indicative* in the main clause becomes a *future active infinitive*.

Translating Ut

When you meet **ut** in a sentence, notice immediately whether the verb that completes it is indicative or subjunctive. If it is *indicative*, **ut** will mean "when," "after," or "as," e.g.:

Ut magistrātum iniit, reprehendit et senātum et plēbem. (19:2–3)
When *he entered upon (his term of) office, he rebuked both the Senate and the plebs.*

If the verb is *subjunctive*, there are several possibilities. The presence of a word such as **tantus, tālis, sīc, adeō,** or **tot** in the main clause suggests that the translation will be "so . . . that," i.e., a *result clause*, e.g.:

Gallī **tantō silentiō** in summum ēvāsērunt **ut** nōn sōlum custōdēs **fallerent,** sed nē canēs quidem **excitārent.** (20:35–37)
*The Gauls climbed onto the top **in such silence that** not only **did they escape the notice of** the guards, but **they awoke** not even the dogs.*

If the main verb means to "tell," "order," "beg," "urge," "persuade," or something similar, an *indirect command* will follow. These are sometimes translated by English infinitives ("to . . .") and sometimes by "that . . . ," e.g.:

Camillus ōrātiōne ācrī cīvibus persuāsit **ut** Rōmam **restituerent.** (20:61–62)
*Camillus in a fierce speech persuaded the citizens **to restore** Rome.*

Gallī . . . postulāvērunt **ut** prō iūre gentium ita violātō lēgātī Rōmānī **dēderentur.** (20:6–8)
*The Gauls . . . demanded **that,** in compensation for such a violation of international law, the Roman ambassadors **should be handed over.***

The **ut** clause may tell *why* the action of the main verb was done. Such *purpose clauses* are usually translated by "(in order) to . . . ," e.g.:

Tarquinius, **ut** rēgnum **reciperet,** ad Lartem Porsenam, Clūsīnum rēgem, fūgit. (14:1–2)
*Tarquinius, **in order to regain** his kingdom, fled to Lars Porsena, the king of Clusiuim.*

PART III

Rome as a World Power

By the year 265 B.C. Rome controlled all of the Italian peninsula south of the Po River. Now that the Romans had come to dominate the Greek cities of southern Italy, they became responsible for protecting the interests of those states. Trade was essential to many of them; they had been fighting for years against Carthage, a city in North Africa, which possessed an extensive trading empire and maintained it with a powerful navy. Thus Rome, in order to protect the interests of her southern Italian clients, was drawn into three wars with Carthage, which are called the Punic Wars. The First Punic War (264–241 B.C.) resulted in the islands of Sicily, Sardinia and Corsica being ceded to Rome. These were Rome's first overseas provinces.

The Carthaginians attempted to compensate for the loss of territory to Rome by expanding their influence in Spain, where they had had colonies for a long time. The general Hamilcar and his followers, who led the Carthaginians in Spain, desired revenge on Rome. After Hamilcar's death, his son Hannibal took over his army and attacked the city of Saguntum, an ally of Rome, thereby precipitating the Second Punic War (218–201 B.C.). Hannibal crossed over from Spain into Italy via the Alps, and for sixteen years he remained on Italian soil. He inflicted several defeats on the Romans but was never able to force the Romans into surrendering. Finally the Romans sent an army to attack Carthage itself. In panic the Carthaginians recalled Hannibal, who was finally defeated at the battle of Zama by Scipio Africanus. The Romans deprived Carthage of all her overseas territory and all her ships, thereby ending forever any real threat from Carthage.

The Punic Wars showed the typical Roman perseverance and toughness. They also marked a turning point for Rome. In order to win the First Punic War, the Romans had to learn how to make use of ships in warfare, something they had never done. They also acquired their first territory outside Italy as a result of this war. They acquired much more territory after the Second Punic War, and from that point on Rome was the dominant power in the western Mediterranean.

1   Cum: *conjunction*, not *preposition* here.
     Pūnicus, -a, um, Punic, Carthaginian.
     Carthāginiēnsis, -is, -e, Carthaginian; (*m. pl.*) the Carthaginians.
2   *contendō, contendere (3), contendī, contentum, to contend, fight.
     M. Atīlius Rēgulus, -ī (*m.*), Marcus Atilius Regulus (consul in 267 and
        256 B.C. and hero of the First Punic War).
3   *nāvālis, -is, -e, naval.
        nāvālī pugnā: this battle took place off Cape Ecnomus on the southern
        shore of Sicily.
4   Hannō, Hannōnis (*m.*), Hanno (leader of the Carthaginians).
5   agere: "to negotiate."
6   dum . . . advenīrent: "until . . . could arrive" (see the grammar note on
        page 97).
     Āfrica, -ae (*f.*), Africa.
7   oportet, oportēre (2, *impersonal*), oportuit, it is right, it is proper, one
        ought.
8   quod . . . fēcissent: *subjunctive in a subordinate clause within indirect
        statement* (see the grammar note on pages 86–87).
10   Poenus, -a, -um, Carthaginian; (*m. pl.*) the Carthaginians.
     catēna, -ae (*f.*), chain.
11   callidus, -a, -um, ingenious, clever, cunning.
12   Sī . . . fēceritis . . . eritis: *future more vivid condition* (see the grammar
        note on page 104).
     nihilō . . . meliōrēs: "better in respect to nothing," "no better."
13   pār parī: "like for like," "tit for tat."
14   conveniō, convenīre (4), convēnī, conventum, to come together; (+ *dat.*) to
        agree, be consistent with.
        conveniēns: *neuter*, modifying respōnsum.
     gravitās, gravitātis (*f.*), severity, harshness, seriousness.
15   *iste, ista, istud, that of yours, that, that very.
        Istō . . . metū: *ablative of separation* (see the grammar note on page
        55).
        Dē pāce . . . nōn convēnit: "Agreement was not reached," *impersonal use
        of the verb* (see the grammar note on pages 153 and 155).
16   ex animō: "sincerely."
     *bellum gerere, to wage war.

22.   Marcus Atilius Regulus

Cum prīmō Pūnicō bellō Rōmānī contrā Carthāginiēnsēs   1   256 B.C.
dē imperiō Siciliae contenderent, M. Atīlius Rēgulus, cōnsul   2
Rōmānus, nāvālī pugnā classem Pūnicam superāvit.   3
Proeliō factō, Hannō, dux Carthāginiēnsis, ad eum vēnit   4
simulāns sē velle dē pāce agere, rē vērā ut tempus extra-   5
heret, dum novae cōpiae ex Āfricā advenīrent. Mīlitēs   6
Rōmānī clāmāre coepērunt Rēgulum idem facere oportēre   7
quod Carthāginiēnsēs paucīs ante annīs in cōnsule quōdam   8
fēcissent. Is enim tamquam in colloquium per fraudem   9
vocātus ā Poenīs comprehēnsus erat et in catēnās coniectus.   10
Iam Hannō timēre incipiēbat, sed perīculum respōnsō cal-   11
lidō reppulit. "Sī hoc fēceritis," inquit, "nihilō eritis Poenīs   12
meliōrēs." Cōnsul tacēre iussit eōs quī pār parī referrī   13
volēbant, et conveniēns gravitātī Rōmānae respōnsum   14
dedit: "Istō tē metū, Hannō, fidēs Rōmāna līberat." Dē   15
pāce, quia Poenus ex animō nōn agēbat et cōnsul bellum   16
gerere quam pācem facere mālēbat, nōn convēnit.   17

Dum + Subjunctive = "until"

You have met the conjunction **dum** meaning "while" (see the grammar
note on page 24). This word also has other meanings, one of which is
"until," e.g.:

> . . . ut tempus extraheret, **dum** novae cōpiae ex Āfricā **advenīrent**.
> (above: 5–6)
> . . . *in order to drag out the time* **until** *new troops* **_could arrive_** *from*
> *Africa.*

When **dum** means "until" and expresses an idea of *anticipation* or
expectation, it is completed by a verb in the *subjunctive*. This can be
translated with the English auxiliary "could."

18   *collēga, -ae (m.), colleague, companion.
     L. Mānlius Vulsō, L. Mānliī Vulsōnis (m.), Lucius Manlius Vulso Longus
        (consular colleague of Regulus in 256 B.C.).
19   castellum, -ī (n.), fort, fortress.
20   Tūnis, Tūnētis (f.), Tunis (a city in Africa, on the site of the modern city
        of Tunis).
21   decem mīlibus passuum: ablative with aberat, "was distant by ten miles."
22   Carthāgō, Carthāginis (f.), Carthage.
23   *vāstō (1), to lay waste, ravage, destroy.
24   hiems, hiemis (f.), winter.

25   *īnsequor, īnsequī (3), īnsecūtus sum, to follow, succeed.
     Lacedaemonius, -a, -um, Lacedaemonian, Spartan.
     Xanthippus, -ī (m.), Xanthippus (Spartan general).
26   perītissimus: remember that the meaning of some adjectives is completed
        by a word or phrase in the genitive case.
     conductī, -ōrum (m. pl.), hired men, mercenaries.
28   mūtō (1), to change.
29   vīcērunt: near Tunis in north Africa.

33   *commūtō (1), to change, exchange.
     iūs iūrandum, iūris iūrandī (n.), oath.
34   adstringō, adstringere (3), adstrīnxī, adstrictum, to bind fast, obligate.
     impetrō (1), to obtain, succeed in one's request.
36   *aliter (adv.), otherwise, differently.
     ac (conj., in comparisons), than, as.
37   illōs . . . habēre: indirect statement, depending on an implied dīxit (see
        the grammar note below).
     *cāsus, -ūs (m.), misfortune, calamity.
38   adulēscentēs . . . senectūte: indirect statement, again depending on an
        implied dīxit, not on negāvit (38).
42   ut: "as," "like," simply introducing a comparison and not a clause.

Transition to Indirect Statement

You know that a verb of saying or thinking often introduces an accusative and infinitive construction (indirect statement). Sometimes
there is no verb of saying or thinking, but the context makes it clear
that someone begins to speak; then the writer suddenly switches to indirect statement. Consider the sentence that begins Nam senātuī
suāsit (opposite: 36). The sentence begins by saying that Regulus ad-
vised the Senate not to make peace with Carthage; then Regulus' words
are given in indirect statement (illōs enim frāctōs tot cāsibus spem
nūllam habēre), but there is no verb of saying to introduce them. You
may wish to insert the words "he said" in your translation.

Deinde Rēgulus et collēga, L. Mānlius Vulsō, in Āfricam 18
prīmī Rōmānōrum ducum trānsiērunt. Ibi, multīs castellīs 19
expugnātīs magnāque praedā captā, Tūnētem occupā- 20
vērunt, quae urbs decem tantum mīlibus passuum ā 21
Carthāgine aberat. Vulsō in Italiam cum parte mīlitum 22
rediit, collēgā ad agrōs vāstandōs relictō. Itaque Rēgulus 23
hiemem in Āfricā ēgit. 24

Īnsequentī annō Lacedaemonius quīdam, nōmine Xan- 25   255 B.C.
thippus, reī mīlitāris perītissimus, Carthāginem cum con- 26
ductīs vēnit. Carthāginiēnsibus celeriter persuāsit ut sē 27
ducem facerent. Quō factō fortūna mūtāta est. Nam nōn 28
sōlum exercitum Rōmānum vīcērunt sed etiam Rēgulum 29
imperātōrem cēpērunt. 30

Paucīs post annīs, cum iterum dē pāce agere cōnstituis- 31   249 B.C.
sent, Rēgulum cum lēgātīs Rōmam mīsērunt quī Rōmānīs 32
pācem suādēret et dē commūtandīs captīvīs ageret; iūre 33
iūrandō autem adstrictus est ut, nisi dē captīvīs impetrāret, 34
redīret ipse Carthāginem. Is, cum Rōmam vēnisset, ēgit 35
aliter ac Poenī mandāverant. Nam senātuī suāsit nē pāx 36
cum Poenīs fieret; illōs enim frāctōs tot cāsibus spem nūl- 37
lam habēre; reddī captīvōs negāvit esse ūtile; adulēscentēs 38
esse et bonōs ducēs, sē iam cōnfectum senectūte; dīxit etiam 39
malum exemplum futūrum esse, sī captīvī Rōmānī redimer- 40
entur. Senātus eō auctōre pācem recūsāvit Poenōsque cap- 41
tīvōs retinuit. Rēgulus ut captīvus coniugem parvōsque 42
nātōs ā sē remōvit Carthāginemque rediit. Ibi crūdēlis- 43
simīs suppliciīs necātus esse dīcitur. 44

Future More Vivid Conditions in Indirect Statement II

The following is a *future more vivid condition*, with a *future indicative*
in the sī-clause and a *future indicative* in the main clause:

Sī captīvī Rōmānī **redimentur**, malum exemplum **erit**.
*If Roman captives **are ransomed**, it **will be** a bad example.*

In indirect statement after a leading verb in the past tense (e.g., **dīxit**),
this becomes:

Dīxit . . . malum exemplum **futūrum esse**, sī captīvī Rōmānī **re-
dimerentur**. (above: 39–41)
*He said . . . that it **would be** a bad example, if Roman captives **were
ransomed**.* (continued on page 100)

2   Hispānia, -ae (f.), Spain.
3   Hamilcar, Hamilcaris (m.), Hamilcar Barca (Carthaginian general in the First Punic War).
5   Sardinia, -ae (f.), Sardinia (a large island to the west of Italy).

    āmīserat: note that the *indicative* is used here because the writer asserts this reason as a fact on his own authority (compare the use of the subjunctive described in the grammar note on page 78).

6   Hannibal, Hannibalis (m.), Hannibal (son of Hamilcar and Carthaginian general in the Second Punic War).

    annōs novem nātus: "aged nine years," "nine years old"; the *acusative of duration of time* is used with the perfect participle of nāscor to indicate age.

8   ōre vultūque: "in face and expression," *ablative of respect.*
11   aptus, -a, -um, suitable, appropriate, adapted.
12   Hasdrubal, Hasdrubalis (m.), Hasdrubal (Carthaginian general and son-in-law of Hamilcar Barca).

    *successor, successōris (m.), successor.

    eī successor: "his successor."
13   cārus: "dear to," with the *datives,* Hasdrubalī . . . exercituī. For the *dative with adjectives,* see the grammar note on page 107.
14   *praeficiō, praeficere (3), praefēcī, praefectum, to put X (*acc.*) in charge of Y (*dative*).

    See the grammar note on page 108.
15   aliō duce: *ablative absolute.*

    confīdō, confīdere (3, *semi-deponent*), confīsus sum, to be confident, have confidence.

Future More Vivid Conditions in Indirect Statement II (continued)

The *future indicative* in the sī-clause becomes an *imperfect subjunctive*, and the *future indicative* in the main clause becomes a *future active infinitive.* Compare the grammar note on pages 93–94, which shows how a *future perfect indicative* in the sī-clause becomes a *pluperfect subjunctive* when the conditional sentence is stated indirectly in secondary sequence.

Now look at the following:

Magna dōna vōbīs dabō, sī Rōmānīs pācem suādēbitis.
I will give you large gifts, if you recommend peace to the Romans.

When this conditional sentence is transformed into the following statement with its main verb in a past tense, the *future indicative* in the sī-clause becomes an *imperfect subjunctive*:

Pyrrhus . . . lēgātīs maga dōna obtulit, sī Rōmānīs pācem suādērent. (21:4–6)
Pyrrhus . . . offered the ambassadors large gifts, if they would recommend peace to the Romans. (See also 14:13–14 , 21:8–10.)

23. Hannibal

After losing Sicily and other territories to Rome, Carthage attempted to compensate for this loss by enlarging her area of influence in Spain, where there had been Carthaginian colonies for some time. This policy led to more conflicts with Rome: the Second Punic War of 218–201 B.C. The next three stories relate some of the events connected with this war.

Carthāginiēnsēs post prīmum Pūnicum bellum imperium opēsque in Hispāniā dīligenter auxērunt. Dux huius operis Hamilcar erat, quī imperātor prīmō bellō fuerat atque indignābātur quod Carthāgō eō bellō Siciliam Sardiniamque āmīserat. 1 237–
2 219 B.C.
3
4
5

Hannibal, eius fīlius, annōs novem nātus patre incitante iūrāvit sē semper hostem futūrum esse populī Rōmānī. Posteā in Hispāniam missus est. Tam similis patrī ōre vultūque erat ut mīlitēs Hamilcarem iuvenem redditum sibi esse crēderent. Ingenium autem erat ad rēs dīversissimās, pārendum atque imperandum, aptum. Nōn minus Hasdrubalī, imperātōrī, quī interfectō Hamilcare eī successor fuit in Hispāniā, quam exercituī cārus erat. Neque Hasdrubal alium quemquam mīlitibus praeficere mālēbat, neque mīlitēs aliō duce plūs cōnfīdēbant aut audēbant. 6
7
8
9
10
11
12 229 B.C.
13
14
15

Hannibal

16   capessō, capessere (3), capessīvī, capessītum, to grasp, enter on, engage
     in.
18   fatīgō (1), to fatigue, tire, wear down.
     frīgus, frīgoris (n.), cold.
19   patientia, -ae (f.), endurance.
     modus: "measure," i.e., the amount he consumed.
     pōtiō, pōtiōnis (f.), drink.
     dēsīderium, -ī (n.), desire, want, need.
20   nātūrālis, -is, -e, natural.
     vigiliae, -ārum (f. pl.), wakefulness.
21   discrīminō (1), to divide, separate, distinguish, mark off.
22   supererat: "was left over from" (+ abl.).
     ea: i.e., quiēs, "sleep."
     mollis, -is, -e, soft.
23   strātus, -ī (m.), blanket, bed.
24   sagulum, -ī (n.), short military coat.
     statiō, statiōnis (f.), station, military guard post, sentry post.
25   vestītus, -ūs (m.), clothes, attire.
     nihil: "in no way."
     aequālis, aequālis (m.), companion of the same age, comrade.
     excellēns, excellentis, excelling, superior.
26   cōnspiciēbantur: "were noticed," "attracted attention."
     pedes, peditis (m.), infantryman, foot-soldier.
27   īdem . . . erat: "he, the same man, was . . ."
     *prīnceps, prīncipis, first.

31   prīstinus, -a, -um, former
32   Saguntīnī, -ōrum (m. pl.), the people of Saguntum (a city on the east
     coast of Spain).
     *socius, -ī (m.), ally, partner.
     Hispāniēnsis, -is, -e, Spanish.
33   Pȳrēnaeus, -a, -um, of the Pyrenees.
35   Tīcīnus, -ī (m.), Ticinus (a tributary of the Po River).
     Trebia, -ae (f.), Trebia (a river in northern Italy).
36   Trasumennus, -ī (m.), Trasimene (a lake in Etruria).
     *lacus, -ūs (m.), lake.
     Āpūlia, -ae (f.), Apulia (a district in southwest Italy).
     Cannae, -ārum (f. pl.), Cannae (a village in Apulia).
37   eō cōnsiliō: "in accordance with this intention," ablative of manner, fol-
     lowed by a purpose clause.
     *lībertās, lībertātis (f.), freedom.
38   sollicitō (1), to stir up, incite.
41   *dēvincō, dēvincere (3), dēvīcī, dēvictum, to conquer, subdue.

Plūrimum audāciae ad perīcula capessenda, plūrimum 16
cōnsiliī inter ipsa perīcula praebēbat. Nūllō labōre aut cor- 17
pus fatīgārī aut animus vincī poterat. Calōris ac frīgoris 18
patientia erat pār. Cibī modus pōtiōnisque dēsīderiō 19
nātūrālī, nōn voluptāte, fīnītus est; tempora vigiliārum 20
somnīque nec diē nec nocte discrīmināta sunt; id quod 21
gerendīs rēbus supererat quiētī datum est; ea neque mollī 22
strātō neque silentiō arcessīta est; multī saepe eum mīlitārī 23
sagulō opertum humī iacentem inter custōdiās statiōnēsque 24
mīlitum cōnspexērunt. Vestītus nihil inter aequālēs excel- 25
lēns; arma atque equī cōnspiciēbantur. Equitum pedi- 26
tumque īdem longē prīmus erat; prīnceps in proelium ībat, 27
ultimus commissō proeliō excēdēbat. 28

Hasdrubale interfectō, Hannibal, nātus annōs vīgintī 29   221 B.C.
septem imperātor creātus, cōnstituit Rōmānōs vincere, ut 30
Carthāginem in prīstinam auctōritātem restitueret. Prī- 31
mum obsidiōne urbem Saguntīnōrum cēpit, quī sociī His- 32   219 B.C.
pāniēnsēs Rōmānōrum erant. Deinde per montēs Pȳrē- 33   218 B.C.
naeōs atque Alpēs iter difficile in Italiam fēcit. Ibi 34
Rōmānōs exercitūs superāvit ad Tīcīnum flūmen, ad Tre- 35   218 B.C.–
biam, ad Trasumennum lacum, in Āpūliā ad Cannās. In 36   216 B.C.
Āpūliam vēnerat eō cōnsiliō, ut spē lībertātis sociōs 37
Rōmānōrum sollicitāret. Quīdam ex sociīs amīcitiam Han- 38
nibalis secūtī sunt, sed multī in fidē Rōmānōrum mān- 39
sērunt. Cum optimī ducēs Rōmānī adversus Hannibalem 40
mitterentur, numquam tamen eum dēvincere potuērunt. 41
Sēdecim annōs in Italiā neque victor neque victus mānsit. 42

Conditional Sentences

Conditional sentences are made up of two halves, one of which begins with the word **sī** "if" or **nisi** "if not," "unless," e.g.:

Rōmānī, **sī** bellum gerunt, plērumque victōrēs sunt.
If the Romans wage war, they are usually the winners.

Some conditional sentences, like the one above, present no particular problems in translating; such sentences are referred to as *simple* or *factual* conditions. The following three types, however, do require special care:

1. Both verbs are in the *future tense*, or the verb of the sī-clause is in the *future perfect* and that of the main clause is in the *future*, e.g.:

    Sī Porsena ad urbem **manēbit, moriētur**.
    *If Porsena **stays** (literally, **will stay**) near the city, he **will die**.*

    Sī Hannibal in Italiam **trānsierit**, Rōmānī maximē **timēbunt**.
    *If Hannibal **crosses** (literally, **will have crossed**) into Italy, the Romans **will be** very **afraid**.*

Use the English *present tense* in translating the sī-clause of sentences of this type; the literal translation ("will stay," "will crossed") is not good English. These are called *future more vivid* conditions.

The *future tense* is used in the sī-clause when the actions of the two clauses take place *at the same time*. The *future perfect tense* is used when the action of the sī-clause is thought of as having been completed *prior* to the action of the main clause.

2. Both verbs are in the *present subjunctive*, e.g.:

    Regulus, sī Carthāginem **redeat, necētur**.
    *If Regulus **should return** to Carthage, he **would be killed**.*
    *If Regulus **returned** to Carthage, he **would be killed**.*

    Carthāginiēnsēs, sī Xanthippum ducem **faciant**, Rōmānōs **vincant**.
    *If the Carthaginians **should make** Xanthippus their leader, they **would defeat** the Romans.*
    *If the Carthaginians **made** Xanthippus their leader, they **would defeat** the Romans.*

Conditional sentences like these present the action as possible but unlikely; they are called *should/would* or *future less vivid* conditions.

3. Both verbs are in the *imperfect* or *pluperfect subjunctive*, e.g.:

Present Contrary to Fact:

Ducēs, sī ex animō **agerent**, dē pāce convenīre **possent**.
If the leaders were negotiating sincerely, they would be able to make an agreement about peace.

Past Contrary to Fact:

Regulus, nisi iūre iūrandō **adstrictus esset**, Carthāginem nōn **redisset**.
If Regulus had not been bound by an oath, he would not have gone back to Carthage.

Sī senātus pācem **fēcisset**, Regulus Rōmae certē **mānsisset**.
If the Senate had made peace, Regulus would certainly have stayed in Rome.

These are called *contrary to fact* conditions, since they present a hypothesis about something that is not or was not true. The *imperfect subjunctive* is used in *present contrary to fact conditions*, and the *pluperfect subjunctive* in *past contrary to fact conditions*.

Remember the basic difference between the indicative and subjunctive moods: the indicative presents something as a fact, while the subjunctive implies that the statement is hypothetical or not real. Hence the subjunctive must be used in future less vivid and contrary to fact conditions.

Exercise 6
Read aloud and translate. Identify the type of condition involved:

1. Sī mīlitēs Rōmānī elephantōs Pyrrhī cōnspexerint, aufugient perterritī.
2. Sī Fabricius pecūniam Pyrrhī accēpisset, Pyrrhus nōn crēdidisset eum esse virum bonum.
3. Nisi Xanthippus dux Carthāginiēnsis factus esset, Rōmānī celeriter bellum cōnfēcissent.
4. Regulus, nisi dē captīvīs impetrāverit, ipse Carthāginem redībit.
5. Nisi Regulus iūrāvisset, necesse eī nōn fuisset Carthāginem redīre.
6. Carthāginiēnsēs, nisi prīmō bellō victī essent, īnsulam Siciliam Rōmānīs nōn dedissent.
7. Hannibal, nisi Rōmānīs inimīcus esset, Alpēs cum exercitū nōn trānsīret.
8. Hannibal, sī dux in Hispāniā fīat, sociōs Rōmānōs aggrediātur.
9. Sī Hannibal oppidum Saguntum aggresus erit, ferentne Rōmānī auxilium?
10. Sī Rōmānī cum Poenīs bellum gerant, necesse sit eīs nāvēs habēre.

1   **clādēs, clādis** (*f.*), loss, defeat, disaster.
2   **Q. Fabius Maximus, -ī** (*m.*), Quintus Fabius Maximus Verrucosus
      Cunctator (elected consul five times and dictator in 217 B.C. against
      Hannibal; the **cognōmen** Verrucosus means "covered with warts").
      M. Minucius Rūfus, -ī (*m.*), Marcus Minucius Rufus (master of the horse
      under Quintus Fabius Maximus in 217 B.C.; killed at the battle of
      Cannae in 216 B.C.).
3   ***magister equitum, magistrī equitum** (*m.*), master of the horse (second in
      command to the dictator).
4   **dēcertō** (1), to fight to the finish.
5   ***intueor, intuērī** (2), **intuitus sum**, to look at, watch.
      *levis, -is, -e, light, slight, minor.
      fortitūdō, fortitūdinis (*f.*), strength, courage.
6   **invidia, -ae** (*f.*), envy, jealousy, ill will.
7   **onerō** (1), to burden, oppress, overwhelm.
8   **ūnī . . . agrō pepercit**: *dative with special intransitive verb* (see the
      grammar note on page 16).
9   **Quīntus, -ī** (*m.*), Quintus (son of Quintus Fabius Maximus).
10   ***redigō, redigere** (3), **redēgī, redāctum**, to drive back, reduce, raise (money
      by selling something).

11   **ratiō, ratiōnis** (*f.*), account, scheme, procedure.
      Fabiānus, -a, -um, relating to Fabius, of Fabius.
12   **cūnctātor, cūnctātōris** (*m.*), one who hesitates or delays; (*here as a*
      cognōmen) the Delayer.
      Rōmānīs grāta: *dative with adjective* (see the grammar note on page
      107).
13   ***absēns, absentis**, absent.
      aliquantum, -ī (*n.*) (+ *partitive genitive*), a certain amount of, a bit.
      aliquantum victōriae: this minor victory took place at Gerunium in
      Apulia.
14   ***adipīscor, adipīscī** (3), **adeptus sum**, to reach, obtain, win.
      lēx lāta est: "a law was passed"; the idiom **lēgem ferre** means to propose
      or pass a law.
      iūs: (*here*) "authority."
15   **aequō** (1), to make equal.
      aequus, -a, -um, calm, level.
16   ***satis** (*adv.*), enough, sufficiently.
      fīdō, fīdere (3, *semi-deponent*), **fīsus sum**, to trust, be confident (that).
      haudquāquam (*adv.*), not at all, by no means.
18   **temere** (*adv.*), by chance, without cause, rashly.

24   **alius dux**: Scipio Africanus, who defeated Hannibal at Zama in 202 B.C.
      (see section 25).
      prōmptus, -a, -um, quick to respond, eager.
26   **cūnctor, cūnctārī** (1), **cūnctātus sum**, to be slow to act, hesitate, delay.

24. Quintus Fabius Maximus

Postquam Rōmānī clādem ad Trasumennum lacum ac- 1   217 B.C.
cēpērunt, Q. Fabius Maximus dictātor creātus est, et M. 2
Minucius Rūfus magister equitum. Cōnsilium erat Fabiī 3
nūllō locō cum hoste dēcertāre, sed fīnēs Rōmānōrum so- 4
ciōrumque intuērī et levibus proeliīs mīlitum fortitūdinem 5
augēre. Hannibal hōc cōnsiliō turbātus dictātōrem invidiā 6
onerāre cōnstituit. Itaque cum ager Fabiī eī mōnstrātus es- 7
set, omnibus agrīs circā vāstātīs, ūnī agrō dictātōris pe- 8
percit. At Fabius, missō Rōmam Quīntō fīliō, agrum vēn- 9
didit pecūniāque redāctā captīvōs Rōmānōs redēmit. 10

Ratiō Fabiāna bellī gerendī, propter quam Fabiō cognō- 11
men Cūnctātor datum est, Rōmānīs grāta nōn erat. Cum 12
Minucius, absente dictātōre, aliquantum victōriae forte 13
adeptus esset, lēx lāta est ut iūs magistrī equitum et dic- 14
tātōris aequārētur. Iniūriam tamen Fabius aequō animō 15
tulit, satis fīdēns haudquāquam cum imperiī iūre artem 16
imperandī aequātam esse. Legiōnēs inter dictātōrem et 17
magistrum dīvīsae sunt. Dēnique Minucius, temere proeliō 18
commissō, ā Fabiō servātus est. Tum sub imperium dic- 19
tātōris rediit legiōnēsque restituit et Fabium patrem appel- 20
lāvit. Rōmae, ut est perlāta fāma eius reī, omnēs Maximum 21
laudibus ad caelum ferēbant. 22

Multīs post annīs, aliīs rēbus interim gestīs, Fabius mor- 23   203 B.C.
tuus est. Quamquam alius dux prōmptior ad proelium 24
Hannibalem dēnique dēvīcit, certum tamen est Fabium rem 25
Rōmānam cōnsiliō cūnctandī restituisse. 26

Dative with Adjectives

The meaning of some adjectives may be completed by a word or phrase
in the *dative case*, e.g.:

Ratiō Fabiāna . . . **Rōmānīs grāta** nōn erat. (above: 11–12)
*Fabius' procedure . . . was not **pleasing to the Romans**.*

Tam **similis patrī** ōre vultūque erat. . . . (23:8–9)
*He was so **similar to his father** in face and expression. . . .*

Nōn minus **Hasdrubalī** . . . quam **exercituī cārus** erat. (23:11–13)
*He was no less **dear to Hadrubal** . . . than **to the army**.*

1 **P. Cornēlius Scīpiō, Scīpiōnis** (*m.*), Publius Cornelius Scipio Africanus
 Major (236–183 B.C.; conqueror of the Carthaginians in the Second
 Punic War).
2 ***praesum, praeesse** (*irreg.*), **praefuī** (+ *dat.*), to be in charge of, be in command of.
  exercituī Rōmānō . . . praefuerat: "had been in charge of the Roman
  army" (see the grammar note below).
3 **circumveniō, circumvenīre** (4), **circumvēnī, circumventum**, to surround.
4 **septendecim**, seventeen.

5 **aedīlitās, aedīlitātis** (*f.*), aedileship (for the functions of the aediles, see
 the note at line 7 below).
6 **lēgitimus, -a, -um**, legitimate, lawful.
7 ***aedīlis, aedīlis** (*m.*), aedile (magistrate in charge of overseeing streets,
 traffic, public buildings, the water and grain supply, and the games).
8 ***favor, favōris** (*m.*), favor, support.

12 **comitia, -ōrum** (*n. pl.*), assembly of the Roman people.
 ēdīcō, ēdīcere (3), **ēdīxī, ēdictum**, to proclaim, announce.
 seniōrēs, seniōrum (*m. pl.*), older men.
14 **profiteor, profitērī** (2), **professus sum**, to declare publicly.
16 **ad ūnum:** "to a man."
 P. Scīpiōnī imperium esse: "that P. Scipio have the command," *dative of
 possession* (see the grammar note on page 7).
18 **dubitō** (1), to doubt, be uncertain.
 num (*introducing a direct question that expects a negative answer*),
  surely . . . not; (*introducing an indirect question*) whether.
19 ***cōntiō, cōntiōnis** (*f.*), public meeting.
20 **disserō, disserere** (3), **disseruī, dissertum**, to discuss, argue, speak.

Dative with Compound Verbs

You know that Latin has many compound verbs. If the root of the compound verb is *intransitive*, you may find an *indirect object* in the *dative*
case completing the meaning of the verb, e.g.:

 . . . quī **exercituī Rōmānō . . . praefuerat.** (opposite: 1–2)
 . . . who **had been in charge of the Roman army**.

If the root of the verb is *transitive*, you may find a *direct object* in
the *accusative* in addition to the *dative indirect object*, e.g.:

 Neque Hasdrubal **alium quemquam mīlitibus praeficere** mālēbat. . . . (23:13–14)
 Neither did Hasdrubal prefer **to put anyone else in charge of his
  soldiers***. . . .*

25. Publius Cornelius Scipio Africanus

P. Cornēlius Scīpiō fīlius erat cōnsulis quī exercituī 1
Rōmānō in proeliō ad Tīcīnum flūmen praefuerat. Fāma est 2 218 B.C.
patrem, cum in eō proeliō vulnerātus ab hostibus circum- 3
venīrētur, ā fīliō septendecim nātō annōs servātum esse. 4

Posteā cum aedīlitātem peteret, tribūnī plēbis resis- 5 214 B.C.
tēbant, quod nōndum ad petendum lēgitima aetās esset. 6
Tum Scīpiō, "Sī mē," inquit, "omnēs Quīrītēs aedīlem facere 7
volunt, satis annōrum habeō." Aedīlis magnō favōre populī 8
nūllō tribūnō resistente creātus est. 9

Quattuor post annīs pater Scīpiōnis et patruus, quī bel- 10
lum in Hispāniā gesserant, intrā diēs trīgintā cecidērunt. 11 211 B.C.
Comitiīs ēdictīs ad imperātōrem creandum omnēs seniōrēs 12 210 B.C.
imperium Hispāniēnse accipere nōlēbant; tum subitō P. 13
Cornēlius Scīpiō, quattuor et vīgintī annōs nātus, professus 14
est sē petere et in superiōre locō unde cōnspicī posset, cōn- 15
stitit. Deinde ad ūnum omnēs P. Scīpiōnī imperium esse in 16
Hispāniā iussērunt. Posteā tamen cīvēs ob aetātem im- 17
perātōris novī dubitāre incipiēbant num rēctē fēcissent. 18
Scīpiō, hōc animadversō, cōntiōnem habuit et tam graviter 19
disseruit ut animōs rūrsus excitāret omnēsque certā spē 20
implēret. 21

26   **mānsuētūdō, mānsuētūdinis** (*f.*), mildness, clemency.
       in (+ *acc.*), (*here*) toward.
       ***comitās, cōmitātis** (*f.*), kindness, friendliness, courtesy.
       ***barbarus, -ī** (*m.*), barbarian, foreigner.
27   **Hispānus, -a, -um**, Spanish.
       Carthāgō Nova, Carthāginis Novae (*f.*), New Carthage (a Carthaginian
          colony in Spain, on the site of the modern Spanish city of Cartagena).
          Carthāgine Novā: the *locative* of **Carthāgō** can be either **Carthāginī**
            or **Carthāgine** (see the grammar note on page 53).
28   **Allucius, -ī** (*m.*), Allucius (chief of the Celtiberians).
       Celtibērī, -ōrum (*m. pl.*), the Celtiberians (a people of central Spain).
31   **beneficium, -ī** (*n.*), kindness.
       remūnerō (1), to repay.
32   **quadringentī, -ae, -a**, four hundred.
       ***revertō, revertere** (3), **revertī, reversum**, to return.
33   **Massīva, -ae** (*m.*), Massiva.
       Āfer, Āfra, Āfrum, African.
34   **avunculus, -ī** (*m.*), uncle.
       Masinissa, -ae (*m.*), Masinissa (king of Numidia, a kingdom in north
          Africa).
       Numidae, -ārum (*m. pl.*), Numidians.
       equitātus, -ūs (*m.*), cavalry.
35   **subsidium, -ī** (*n.*), aid, support, help.
       subsidiō Carthāginiēnsibus: "to help the Carthaginians," *double dative*
          (see the grammar note below).

36   **spectāre**: (*here*) "to direct his vision toward," "to aim at."
37   **prius** (*adv.*), first.
       Syphāx, Syphācis (*m.*), Syphax (king of Numidia).
40   ***portus, -ūs** (*m.*), port, harbor.
41   **Hasdrubal, Hasdrubalis** (*m.*), Hasdrubal (Carthaginian commander in
          Spain from 214 to 206 B.C.; not the same as the Hasdrubal mentioned
          at 23:12).
44   **eōdem lectō accubuērunt**: referring to the ancient custom of reclining
          while dining.
       īnsum, inesse (*irreg.*), **īnfuī** (+ *dat.*), to be in.
          For the *dative with compound verbs*, see the grammar note on page
          108.

Double Dative

You may encounter sentences that contain two nouns or a noun and a
pronoun in the *dative case*, e.g.:

    ... **subsidiō Carthāginiēnsibus** vēnerat. (opposite: 34–35)
    ... *had come **to be of help with reference to the Carthaginians**.*
    ... *had come **to help the Carthaginians**.*

Quīnque annōs in Hispāniā bellum adversus Car- 22   210–
thāginiēnsēs continuō cursū victōriārum gessit. Exercitūs 23   206 B.C.
hostium ex Hispāniā expulit et amīcitiās gentium His- 24
pāniēnsium sibi conciliāvit. Multa nārrantur dē Scīpiōnis 25
mānsuētūdine in miserōs et dē cōmitāte in hostēs ac bar- 26
barōs. Virginem Hispānam captam Carthāgine Novā, quae 27
Alluciō, prīncipī Celtibērōrum, dēspōnsa erat, spōnsō trā- 28
didit. Magnum quoque aurī pondus, quod virginis parentēs 29
ad redimendam fīliam attulērunt, spōnsō dedit. Allucius, 30
ut beneficium remūnerārētur, domum profectus ad 31
Scīpiōnem cum dēlēctīs mīlle et quadringentīs equitibus re- 32
vertit. Massīvam adulēscentem, captīvum Āfrum, restituit 33
avunculō, Masinissae, Numidārum rēgī, quī cum equitātū 34
subsidiō Carthāginiēnsibus vēnerat. 35

Scīpiō, receptā Hispāniā, glōriam cōnficiendī bellī spec- 36
tāre coepit. Cōnstituit prius conciliāre rēgēs Āfrōs, Syphā- 37
cem et Masinissam, quī sociī Carthāginiēnsium erant. 38
Syphāx colloquium cum duce Rōmānō postulāvit. Scīpiō ab 39
Carthāgine Novā profectus forte invectus est in rēgium por- 40
tum eō ipsō tempore quō Hasdrubal, dux Carthāginiēnsis, 41
quī Hispāniā pulsus erat. Rōmānus et Carthāginiēnsis, 42
quamquam hostēs erant, ā Syphāce in hospitium invītātī 43
eōdem lectō accubuērunt. Tanta autem inerat comitās 44
Scīpiōnī ut Hasdrubal nōn minus quam Syphāx Rōmānum 45
admīrārētur. Scīpiō cum Syphāce foedere factō Novam 46
Carthāginem rediit. 47

Double Dative (continued)

The first dative, **subsidiō**, is a *dative of purpose* (see the grammar note
on page 77); the second, **Carthāginiēnsibus**, is a *dative of reference*.
The two together are called a *double dative*.
    Here is another example:

    ... eum ... **nōbīs praesidiō** futūrum esse. (9:20)
    ... *that he will* ... *be* **a means of defense** **with reference to us**.
    ... *that he will* ... *be* **our** **defense**.
    ... *that he will* ... **defend** **us**.

49   **maiestās, maiestātis** (*f.*), majesty, dignity, grandeur.
50   **Numida**: "the Numidian," i.e., Masinissa.
52   **Rōmānōs, sī . . . mitterent, . . . captūrōs esse**: *future more vivid condition in indirect statement* (see the grammar note on pages 99–100).

57   ***prōvincia, -ae** (*f.*), province, sphere of administration.
     *dēcernō, dēcernere (3), **dēcrēvī, dēcrētum**, to determine, decide, settle, decree, assign.
     permissum: supply **est**: "it was permitted to him," "he was permitted," *impersonal passive of special intransitive verb* with *dative* (**eī**) (see the grammar notes on pages 16 and 72–73).
58   ***inimīcus, -ī** (*m.*), (personal or political) enemy.
59   **nūntiātum est**: "it was reported," "a report was brought," *impersonal passive* (see the grammar note on pages 76–77.
     Syrācūsae, -ārum (*f. pl.*), Syracuse (a city in Sicily).
60   **amoenitās, amoenitātis** (*f.*), charm.
     *licentia, -ae (*f.*), license, liberty.
62   ***dēcurrō, dēcurrere** (3), **dēcurrī, dēcursum**, to run down, perform military drills.
     simulācrum, -ī (*n.*), likeness, imitation, sham-appearance.
     simulācrum nāvālis pugnae: "a mock naval battle."
63   ***ēdō, ēdere** (3), **ēdidī, ēditum**, to put forth, publish, show, display, put on.
     armāmentārium, -ī (*n.*), arsenal, armory.
     horreum, -ī (*n.*), barn for storing grain, granary.
     apparātus, -ūs (*m.*), equipment.
66   **cēnseō, cēnsēre** (2), **cēnsuī, cēnsum**, to recommend, decide, decree.

Posteā iter longum per Hispāniam fēcit, ut cum Ma- 48
sinissā quoque colloquerētur, quem cōmitāte atque ma- 49
iestāte facile conciliāvit. Numida grātiās ēgit quod Scīpiō 50
frātris fīlium remīsisset dīxitque sē velle in fidē atque 51
amīcitiā populī Rōmānī esse; Rōmānōs, sī Scīpiōnem ducem 52
in Āfricam mitterent, brevī tempore Carthāginem captūrōs 53
esse. Scīpiō, fidē datā acceptāque, in castra rediit atque 54
mox Rōmam profectus est. 55

Cum ibi cōnsul ingentī favōre factus esset, Sicilia eī 56 205 B.C.
prōvincia dēcrēta est permissumque ut in Āfricam trān- 57
sīret. Dum in Siciliā bellum parat, Rōmam ab inimīcīs eius 58
nūntiātum est imperātōrem exercitumque Syrācūsārum 59
amoenitāte licentiāque corrumpī. Lēgātīs ā senātū Syrā- 60
cūsās ad haec cognōscenda missīs, Scīpiō mīlitēs in terrā 61
dēcurrentēs, classem in portū simulācrum nāvālis pugnae 62
ēdentem, armāmentāria, horrea, bellī alium apparātum os- 63
tendit; tantaque admīrātiō lēgātōs cēpit ut satis crēderent 64
aut illō duce atque exercitū vincī Carthāginiēnsēs aut nūllō 65
aliō posse. Senātus igitur cēnsuit ut Scīpiō quam prīmum 66
in Āfricam trānsīret. 67

The Second Punic War

68 Scīpiōnī . . . sē coniūnxit: *dative* and *accusative* with a *compound verb*
    (see the grammar note on page 108).
70 *dēficiō, dēficere (3), dēfēcī, dēfectum, to run short, be lacking, defect.
71 *salūs, salūtis (f.), greetings, welfare, safety, survival.

73 frendō, frendere (3), to gnash the teeth.
    temperō (1), to abstain from (ab + *abl.*).
74 audīsse: = audīvisse.
75 victōrem: the *noun* is here used as an *adjective*.
    Cannēnsis, -is, -e, relating to Cannae, at Cannae.
76 Zama, -ae (f.), Zama (a town in Numidia).
    quīnque diērum iter: "journey of five days," "five-day journey," *genitive of
    description* (see the grammar note on page 138).
77 ab Carthāgine: "from Carthage"; normally prepositions are not used in
    place constructions with names of cities (see the grammar note on
    pages 52–53). However, when both ends of a journey or when dis-
    tances between cities are mentioned, the preposition ab may be used,
    e.g., Scīpiō ab Rōmā Carthāginem vēnit, "Scipio went from Rome to
    Carthage." So here, we have quae urbs quīnque diērum iter ab
    Carthāgine abest, "which city is a five-day journey from Carthage."
    See 21:21–22 for another example.
    speculātor, speculātōris (m.), spy, explorer.
79 circumdūcō, circumdūcere (3), circumdūxī, circumductum, to lead around

84 dēfīgō, dēfīgere (3), dēfīxī, dēfīxum, to fix, astound, stupefy.
    *condiciō, condiciōnis (f.), agreement, terms, condition.
    nōn convēnisset: "agreement was not reached," *impersonal use of the
    verb* (see the grammar note on pages 153 and 155).
85 sē recipere, to retreat, withdraw.
    *renūntiō (1), to report, bring back word.
    dēcernendum esse: "that it had to be decided," *impersonal passive peri-
    phrastic* in *indirect statement* (see the grammar note on page 60).

Scīpiōnī in Āfricam advenientī Masinissa sē coniūnxit   68   204 B.C.
cum parvā manū equitum. Syphāx, quī ā Rōmānīs ad   69
Poenōs dēfēcerat, captus est Rōmamque missus. Dēnique   70
Carthāginiēnsēs, salūte dēsperātā ob multās victōriās   71
Scīpiōnis, Hannibalem ex Italiā revocāvērunt.   72   203 B.C.

Frendēns gemēnsque ac vix ā lacrimīs temperāns dīcitur   73
lēgātōrum verba audīsse. Respexit saepe Italiae lītora, sē   74
accūsāns quod nōn victōrem exercitum statim ab Cannēnsī   75
pugnā Rōmam dūxisset. Zamam vēnit, quae urbs quīnque   76   202 B.C.
diērum iter ab Carthāgine abest. Inde praemissī specu-   77
lātōrēs exceptī sunt ab custōdibus Rōmānīs et ad Scīpiōnem   78
dēductī. Ille autem iussit eōs per castra circumdūcī et ad   79
Hannibalem dīmīsit.   80

Deinde, quaerente colloquium Hannibale, diēs locusque   81
cōnstituitur. Itaque congressī sunt duo maximī suae   82
aetātis ducēs. Paulīsper tacuērunt admīrātiōne mūtuā   83
dēfīxī. Cum vērō dē condiciōnibus pācis inter eōs nōn con-   84
vēnisset, ad suōs sē recēpērunt renūntiantēs armīs dēcer-   85
nendum esse. Commissō deinde proeliō Hannibal victus   86
cum paucīs equitibus fūgit.   87

Scipio Africanus

88　**quae . . . facerent**: *relative clause of characteristic* (see the grammar note below).

90　**terrā marīque**: "on land and sea," *ablative of place where* without a preposition (this idiomatic phrase is an exception to the rules for place constructions given in the grammar note on pages 52–53).

　　pariō, parere (3), **peperī, partum**, to give birth to, produce, accomplish, obtain.

91　**pāce . . . victōriā**: *ablative of cause* with **laetam**.

92　**habendōs**: the verb **habēre** here means "to offer."

93　*****effundō, effundere** (3), **effūdī, effūsum**, to pour out.

　　effūsae sunt: "poured out"; the *passive voice* is here used to give the *transitive* verb an *intransitive* force.

　　agrestis, -is, -e, rustic; (*as a noun*) peasant.

94　*****triumphus, -ī** (*m.*), victory parade, triumph.

　　Triumphō . . . clārissimō: "With the most splendid . . . ," *ablative of manner*, describing the *attendant circumstances*.

95　**Āfricānus, -a, -um**, African; (*as a cognōmen*) Africanus.

Relative Clauses of Characteristic

A relative clause with its verb in the *subjunctive* may characterize something as typical of a group, e.g.:

> . . . eīs condiciōnibus **quae** Rōmānōs suae partis orbis terrārum dominōs **facerent**. (opposite: 88–89)
> . . . *under those conditions **that would make** the Romans masters of their part of the world.*

In this example, the conditions imposed on the Carthaginians are characterized as belonging to that large general class of conditions that would tend to increase the power of Rome.

If the indicative **fēcērunt** had been used instead of the subjunctive **facerent**, the translation would be "under those conditions **that actually made** the Romans masters of their part of the world."

The subjunctive in relative clauses of characteristic makes such clauses *descriptive* rather than *particularizing*. Consider these examples that you have already met:

> . . . monumentō **quod esset**, templum Fortūnae muliebrī aedificātum dēdicatumque est. (18:27–28)
> . . . *and a temple, **which would (be of a type to) serve** as a memorial, was built and dedicated to Fortuna Muliebris.*

> . . . tribūnōs plēbeiōs, **quī** auxilium plēbī adversus cōnsulēs **ferrent**. (17:13–14)
> . . . *tribunes of the plebs, **who would help** the plebeians against the consuls.*

Pāx Carthāginiēnsibus data est eīs condiciōnibus quae 88   201 B.C.
Rōmānōs suae partis orbis terrārum dominōs facerent. 89
Pāce terrā marīque partā, Scīpiō exercitū in nāvēs impositō 90
Rōmam profectus est. Per Italiam laetam pāce nōn minus 91
quam victōriā iter fēcit. Nōn urbēs modo ad habendōs 92
honōrēs effūsae sunt, sed agrestium etiam turba viās ob- 93
sidēbat. Triumphō omnium clārissimō urbem est invectus 94
cognōmenque Āfricānum sibi sūmpsit. 95

Under the terms of the peace treaty, Carthage ceded all of her overseas territory to Rome, paid a large fine, and had to destroy the navy that had been the mainstay of her power. Rome became the undisputed master of the western Mediterranean. The Romans, however, never forgot how close they came to being defeated by Hannibal; they remained extremely distrustful of Carthage. Finally, under the pretext that Carthage was beginning to reassert itself, they declared war and destroyed the city completely. This was the Third Punic War, 149–146 B.C.

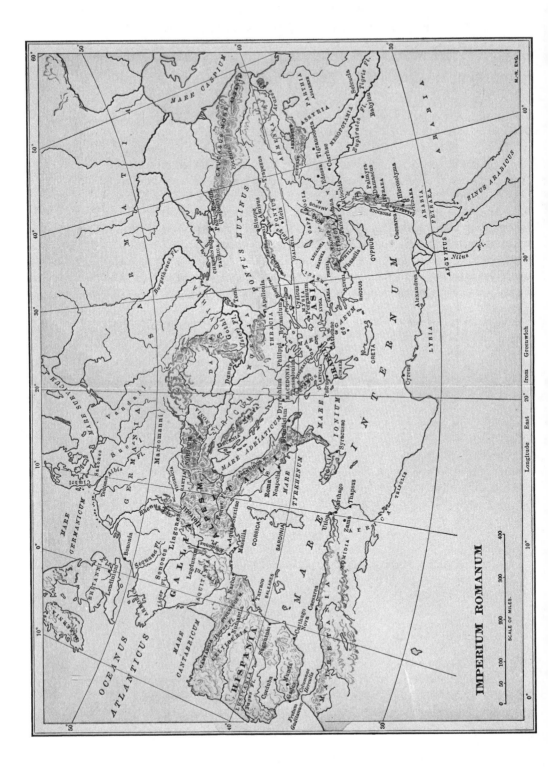

IMPERIUM ROMANUM

SCALE OF MILES.

PART IV

The Last Years of the Republic

The Punic Wars had several consequences for Roman society. The first was that large amounts of money began flowing into Rome from her overseas provinces, making the senatorial class wealthier than ever before. A second and related consequence was a strain on the system of government. This system, which had been designed for a small city-state, was not well suited to governing an empire. Finally, the condition of the farmers became considerably worse. Many farms were destroyed by Hannibal during his sixteen-year occupation of Italy; in addition, some men were away so long on military service that their land fell into disuse or was taken for non-payment of taxes. After Hannibal was defeated, many veterans could not or did not want to return to the country. Instead, they moved to Rome and formed a large group of semi-unemployed citizens. The empty land was taken over by large estates called **lātifundia**, owned by senators and worked by slaves.

These conditions were a source of concern because free peasant farmers had always formed the backbone of the Roman army (a man had to own land to serve in the army!) and because the large numbers of urban poor were a potential source of social unrest. The first story in this part describes how two brothers, Tiberius and Gaius Gracchus, tried to help the landless citizens. While the Gracchi were undoubtedly well-intentioned, their actions opened the door to a whole series of illegal actions by various politicians.

Subsequent political strife often took the form of conflicts between the **populārēs** (those who favored measures to benefit ordinary people) and the **optimātēs** (those who wanted to maintain the power of the senatorial aristocracy). Individual politicians often exploited the tension between **populārēs** and **optimātēs** to enhance their own positions.

The period 133–31 B.C. is dominated by a string of politicians and generals—the Gracchi, Marius, Sulla, Pompey, Caesar, Antony, and Octavian—whose actions caused great suffering for the Roman people. This period, the Late Republic, saw the expansion of the Roman empire in the eastern half of the Mediterranean; at the same time, it saw the disintegration of government at home and the outbreak of civil warfare. The form of government had to be fundamentally changed before the civil wars could be brought to an end. This was accomplished by Octavian, who was given the title Augustus and ushered in a period of autocratic rule known as the Empire.

1   **Tiberius Gracchus, -ī** (*m.*), Tiberius Sempronius Gracchus (163–133 B.C.;
     son of the consul Tiberius Sempronius Gracchus and Cornelia and
     grandson of Publius Scipio Africanus, victor over Carthage in the
     Second Punic War).
     Gaius Gracchus, -ī (*m.*), Gaius Sempronius Gracchus (154–121 B.C.;
     younger brother of Tiberius).
2   **adulēscentia, -ae** (*f.*), youth.
3   **indolēs, indolis** (*f.*), inborn quality, nature, character.
4   ***accēdō, accēdere** (3), **accessī, accessum**, to agree with, enter upon, be
     added to.
     ēducātio, ēducātiōnis (*f.*), rearing, education.
     ***dīligentia, -ae** (*f.*), diligence, faithfulness.
     Cornēlia, -ae (*f.*), Cornelia (daughter of Publius Scipio Africanus and
     mother of Tiberius and Gaius Gracchus and of ten other children; all of
     her children except for Tiberius, Gaius, and a daughter Sempronia died
     in childhood).
5   **ā puerīs**: "from boyhood."
     ērudiō (4), to instruct, educate.
6   ***ōrnāmentum, -ī** (*n.*), equipment, distinction, pride and joy; (*pl.*), jewelry,
     jewels.
     ***īnstituō, īnstituere** (3), **īnstituī, īnstitūtum**, to establish, appoint, teach,
     train.
     meritō (*adv.*), deservedly, rightly.
7   ***sapiēns, sapientis**, wise, sensible.
     Campānus, -a, -um, Campanian, from Campania (a rich agricultural
     province of Italy south of Latium).
8   ***hospita, -ae** (*f.*), hostess, female guest.
     saeculum, -ī (*n.*), generation, century, age.
     illō saeculō: *ablative of time when.*
9   **ostentō** (1, *frequentative*), to show, display ostentatiously.
     This is a *frequentative* or *intensive verb*, made from the supine stem of
     ostendō, "to show." Frequentative or intensive verbs end in **-tō** or **-itō**
     and belong to the first conjugation. They usually denote repeated or
     eager action. Compare the use of the frequentative **ostentāret** here
     of Cornelia's friend ostentatiously displaying her jewels with the use
     of **ostendēns** of Cornelia showing her children with modest pride in
     line 11.
     muliebriter (*adv.*), like a woman, in a womanly way.
     ***trahō, trahere** (3), **trāxī, tractum**, to drag, pull, prolong, keep (a person)
     waiting, delay.

26. Tiberius and Gaius Gracchus

You will notice that the author of the following passage is quite hostile toward the Gracchi and their reforms. This is the attitude that almost all Roman historians took, since they themselves belonged to the upper class, whose interests had been threatened by the Gracchan program. Modern historians have found it difficult to provide accurate and objective accounts of the Gracchi, since all our primary sources are slanted toward the senatorial viewpoint.

Notice also some of the subtle ways in which the author attempts to influence the attitudes of his readers. What good qualities does he attribute to the Gracchi? How does he use these good qualities to make the reader take a negative view of the Gracchi?

Tiberius et Gaius Gracchī Scīpiōnis Āfricānī ex fīliā 1
nepōtēs erant. Hōrum adulēscentia bonīs artibus et magnā 2
omnium spē exācta est; ad ēgregiam enim indolem optima 3
accēdēbat ēducātiō. Erant enim dīligentiā Cornēliae mātris 4
ā puerīs doctī et Graecīs litterīs ērudītī. Maximum mā- 5
trōnīs ōrnāmentum esse līberōs bene īnstitūtōs meritō 6
putābat māter illa sapientissima. Cum Campāna mātrōna, 7
apud illam hospita, ōrnāmenta sua, illō saeculō pulcher- 8
rima, ostentāret eī muliebriter, Cornēlia trāxit eam ser- 9
mōne, quōusque ē scholā redīrent līberī. Quōs reversōs 10
hospitae ostendēns, "Haec," inquit, "mea ōrnāmenta sunt." 11
Nihil quidem hīs adulēscentibus neque ā nātūrā neque ā 12
doctrīnā dēfuit; sed ambō rem pūblicam, quam tuērī poter- 13
ant, perturbāre māluērunt. 14

---

10 **quōusque:** equivalent to **dum,** "until," with the *subjunctive,* expressing *anticipation* or *expectation* (see the grammar note on page 97).
   *****schola, -ae** (f.), school.
   revertor, revertī (3), **reversus sum,** to return.
   Note that this verb is found as either *regular* (see 25:32–33) or *deponent* (as here).

12 **Nihil . . . hīs adulēscentibus . . . dēfuit:** "Nothing was lacking for these young men," "These young men lacked nothing."13 **doctrīna, -ae** (f.), education, learning.
   *****tueor, tuērī** (2), **tūtus sum,** to see, look after, defend, protect.
   poterant: "would have been able (but did not)"; the *imperfect indicative* of **posse** here expresses an *unrealized possibility,* as if it were the verb in the main clause of a *contrary to fact condition,* e.g., ". . . they would have been able to defend, if they had so wished."

16 **dēscīscō, dēscīscere** (3), **dēscīvī, dēscītum**, to revolt, break alliance with, fall away from.
 profūsus, -a, -um, lavish, extravagant.
 *__largītiō, largītiōnis__ (*f.*), distribution of gifts, land, or doles, largess, bribery.

17 **agrōs plēbī dīvidēbat**: upon becoming tribune, Tiberius succeeded in passing the **Lēx Semprōnia agrāria**, his agrarian bill, by which provisions of previous agrarian bills were to be implemented and some land would be taken from those presently occupying it and distributed to the poor.
 colōnia, -ae (*f.*), colony, settlement.
 repleō, replēre (2), **replēvī, replētum**, to fill (up).

18 **tribūnicius, -a, -um**, tribunician, tribune's.
 *__potestās, potestātis__ (*f.*), power.
 prōrogō (1), to prolong, extend.

19 **dictitō** (1, *frequentative*), to say repeatedly.
 dictitāsset: = **dictitāvisset**.
 *__interimō, interimere__ (3), **interēmī, interēmptum**, to do away with, abolish, destroy, kill.
  interēmptō ... vidēbātur: the exaggerated language here reflects the fears of the entrenched aristocracy when faced with the prospect of having to forfeit land that it held in violation of previous agrarian legislation more than it reflects any actual plans of Tiberius Gracchus.

21 **Quā rē**: "Because of which thing," "Therefore."
 dēlīberō (1), to ponder, consult, think seriously about.
 quisnam, quaenam, quidnam (*interrogative*), who, what.

23 **commendō** (1), to entrust, commit.

24 **nōbilitās, nōbilitātis** (*f.*), aristocracy, nobility.
 *__diadēma, diadēmatis__ (*n.*), diadem, crown.
 sēgniter (*adv.*), half-heartedly, feebly.
  sēgniter cessante: "was feebly doing nothing" (when decisive action was desired by others).

25 **Scīpiō Nāsīca, Scīpiōnis Nāsīcae** (*m.*), Publius Cornelius Scipio Nasica Serapio (cousin of Tiberius Gracchus; served as consul in 138 B.C. and supported the conservative faction in Roman politics).
 cōnsōbrīnus, -ī (*m.*), first cousin.

26 **cognātiō, cognātiōnis** (*f.*), relationship by birth, family relationship.
 praeferō, praeferre (*irreg.*), **praetulī, praelātum** (+ *dat.*), to carry in front, prefer X (*acc.*) to Y (*dat.*).

27 **prōclāmō** (1), to shout forth.
 Quī: i.e., **Eī quī**, "Those who ... ," *relative pronoun without an antecedent* (see the grammar note on page 125).

28 **sequantur**: "let them follow," *jussive subjunctive* (see the grammar note on page 28).
 dein: = **deinde**.
 optimātēs, optimātium (*m. pl.*), optimates (the conservative senatorial faction), aristocracy, nobility.

Tiberius Gracchus, tribūnus plēbis creātus, ā senātū ₁₅ 133 B.C.
dēscīvit; populī favōrem profūsīs largītiōnibus sibi concil- ₁₆
iāvit; agrōs plēbī dīvidēbat, prōvinciās novīs colōniīs replē- ₁₇
bat. Cum autem tribūniciam potestātem sibi prōrogārī vel- ₁₈
let et palam dictitāsset, interēmptō senātū omnia per ₁₉
plēbem agī dēbēre, viam sibi ad rēgnum parāre vidēbātur. ₂₀
Quā rē cum convocātī patrēs dēlīberārent quidnam facien- ₂₁
dum esset, statim Tiberius Capitōlium petit, manum ad ca- ₂₂
put referēns, quō signō salūtem suam populō commendābat. ₂₃
Hoc nōbilitās ita accēpit, quasi diadēma posceret, sēg- ₂₄
niterque cessante cōnsule, Scīpiō Nāsīca, cum esset cōn- ₂₅
sōbrīnus Tiberiī Gracchī, patriam cognātiōnī praeferēns ₂₆
sublātā dextrā prōclāmāvit: "Quī rem pūblicam salvam esse ₂₇
volunt, mē sequantur!" Dein optimātēs, senātus atque ₂₈
equestris ōrdinis pars maior in Gracchum irruunt, quī ₂₉
fugiēns dēcurrēnsque clīvō Capitōlīnō frāgmentō subselliī ₃₀
ictus vītam, quam glōriōsissimē dēgere potuerat, immātūrā ₃₁
morte fīnīvit. Mortuī Tiberiī corpus in flūmen prōiectum ₃₂
est. ₃₃

---

29 *equester, equestris, equestre, equestrian, belonging to the equestrian or-
       der.
     *ōrdō, ōrdinis (m.), row, rank, class.
       equestris ōrdinis: the equestrian order or the knights (equitēs) repre-
          sented a midddle class between the plebeians and the senators and
          included many wealthy businessmen.
     *irruō, irruere (3), irruī, to rush on, attack.
30   clīvus, -ī (m.), slope.
       clīvus Capitōlīnus, -ī (m.), clivus Capitolinus (the name of the road that
          ascended the Capitoline Hill).
     frāgmentum, -ī (n.), fragment, piece.
     subsellium, -ī (n.), seat in the senate, bench.
31   īciō, īcere (3), īcī, ictum, to hit, strike.
     dēgō, dēgere (3), dēgī, to spend, pass (time).
       dēgere potuerat: "he could have spent"; compare poterant in line 13
          and the note.
     immātūrus, -a, -um, immature, premature.
32   *prōiciō, prōicere (3), prōiēcī, prōiectum, to throw forth.

34   **furor**: this term was often used by members of the senatorial class to attack anyone who supported agrarian reform and popular causes.

35   **tribūnātus, -ūs** (*m.*), tribuneship.

adeptus: from **adipīscor**.

seu . . . seu *or* **sīve . . . sīve**, either . . . or, whether . . . or.

frāternus, -a, -um, of a brother, brother's.

39   **Italicus, -a, -um**, Italian.

40   **contentiō, contentiōnis** (*f.*), struggle, effort.

obsistō, obsistere (3), **obstitī, obstitum** (+ *dat.*), to resist, oppose.

***bonī, -ōrum** (*m. pl.*), good men, patriotic men.

This word is part of the stock political vocabulary of the nobility or patricians and is used of those who support the interests of the conservative senatorial faction.

41   **Pīsō, Pīsōnis** (*m.*), Lucius Calpurnius Piso Frugi (a member of a famous patrician family; served as consul in 133 B.C. and wrote a history of Rome).

42   **frūmentārius, -a, -um**, of or pertaining to grain.

44   **compellō** (1), to address, rebuke, reproach.

45   **Quī**: *adverb*, "How . . . ?"

***cōnstat**: "it is consistent," *impersonal* (see the grammar note on pages 153 and 155).

> **Quī tibi cōnstat . . . ?**: "How is it consistent for you . . . ?" "How are you being consistent . . . ?"

cum: *conjunction*, "since," not *preposition* here.

eā lēge: "in accord with . . ."

46   **dissuādeō, dissuādēre** (2), **dissuāsī, dissuāsum**, to object to, oppose.

Nōlim: "I would not wish/want," *potential subjunctive* (see the grammar note on page 29).

> **Nōlim . . . tibi . . . liceat**: "I would not wish that it be allowed to you," "I would wish that you not be allowed."

48   **apertē** (*adv.*), openly.

49   **dēclārō** (1), to proclaim, announce officially, declare.

50   ***patrimōnium, -ī** (*n.*), patrimony, inheritance, estate, property.

dissipō (1), to disperse, squander.

Gaium Gracchum īdem furor, quī frātrem Tiberium, oc- 34   123 B.C.
cupāvit. Tribūnātum enim adeptus, seu vindicandae frā- 35
ternae necis, seu comparandae rēgiae potentiae causā, 36
pessima coepit inīre cōnsilia; maximās largītiōnēs fēcit; 37
aerārium effūdit; lēgem dē frūmentō plēbī dīvidendō tulit; 38
cīvitātem omnibus Italicīs dabat. Hīs Gracchī cōnsiliīs 39
quantā poterant contentiōne, obsistēbant omnēs bonī, in 40
quibus māximē Pīsō, vir cōnsulāris. Is cum multa contrā 41
lēgem frūmentāriam dīxisset, lēge tamen lātā, ad frūmen- 42
tum cum cēterīs accipiendum vēnit. Gracchus, ubi animad- 43
vertit in cōntiōne Pīsōnem stantem, eum sīc compellāvit au- 44
diente populō Rōmānō: "Quī tibi cōnstat, Pīsō, cum eā lēge 45
frūmentum petās, quam dissuāsistī?" Cui Pīsō, "Nōlim qui- 46
dem, Gracche," inquit, "mea bona tibi virītim dīvidere 47
liceat; sed sī faciēs, partem petam." Quō respōnsō apertē 48
dēclārāvit vir gravis et sapiēns, lēge, quam tulerat Grac- 49
chus, patrimōnium pūblicum dissipārī. 50

Relative Pronouns and Linking Quī

You have met the *relative pronoun* **quī, quae, quod** many times with the meaning "who" or "that." In this sense the word usually occurs within a sentence, following its *antecedent*, and not at the beginning of the sentence, e.g.:

> . . . in Gracchum irruunt, **quī** fugiēns dēcurrēnsque. . . . (26:29–30)
> . . . *they rush at Gracchus,* **who,** *as he was fleeing and running down.* . . .

Sometimes the relative pronoun *will* be found at the beginning of a sentence with no antecedent expressed, e.g.:

> **"Quī** rem pūblicam salvam esse volunt. . . ." (26:27–28)
> *"(Those)* **who** *want the state to be safe. . . ."*

Here the word **eī** "those" may be supplied as an antecedent.

Quite often a form of the relative pronoun is found at the beginning of a sentence and refers to someone or something in the previous sentence, thus linking the two sentences together. An example of this is seen in the two sentences in lines 43–48 above. The relative pronoun **Cui** at the beginning of the second sentence (line 46) refers to Gracchus, the subject of the first sentence, and may be translated "To **whom**" or "**And** to **him**." This is called *linking quī.*

(*continued on next page*)

51 **Opīmius, -ī** (*m.*), Lucius Opimius (consul 121 B.C. and the first to interpret a decree of the Senate as a so-called **senatūs cōnsultum ultimum**; see the note on line 52 below).

52 **dētrīmentum, -ī** (*n.*), loss, damage.

dētrīmentum capere, to incur or suffer harm.

nē quid dētrīmentī rēs pūblica caperet: this was the official wording of the so-called **senatūs cōnsultum ultimum** or **senatūs cōnsultum dē rē pūblicā dēfendendā**, which gave the magistrates the authority to take forceful and summary action against enemies of the state, without trial or right of appeal.

quod: "(a provision) that."

54 **familiā**: i.e., his household slaves.

Aventīnus, -ī (*m.*), Aventine (Hill) (one of the seven hills of Rome).

56 ***iugulum, -ī** (*n.*), throat.

57 ***sēmet**: emphatic form of **sē**.

super (*prep. + acc.*), above, upon.

60 **Septimuleius, -ī** (*m.*), Septimuleius (a friend of Gaius Gracchus).

61 **rependō, rependere** (3), **rependī, repēnsum**, to weigh out, exchange for, pay for (by weight).

repēnsum: supply **esse**.

fertur: "is said."

Sunt quī: "(There) are (those) who."

īnfundō, īnfundere (3), **īnfūdī, īnfūsum**, to pour in.

plumbum, -ī (*n.*), lead.

62 **efficiō, efficere** (3), **effēcī, effectum**, to bring about, make.

quō . . . efficerētur: *purpose clause* containing a *comparative adjective* and introduced by **quō** (see 21:27 and note).

expleō, explēre (2), **explēvī, explētum**, to fill up.

explēsse: = **explēvisse**.

Relative Pronouns and Linking Quī (continued)

The relative word may also serve as an adjective rather than a pronoun in this linking **quī** construction, e.g.:

Quō respōnsō. . . . (26:48)
*Through **which** answer. . . .*
*And through **this** answer. . . .*

While Latin frequently begins sentences with linking **quī**, English normally does not begin sentences with relative pronouns or relative adjectives. Thus, the better English translations given on the previous page and above are "And to him" and "And through this answer."

Dēcrētum ā senātu est, ut vidēret cōnsul Opīmius, nē 51   121 B.C.
quid dētrīmentī rēs pūblica caperet; quod nisi in maximō 52
discrīmine dēcernī nōn solēbat. Gaius Gracchus, armātā 53
familiā, Aventīnum occupāvit. Cōnsul, vocātō ad arma 54
populō, Gaium aggressus est, quī pulsus profūgit et, cum 55
iam comprehenderētur, iugulum servō praebuit, quī 56
dominum et mox sēmet ipsum super dominī corpus in- 57
terēmit. Ut Tiberiī Gracchī anteā corpus, ita Gaiī mīrā 58
crūdēlitāte victōrum in Tiberim dēiectum est; caput autem 59
ā Septimuleiō, amīcō Gracchī, ad Opīmium relātum aurō 60
repēnsum fertur. Sunt quī trādunt īnfūsō plumbō eum 61
partem capitis, quō gravius efficerētur, explēsse. 62

1   **C. Marius, -ī** (*m.*), Gaius Marius (157–86 B.C.; a plebeian by birth, served as tribune in 119, as praetor in 115, and as consul seven times).
      locus, -ī (*m.*), place, rank, birth.
      *****stīpendium, -ī** (*n.*), military service.

2   **Scīpiō, Scīpiōnis** (*m.*), Publius Cornelius Scipio Aemilianus Africanus Numantinus (185–129 B.C.; adoptive grandson of the Scipio who defeated Carthage in the Second Punic War and himself a prominent general; after defeating Carthage in the Third Punic War, 149–146 B.C., he was sent to Spain and crushed a rebellion at Numantia in 134–133 B.C.; Marius served under Scipio during this Spanish campaign).
      *****imprīmīs** (*adv.*), especially.

3   **sī . . . accidisset, rem pūblicam . . . inventūram esse**: *future more vivid condition in indirect statement* (see the grammar note on pages 93–94).

5   **spīritus, -ūs** (*m.*), breath, inspiration, spirit.

6   **dignus, -a, -um** (+ *abl.*), worthy of.
      concipiō, concipere (3), **concēpī, conceptum**, to take up, conceive.

7   **Q. Metellus, -ī** (*m.*), Quintus Caecilius Metellus Numidicus (commander of the Roman forces against Jugurtha until Marius replaced him).
      Numidia, -ae (*f.*), Numidia (a country in north Africa).

8   **Iugurtha, -ae** (*m.*), Jugurtha (king of Numidia).

9   **apud populum**: "before the people."
      dūcō, dūcere (3), **dūxī, ductum**, to lead, take, bring; (*here*) to draw out, prolong.
      sī . . . fēcissent, . . . captūrum esse: *future more vivid condition in indirect statement* (see the grammar note on pages 93–94).

12   **Bocchus, -ī** (*m.*), Bocchus (king of the Gaetuli).
      Gaetūlī, -ōrum (*m. pl.*), the Gaetulians (a people of northwest Africa along the Sahara Desert).

13   **Sulla, -ae** (*m.*), Lucius Cornelius Sulla Felix (138–78 B.C.; later he became a prominent general and dictator; see section 28).

14   *****quaestor, quaestōris** (*m.*), quaestor (quaestors were financial officers in charge of the treasury in Rome and in charge of financial affairs in the provinces, serving under the praetors or governors).

Ablative of Comparison

The *ablative case* may be used with a comparative adjective or adverb to express a comparison, e.g.:

> . . . nūllum alium successōrem **Mariō meliōrem**. . . . (opposite: 4–5)
> . . . no other successor **better than Marius**. . . .

As an alternative, the word **quam**, "than," may be used:

> . . . nūllum alium successōrem **meliōrem quam Marium**. . . .

27. Gaius Marius

The inflammatory actions taken by the Gracchi brothers, although undoubtedly well intentioned, and the harsh response of the senatorial party marked the beginning of a difficult period for Rome. More and more, ambitious politicans disregarded not only the legalities of the Roman constitution but even the welfare of the Roman people in their search for power and prestige. Marius, whose story is told in this section, was the first in a series of military strongmen who came to power during the last century of the Republic.

C. Marius humilī locō nātus, prīma stīpendia in His-   1   134–
pāniā duce Scīpiōne fēcit. Imprīmīs Scīpiōnī ob ēgregiam   2   133 B.C.
virtūtem cārus erat; Scīpiō enim dīxit, sī quid sibi accidis-   3
set, rem pūblicam nūllum alium successōrem Mariō meli-   4
ōrem inventūram esse. Quā laude excitātus Marius spīr-   5
itūs dignōs rēbus quās posteā gessit concēpit.   6

Posteā lēgātus fuit Q. Metellī, quī bellum in Numidiā   7   109 B.C.
contrā Iugurtham rēgem gerēbat. Rōmam missus Metellum   8
apud populum incūsāvit, quod bellum dūceret; sī sē cōn-   9
sulem fēcissent, brevī tempore aut vīvum aut mortuum   10
Iugurtham captūrum esse. Itaque cōnsul creātus in Nu-   11   107 B.C.
midiam rediit atque superāvit Bocchum, rēgem Gae-   12
tulōrum, ad quem Iugurtha profūgerat. Deinde Sulla,   13
quaestor Mariī, persuāsit Bocchō ut Iugurtham trāderet.   14   105 B.C.

15   **Gallia, -ae** (*f.*), Gaul.
16   **Teutonēs, Teutonum** (*m. pl.*), the Teutons (a northern Germanic tribe
      that migrated westward with the Cimbri).
         vīcit Teutonēs: at Aquae Sextiae in 102 B.C.
      Germānicus, -a, -um, Germanic.
      Cimbrī, -ōrum (*m. pl.*), the Cimbri (a Germanic tribe).
17   **vallis, vallis** (*f.*), valley.
18   **quibus . . . nūlla cōpia erat**: *dative of possession* (see the grammar note
      on page 7).
19   **flāgitō** (1), to demand.
20   **ēn** (*interjection*), come on!
      illīc (*adv.*), there.
22   **nōnāgintā**, ninety.

23   **victī sunt**: at Vercellae in 101 B.C.
24   **Camertēs, Camertium** (*m. pl.*), the Camertes (inhabitants of
      Camerinum, a town in Umbria).
27   ***cīvīlis, -is, -e**, civil.
      iūs cīvīle, iūris cīvīlis (*n.*), civil law.
28   **exaudiō** (4), to hear clearly, listen to.

29   ***factiōnem populārem**: "the faction of the **populārēs**." The **populārēs** were
      supporters of political causes that appealed to the common people, as
      opposed to the **bonī** or **optimātēs**, who supported the political causes of
      the senatorial aristocracy.
30   **senēscō, senēscere** (3), **senuī**, to grow old.
31   ***nōbilēs, nōbilium** (*m. pl.*), aristocrats, nobles, patricians.
      ***cōnsulātus, -ūs** (*m.*), consulship.
32   **Mithridāticus, -a, -um**, Mithridatic, of or related to Mithridates (king of
      Pontus).
         bellō Mithridāticō: "the war against Mithridates"; Rome waged a se-
         ries of wars from 88 to 63 B.C. against Mithridates, king of Pontus,
         who threatened Roman interests in Asia Minor. The kingdom of
         Pontus is to the east of Bithynia in northeastern Asia Minor.
33   **abrogō** (1), to repeal.
36   **fugō** (1), to put to flight, drive away.
      aliquamdiū (*adv.*), for some time.
      ***palūs, palūdis** (*f.*), swamp, marsh.
37   **nāvicula, -ae** (*f.*), small ship.

The campaigns of Marius against the Teutons
and the Cimbri and of Sulla against Mithridates

Marius iterum cōnsul creātus in Galliam profectus est,   15   102 B.C.
ubi vīcit Teutonēs, gentem Germānicam, quī cum Cimbrīs   16
novās sēdēs quaerēbant. Cum Teutonēs vallem flūmenque   17
medium tenērent, mīlitēsque Rōmānī, quibus aquae nūlla   18
cōpia erat, aquam flāgitārent, Marius, "Virī," inquit, "estis;   19
ēn, illīc aquam habētis." Mīlitēs ita concitātī tam ācriter   20
pugnāvērunt ut ducenta mīlia hostium caederentur et   21
nōnāgintā caperentur.   22

Īnsequentī annō, Cimbrī etiam proeliō ā Mariō victī   23   101 B.C.
sunt. In ipsā pugnā Marius duās cohortēs Camertium, quī   24
mīrā virtūte vim Cimbrōrum sustinēbant, contrā lēgem   25
cīvitāte dōnāvit. Dē quā rē posteā reprehēnsus sē ex-   26
cūsāvit, quod inter armōrum strepitum verba iūris cīvīlis   27
exaudīre nōn potuisset.   28

Marius, quī semper factiōnem populārem in rē pūblicā   29
secūtus erat, cum senēsceret, invidēre coepit Sullae, quī   30
dux nōbilium erat. Itaque, cum Sulla in cōnsulātū bellō   31   88 B.C.
Mithridāticō praefectus esset, tribūnus quīdam lēge im-   32
perium Sullae abrogāvit Mariōque bellum dētulit. Quā rē   33
commōtus Sulla, quī ex Italiā nōndum excesserat, Rōmam   34
cum exercitū rediit et urbe occupātā tribūnum interfēcit   35
Mariumque fugāvit. Marius aliquamdiū in palūde latuit;   36
acceptā nāviculā in Āfricam trānsiit et in agrum Carthā-   37
giniēnsem pervēnit.   38

39   **locīs**: "regions."
     sōlitārius, -a, -um, solitary, lonely.
40   **Sextilius, -ī** (*m.*), Sextilius (a praetor).
     *****praetor, praetōris** (*m.*), praetor (in Rome, a magistrate concerned with the administration of justice; in a province, the chief administrative officer, the governor).
     *****obtineō, obtinēre** (2), **obtinuī, obtentum**, to get hold of, be in charge of.
41   **laesisset**: *subjunctive* in a *relative clause of characteristic* (see the grammar note on page 116).
     hūmānitās, hūmānitātis (*f.*), compassion, kindness.
42   **dēcēdō, dēcēdere** (3), **dēcessī, dēcessum**, to withdraw.
43   *****animadvertō, animadvertere** (3), **animadvertī, animadversum**, to notice, punish, inflict capital punishment upon (+ **in** + *acc.*).
     in sē animadvertī: "punishment to be inflicted against himself," i.e., to be put to death.
     vellet: *subjunctive* because its clause is part of the *accusative and infinitive construction* with **iussit** (see the grammar note on pages 86–87).
     torvus, -a, -um, grim, fierce, stern.
44   **ecquid** (*introducing an indirect question*), whether . . . anything.

48   **Cinna, -ae** (*m.*), Lucius Cornelius Cinna (a supporter of Marius and opponent of Sulla; consul in 87, 86, 85, and 84 B.C.).
50   **rapīna, -ae** (*f.*), rapine, pillaging.
     *****adversus, -a, -um**, opposite.
51   **afficiō, afficere** (3), **affēcī, affectum**, to treat, afflict.
52   *****totidem** (*indeclinable adj.*), just so many, just as many.
55   **laetitia, -ae** (*f.*), joyfulness, gladness.
     sī comparentur . . . sit: *should/would* or *future less vivid condition* (see the grammar note on page 104).
56   **vitium, -ī** (*n.*), fault, vice.
     dictū: "to say," *supine* in the *ablative* with **facile** (see the grammar note below).
57   **perniciōsus, -a, -um**, pernicious, ruinous.
     fuerit: *perfect subjunctive* in an *indirect question*.

Supine in the Ablative Case

The *supine* (the 4th principal part of the verb) may be used as a 4th declension noun. This usage is limited to the accusative and ablative cases. Supines are often found in the ablative (*ablative of respect*) with an adjective, e.g.:

   . . . haud **facile** sit <u>**dictū**</u>. . . . (opposite: 56)
   . . . *it would not be* **easy** <u>**with respect to saying**</u>. . . .
   . . . *it would not be* **easy** <u>**to say**</u>. . . .

The best translation is an English infinitive. Here is another example:

   Rēs erat **mīrābilis** <u>**vīsū**</u>.
   The thing was **wonderful** <u>**to see**</u>.

Ibi cum in locīs sōlitāriīs sedēret, vēnit ad eum līctor 39
Sextiliī praetōris, quī tum Āfricam obtinēbat. Ab hōc, quem 40
numquam laesisset, Marius hūmānitātis aliquod officium 41
exspectābat; at līctor dēcēdere eum dē prōvinciā iussit, nisi 42
in sē animadvertī vellet; torvēque intuentem et vōcem nūl- 43
lam ēmittentem Marium rogāvit tandem, ecquid renūntiārī 44
praetōrī vellet. Marius, "Nūntiā," inquit, "tē vīdisse C. Ma- 45
rium in Carthāginis ruīnīs sedentem." 46

Cum Sulla ad bellum Mithridāticum profectus esset, 47
Marius revocātus ā Cinnā in Italiam rediit, calamitāte in- 48
cēnsus magis quam frāctus. Cum exercitū Rōmam ingres- 49   87 B.C.
sus eam caedibus et rapīnīs vāstāvit; omnēs adversae fac- 50
tiōnis nōbilēs variīs suppliciōrum generibus affēcit. 51
Quīnque diēs continuōs totidemque noctēs illa licentia 52
scelerum omnium dūrāvit. Tandem Marius, senectūte et 53
labōribus cōnfectus in morbum incidit et ingentī omnium 54
laetitiā mortuus est. Cuius virī sī comparentur cum vir- 55   86 B.C.
tūtibus vitia, haud facile sit dictū utrum bellō melior an 56
pāce perniciōsior fuerit. 57

A lictor carrying the **fascēs**,
symbol of a magistrate's authority

1 **Iugurthīnus, -a, -um**, Jugurthine.
   bellō Iugurthīnō: see 27:7–14.
2 ***quaestūra, -ae** (f.), quaestorship.
   lūxuriōsus, -a, -um, luxuriant, extravagant.
3 **molestē ferre**, to be annoyed, be disgruntled.
4 ***obveniō, obvenīre** (4), **obvēnī, obventum** (+ dat.), to fall to the lot of, be assigned to.
6 **ēniteō** (2), to shine forth, be distinguished.
   Cimbricus, -a, -um, of or involving the Cimbri (a Germanic tribe defeated by Marius).
     Bellō Cimbricō: see 27:23–28.
7 **opera, -ae** (f.), effort, service, assistance.
   pulsō in exilium Mariō: see 27:31–38.
8 **Mithridātēs, Mithridātis** (m.), Mithridates VI (king of Pontus; see the notes to line 32 on page 130).
9 **Ponticus, -a, -um**, of Pontus (the kingdom of Mithridates in northeastern Asia Minor).
   virtūte ēgregiā: "of outstanding courage," *ablative of description* (see the grammar note below).
10 **odium, -ī** (n.), hatred.
   odiō: *ablative of respect* with **īnferior**.
   in: (here) "against."
   īnferior, īnferius, gen. **īnferiōris**, lower, inferior, less.
   *efficiō, efficere (3), **effēcī, effectum**, to bring about.
     Effēcerat . . . ut . . . interficerentur: "He had brought it about that. . . .," *result clause as object of a verb of effort* (see the grammar note on pages 136–137).
12 **illīus**: i.e., of Mithridates.
   praefectus, -ī (m.), officer, general.
13 **superāvit**: at Athens and Chaeronea in 86 B.C.
14 ***fundō, fundere** (3), **fūdī, fūsum**, to pour out, rout, defeat.
   oppressisset . . . nisi . . . māluisset: "he would have conquered him completely, if he hadn't preferred. . . .," *past contrary to fact condition* (see the grammar note on page 105).
16 **quāliscumque, quāliscumque, quālecumque**, of whatever kind, whatever, any at all.
17 **multō** (1), to punish, fine.
18 **paternus, -a, -um**, father's, paternal.
   contentus, -a, -um (+ abl.), content with.

Ablative of Description

A noun in the *ablative case*, modified by an adjective, may describe a *quality* or *characteristic*, e.g.:

   Mithridātēs enim . . . **virtūte ēgregiā** . . . (opposite: 9–10)
   For Mithridates . . . (a man) **of outstanding courage** . . .

This is called the *ablative of description*. Note that it is sometimes useful to add a phrase such as "a man" in your translation.

28.   Lucius Cornelius Sulla

L. Cornēlius Sulla, quī bellō Iugurthīnō quaestor Mariī   1   107 B.C.
cōnsulis fuit, usque ad quaestūram vītam lūxuriōsam   2
ēgerat. Marius molestē tulisse trāditur, quod sibi gravissi-   3
mum bellum gerentī quaestor voluptātī dēditus sorte ob-   4
vēnisset. Eiusdem virtūs tamen, postquam in Āfricam   5
vēnit, ēnituit. Bellō Cimbricō lēgātus cōnsulis fuit et   6   101 B.C.
bonam operam ēdidit. Cōnsul ipse deinde factus, pulsō in   7   88 B.C.
exilium Mariō, adversus Mithridātem profectus est.   8
Mithridātēs enim, Ponticus rēx, vir bellō ācerrimus, virtūte   9
ēgregiā, odiō in Rōmānōs nōn īnferior Hannibale fuit. Ef-   10
fēcerat igitur ut omnēs in Asiā cīvēs Rōmānī eādem diē   11
atque hōrā interficerentur. Ac prīmō Sulla illīus praefectōs   12
duōbus proeliīs in Graeciā superāvit; deinde in Asiā   13   86 B.C.
Mithridātem ipsum fūdit; oppressisset quoque nisi in Ital-   14   85 B.C.
iam ad bellum cīvīle adversus factiōnem populārem redīre   15
properāns quālemcumque pācem facere māluisset, Mith-   16
ridātem tamen pecūniā multāvit; dē Asiā aliīsque prōvinciīs   17
quās occupāverat dēcēdere paternīsque fīnibus contentum   18
esse coēgit.   19

A coin commemorating the consulship of Sulla and Rufus in 88 B.C. (above: 7). The legends read SVLLA COS and Q · POM · RVFI · RVFVS · COS, that is, **Sulla cōnsul** and **Q. Pompōnius Rūfī [fīlius] Rūfus cōnsul.**

20   **mōtus, -ūs** (*m.*), movement, change, rebellion.
23   **vel**, or, even.
      sponte, of their own accord, voluntarily.
24   **inermis, -is, -e**, unarmed, defenseless, harmless.
26   **ēnumerō** (1), to count up.
      *passim (*adv.*), here and there, everywhere.
      quisquis, quidquid, whoever, whatever.
27   **admoneō** (2), to suggest, warn, urge.
      Fūfidius, -ī (*m.*), Fufidius.
28   **quibus**: "(some) whom . . ."
      inaudītus, -a, -um, unheard of.
29   **tabula, -ae** (*f.*), tablet, list.
      prōscrīptiō, prōscrīptiōnis (*f.*), proscription.
        Proscription was a process whereby men such as Sulla and later the
          triumvirs, Antony, Lepidus, and Octavian, would publish lists of
          their political enemies, who were thereby branded as outlaws, whose
          property could be confiscated, and who could be murdered with im-
          punity by soldiers or citizens. Sulla used his authority as **dictātor** to
          legalize this systematic elimination of his political opponents.
31   **adiciō, adicere** (3), **adiēcī, adiectum**, to add.
32   **caesōrum**: "of those who had been slaughtered."

33   ***saeviō, saevīre** (4), **saeviī, saevītum**, to be fierce, be savage, be brutal.
      *dīmicō (1), to fight, struggle.
34   ***magnitūdō, magnitūdinis** (*f.*), greatness, large number, size.
35   ***prōscrīptī, -ōrum** (*m. pl.*), proscribed.
      innoxius, -a, -um, innocent.
36   ***fundus, -ī** (*m.*), farm.
37   **adscrībō, adscrībere** (3), **adscrīpsī, adscrīptum**, to add by writing, enroll,
      register.
38   **persequor, persequī** (3), **persecūtus sum**, to pursue, chase, hunt down.

Result Clause as Object of a Verb of Effort

Most of the result clauses that you have met so far are adverbial (see
the grammar note on page 56), e.g.:

> Rōmānī . . . **ita** scelere quōdam Sex. Tarquiniī concitātī sunt **ut rē-
> giam** familiam in exilium pellere **statuerent**. (12:1–4)
> *The Romans . . . were **so** aroused by a certain crime of Sextus Tar-
> quinius **that they decided** to drive the royal family into exile.*

The result clause is here said to be *adverbial* because it describes the
result of the action of the verb of the main clause: "The Romans . . .
were so aroused that they. . . ."

     Another kind of result clause serves as the *object* of the verb of the
main clause instead of serving as an *adverb*, e.g.:

Sulla propter mōtūs urbānōs cum victōre exercitū Rō- 20   83 B.C.
mam properāvit; eōs quī Mariō favēbant omnēs superāvit. 21
Nihil autem eā victōriā fuit crūdēlius. Sulla, urbem ingres- 22
sus et dictātor creātus, vel in eōs quī sē sponte dēdiderant 23   82 B.C.
iussit animadvertī. Quattuor mīlia dēditōrum inermium 24
cīvium in circō interficī iussit. Quis autem illōs potest 25
ēnumerāre quōs in urbe passim quisquis voluit occīdit? 26
Dēnique admonuit eum Fūfidius quīdam vīvere aliquōs 27
dēbēre, ut essent quibus imperāret. Novō et inaudītō ex- 28
emplō tabulam prōscrīptiōnis prōposuit, quā nōmina eōrum 29
quī occīdendī essent continēbantur; cumque omnium orta 30
esset indignātiō postrīdiē plūra etiam nōmina adiēcit. 31
Ingēns caesōrum fuit multitūdō. 32

Nec sōlum in eōs saevīvit quī armīs contrā sē dīmicāve- 33
rant, sed etiam quiētōs cīvēs propter pecūniae mag- 34
nitūdinem prōscrīptōrum numerō adiēcit. Cīvis quīdam in- 35
noxius, cui fundus in agrō Albānō erat, legēns prōscrīptō- 36
rum nōmina sē quoque vīdit adscrīptum. "Vae," inquit, "mi- 37
serō mihi! Mē fundus Albānus persequitur." Neque longē 38
prōgressus ā quōdam quī eum āgnōverat interfectus est. 39

Result Clause as Object of a Verb of Effort (*continued*)

Effēcerat . . . **ut** omnēs in Asiā cīvēs Rōmānī . . . **interficerentur.**
     (28:11–12)
*He had brought [it] about **that** all the Roman citizens in Asia **were
killed**. . . .*

The **ut** clause here serves as the direct object of the verb **effēcerat**, and
as such it performs the same function in the sentence as a noun or a
substantive in the accusative case. Subordinate clauses that serve as
substantives are called *substantive clauses* (as opposed to *adverbial
clauses*), and the **ut** clause is here called a *substantive clause of result*
to distinguish it from *adverbial* clauses of result such as the clause in
the example on page 136.

40   **partibus**: "(political) faction."
      Fēlīcem: "Lucky," "Fortunate."
      ēdictum, -ī (*n.*), decree, edict.
41   **partus, -ūs** (*m.*), birth.
42   **Faustum . . . Faustam**: "Lucky," "Fortunate," from the adjective **faustus,**
         -a, -um, which is related to the verb **favēre**, "to favor."
43   **repente** (*adv.*), suddenly, unexpectedly.
44   **exspectātiō, exspectātiōnis** (*f.*), expectation.
      dēmittō, dēmittere (3), **dēmīsī, dēmissum**, to send away, dismiss.
45   **dēambulō** (1), to go for a walk, take a stroll.
46   ***modo** (*adv.*), only, just now, recently.
48   ***dignitās, dignitātis** (*f.*), dignity, authority, prestige.
50   **foris, foris** (*f.*), door; (*pl.*) double doors.
      exsecror, exsecrārī (1), **exsecrātus sum**, to curse.
      potēns, potentis, powerful, strong.
52   **plācō** (1), to calm, quiet, placate.
      contumēlia, -ae (*f.*), mistreatment, insult.
53   **efficiet ut nēmō dēpōnat**: *result clause as object of a verb of effort* (see the
         grammar note on pages 136–137).
54   **posthāc** (*adv.*), hereafter, in the future.

56   **ingentis animī**: *genitive of description* (see the grammar note below).
59   **urbem**: i.e., Rome.
60   **inundō** (1), to flood.
62   **ēruō, ēruere** (3), **ēruī, ērutum**, to uproot, dig out.
      cinis, cineris (*m.*), ash; (*pl.*) ashes of the dead.

Genitive of Description

A noun in the *genitive case*, modified by an adjective, will sometimes be found indicating a *size* or *measure* or describing a *quality*,
e.g.:

> . . . **quīnque diērum** iter . . . (25:76–77)
> . . . *journey **of five days*** . . .
> . . . ***five-day*** journey . . .

> . . . vir **ingentis animī** . . .   (opposite: 56)
> . . . a man **of great zeal** . . .
> . . . a **very zealous** man . . .

This is called the *genitive of description*. An English adjective is sometimes the best translation.

The ablative case will also be found in phrases describing *qualities*
or *characteristics* (see the grammar note on page 134).

Sulla, oppressīs inimīcōrum partibus, Fēlīcem sē ēdictō 40
appellāvit; cumque eius uxor geminōs eōdem partū ēdidis- 41
set, puerum Faustum puellamque Faustam nōminārī 42
voluit.   Sed paucīs post annīs repente contrā omnium 43   79 B.C.
exspectātiōnem dictātūram dēposuit. Dēmissīs līctōribus, 44
diū in forō cum amīcīs dēambulāvit. Stupēbat populus eum 45
prīvātum vidēns, cuius potestās modo tam metuenda 46
fuerat. Quamquam iam prīvātus erat, nōn sōlum salūs, sed 47
etiam dignitās manēbat—quī tot cīvēs occīderat. Ūnus 48
adulēscēns fuit quī audēret querī et Sullam redeuntem 49
usque ad forēs domūs exsecrārī. Atque ille, cuius īram po- 50
tentissimī virī maximaeque cīvitātēs nec effugere nec 51
plācāre potuerant, ūnīus adulēscentis contumēliās aequō 52
animō tulit, id tantum in līmine dīcēns: "Hic adulēscēns ef- 53
ficiet ut nēmō posthāc tāle imperium dēpōnat." 54

Sulla in vīllā voluptātibus dēditus reliquam vītam ēgit. 55
Ibi morbō correptus mortuus est, vir ingentis animī, cu- 56   78 B.C.
pidus voluptātum, sed glōriae cupidior. Ante victōriam 57
laudandus erat, sed in eīs quae secūta sunt numquam satis 58
reprehēnsus; urbem enim et Italiam cīvīlis sanguinis 59
flūminibus inundāvit. Nōn sōlum in vīvōs saeviit, sed nē 60
mortuīs quidam pepercit. Nam Gaiī Mariī, cuius quaestor 61
fuerat, ērutōs cinerēs in flūmen prōiēcit. Quā crūdēlitāte 62
factōrum ēgregiōrum glōriam corrūpit. 63

1 **Gnaeus Pompeius, -ī** (*m.*), Gnaeus Pompeius Magnus (Pompey the Great, 106–48 B.C.).

4 **saltus, -ūs** (*m.*), leaping, jumping.
lūctor, lūctārī (1), **lūctātus sum**, to wrestle.

5 ***reliquiae, -ārum** (*f. pl.*), remains.

6 **contendō, contendere** (3), **contendī, contentum**, to contend, fight, advance go quickly.

7 **adiungō, adiungere** (3), **adiūnxī, adiūnctum**, to join to, add to.

10 **Numidiam . . . dēvīcisset**: in Sicily and then Numidia (in Africa), Pompey defeated the forces of supporters of Marius, Sulla's opponent.

13 **incrēdibilis, -is, -e**, incredible.

14 **obviam īre** (+ *dat.*), to go to meet.

15 **nihilō minus** (*adv.*), nevertheless, none the less.

16 **neque verō**: "nor indeed."

17 **prōpositum, -ī** (*n.*), intention, objective.
***dēterreō** (2), to frighten away, discourage, deter.

18 **adōrō** (1), to worship.
occidō, occidere (3), **occidī, occāsum**, to fall down, set.

19 ***significō** (1), to indicate, mean, signify.

20 **"Triumphet!"**: *jussive subjunctive* (see grammar note on page 28).

29. Gnaeus Pompeius Magnus

Gnaeus Pompeius bellō cīvīlī annōs vīgintī trēs nātus 1   83 B.C.
partēs Sullae secūtus est brevīque tempore sē ducem perī- 2
tum praebuit. Imprīmīs mīlitibus cārus erat, quod nūllum 3
labōrem vītābat atque cum omnibus saltū, cursū, lūctandō 4
certābat. Coāctīs reliquiīs eius exercitūs cui pater prae- 5
fuerat ad Sullam ex Asiā advenientem contendit, et in 6
itinere trēs hostium exercitūs aut superāvit aut sibi ad- 7
iūnxit. Sulla imperātōrem tum salūtāvit semperque max- 8
imō honōre habuit. 9

Paulō post cum Numidiam intrā diēs quadrāgintā dēvī- 10   82 B.C.
cisset, ā Sullā iussus est exercitum dīmittere atque cum 11
ūnā legiōne successōrem exspectāre. Quamquam aegrē id 12
ferēbat, pāruit tamen et Rōmam rediit. Eī advenientī in- 13
crēdibilis hominum multitūdō obviam iit; Sulla quoque lae- 14
tus eum excēpit et Magnī cognōmine salūtāvit. Nihilō mi- 15
nus Pompeiō triumphum petentī restitit; neque vērō Pom- 16
peius eā rē ā prōpositō dēterritus est aususque dīcere 17
plūrēs adōrāre sōlem orientem quam occidentem; quae vōx 18
significābat Sullae potentiam minuī, Pompeiī crēscere. Eā 19
vōce audītā Sulla audāciā adulēscentis percussus, "Tri- 20
umphet! Triumphet! Triumphet!" clāmāvit. 21   81 B.C.

Pompey

22   **extraōrdinārius, -a, -um,** extraordinary.
      imperium extraōrdinārium: this extraordinary command was conferred
      upon Pompey by the Gabinian Law, passed in 67 B.C. with the sup-
      port of the **populārēs** against strong senatorial opposition.
23   ***praedō, praedōnis** (*m.*), robber, pirate.

28   **in Asiam . . . missus est:** the Manilian Law of 66 B.C. conferred this new
      mission upon Pompey. The bill was supported by the equestrian order
      against senatorial opposition. Cicero delivered an oration in favor of
      the law, his *De lege Manilia.* The bill transferred command of the war
      against Mithridates of Pontus and Tigranes of Armenia from Lucullus,
      who had supported Sulla's operations in the East, to Pompey.
30   **iam contendēbant:** note this use of **iam** + *imperfect indicative,* "had been
      contending (and were still contending)."
31   **facultās, facultātis** (*f.*), opportunity.
33   **saltus, -ūs** (*m.*), mountain-pass.
      intercipiō, intercipere (3), **intercēpī, interceptum,** to intercept, cut off.
34   **ā tergō:** "in the rear," "at their backs"; note that the Latin expression
      suggests the direction from which the moonlight comes, while the
      English expression states where it is; compare the commonplace ex-
      pressions **ā dextrā** "on the right" and **ā sinistrā** "on the left."
35   **dēcipiō, dēcipere** (3), **dēcēpī, dēceptum,** to deceive.
36   **Pontus, -ī** (*m.*), Pontus (the kingdom of Mithridates between Bithynia
      and Armenia).
39   **medicāmentum, -ī** (*n.*), medicine, antidote.

41   **Tigrānēs, Tigrānis** (*m.*), Tigranes the Great (king of Armenia).
      Armenia, -ae (*f.*), Armenia (a country to the east of Asia Minor, beyond
      the kingdom of Pontus).
42   **genū, -ūs** (*n.*), knee.
      prōcumbō, prōcumbere (3), **prōcubuī, prōcubitum,** to fall down.
43   **abiciō, abicere** (3), **abiēcī, abiectum,** to throw down, give up.
44   **Iūdaeus, -a, -um,** Jewish; (*m. pl.*) the Jews.
      Hierosolyma, -ōrum (*n. pl.*), Jerusalem.

Paucīs post annīs imperium extraōrdinārium Pompeiō dēlātum est, ut opprimeret praedōnēs, quī omnia maria īnfesta reddēbant et quāsdam etiam Italiae urbēs dīripuerant. Hoc bellum tantā celeritāte cōnfēcit ut intrā quadrāgintā diēs omnēs praedōnēs aut interficerentur aut sē dēderent. 22   67 B.C.
23
24
25
26
27

Statim in Asiam magnō exercitū missus est contrā Mithridātem, Ponticum rēgem, quōcum Rōmānī aliquot annōs iam contendēbant. Rēx diū castrīs sē continuit neque pugnandī facultātem dedit. Cum autem frūmentum dēficere coepisset, fugere cōnātus est. At Pompeius secūtus hostem tertiā nocte in saltū quōdam intercēpit lūnāque adiuvante fūdit. Nam cum Rōmānī lūnam ā tergō habērent, hostēs longīs umbrīs corporum Rōmānōrum deceptī in umbrās tēla coniēcērunt. Victus Mithridātēs in Pontum profūgit. Posteā dēspērātīs fortūnīs venēnō vītam fīnīre frūstrā cōnātus est; adversus enim venēna multīs anteā medicāmentīs corpus firmāverat. Impetrāvit inde ā mīlite Gallō ut sē gladiō interficeret. 28   66 B.C.
29
30
31
32
33
34
35
36
37   63 B.C.
38
39
40

Cum Tigrānēs, rēx Armeniae, celeriter sē dēdisset atque ad genua victōris prōcubuisset, Pompeius eum benignīs verbīs allocūtus est et diadēma, quod abiēcerat, capitī repōnere iussit. Inde Rōmānōrum prīmus Iūdaeōs vīcit Hierosolymaque, caput gentis, cēpit sānctissimamque partem templī iūre victōris ingressus est. 41   64 B.C.
42
43
44   63 B.C.
45
46

A coin issued in honor of Pompey's victory over the pirates (above: 22–27). Neptune's face bears a strong resemblance to that of Pompey.

47   **triumphum agere**, to celebrate a triumph.
      ex Asiā: "from (his victory in) Asia."
48   *****illūstris, -is, -e**, bright, distinguished, illustrious.
50   *****sīcut** (*conj.*), as, just as, like.
      subigō, subigere (3), **subēgī, subāctum**, to subdue.
51   **redīsset**: = **rediisset**.

52   **Caesar, Caesaris** (*m.*), Gaius Julius Caesar (100–44 B.C.; Roman general
      and statesman whose career will be described in section 30).
53   **hic . . . ille**: "the latter . . . the former."
54   **exārdēscō, exārdēscere** (3), **exārsī, exārsum**, to catch fire, be provoked,
      flare up.
      Caesar . . . vēnit: this was Caesar's famous crossing of the Rubicon on
      January 10, 49 B.C., an action that precipitated civil war.
55   **Thessalia, -ae** (*f.*), Thessaly (the northernmost part of Greece).
57   **Pharsālus, -ī** (*f.*), Pharsalus (a town in Thessaly).
58   **Ptolemaeus, -ī** (*m.*), Ptolemy XIII (king of Egypt; about thirteen years of
      age).
      Aegyptus, -ī (*f.*), Egypt.
      cui tūtor . . . datus erat: "to whom he (Pompey) had been assigned (as a)
      guardian." Ptolemy's father, Ptolemy XII, had been on good terms with
      the Romans, who in fact supported him when his subjects tried to drive
      him from the throne. He therefore asked the Romans to ensure the
      welfare of his children, who were relatively young when he died; this
      task was assigned to Pompey.
61   *****praecīdō, praecīdere** (3), **praecīdī, praecīsum**, to lop off, cut off.
      truncus, -ī (*m.*), trunk , torso.
      Nīlus, -ī (*m.*), Nile River.

64   **exitus, -ūs** (*m.*), end, close.

Regressus in Italiam triumphum ex Asiā ēgit, cum anteā 47   62 B.C.
ex Āfricā et ex Hispāniā triumphāvisset. Triumphus il- 48
lūstrior fuit grātiorque populō, quod Pompeius nōn armā- 49
tus, sīcut Sulla, ad Rōmam subigendam, sed dīmissō ex- 50
ercitū redīsset. 51

Posteā, ortā inter Pompeium et Caesarem gravī dissēn- 52
siōne, quod hic superiōrem, ille parem ferre nōn poterat, 53
bellum cīvīle exārsit. Caesar īnfestō exercitū in Italiam 54   49 B.C.
vēnit. Pompeius, relictā urbe ac deinde Italiā ipsā, Thes- 55
saliam petīvit et cum eō cōnsulēs senātūsque magna pars; 56
quem īnsecūtus Caesar apud Pharsālum aciē fūdit. Victus 57   48 B.C.
Pompeius ad Ptolemaeum, Aegyptī rēgem, cui tūtor ā 58
senātū datus erat, profūgit; ille Pompeium interficī iussit. 59
Ita Pompeius sub oculīs uxōris et līberōrum interfectus est, 60
caput praecīsum, truncus in Nīlum coniectus. Deinde caput 61
ad Caesarem dēlātum est, quī eō vīsō lacrimās nōn conti- 62
nuit. 63

Is fuit Pompeiī vītae exitus post trēs cōnsulātūs et toti- 64
dem triumphōs. 65

1   **nōbilissimā . . . familiā**: "from the very noble family," *ablative of source*
     with **nātus**.
     Iūliī, -ōrum (*m. pl.*), Julii (the members of the Julian family, which
     traced its origin back to Iulus, also known as Ascanius, the son of
     Aeneas; at the time of Caesar's birth, the family had not been
     politically important for some time).
2   **agēns annum . . .** : "being in his . . . year."
     Ā puerō: "From boyhood."
3   **eō magis**: "all the more."
4   **Iūlia, -ae** (*f.*), Julia (Caesar's aunt).
     amita, -ae (*f.*), aunt (father's sister).
5   **Cornēlia, -ae** (*f.*), Cornelia (daughter of Cinna, who was a supporter of
     Marius; wife of Caesar).
     uxōrem dūcere, to marry.
6   **inimīcus, -a, -um**, unfriendly, hostile.
7   ***repudiō** (1), to reject, divorce.
10   **quārtāna, -ae** (*f.*), quartan fever.
     labōrābat: this verb can mean "to suffer" as well as "to work."
11   **latebrae, -ārum** (*f. pl.*), hiding place.
13   **affīnis, affīnis** (*m.* or *f.*), in-law.
     ***venia, -ae** (*f.*), kindness, favor, forgiveness.
14   ***cōnstat**: "it is agreed," *impersonal* (see the grammar note on pages 153
     and 155).
16   **partibus exitiō**: *double dative* (see the grammar note on pages 110–111).

18   **expugnātiō, expugnātiōnis** (*f.*), assault.
19   **Mytilēnae, -ārum** (*f. pl.*), Mytilene (capital of the island of Lesbos).
     corōna, -ae (*f.*), crown, garland.
         corōna cīvica: a crown or garland of oak leaves awarded for saving the
         life of a fellow soldier.
     Rhodus, -ī (*f.*), Rhodes (an island off the coast of Asia Minor).
20   **per ōtium**: "at leisure."
     Apollōnius Molō, Apollōniī Molōnis (*m.*), Apollonius Molon (a teacher of
     rhetoric at Rhodes in the first century B.C.).
21   **opera, -ae** (*f.*), effort.
     operam dare (+ *dat.*), to give attention to, devote oneself to.
23   ***spatium, -ī** (*n.*), space, time, period.
     sē gerere, to carry oneself, behave.
24   **praedōnibus . . . terrōrī venerātiōnīque**: *double dative* (see the grammar
     note on pages 110–111).
     pariter (*adv.*), equally.
     venerātiō, venerātiōnis (*f.*), veneration, reverence, respect.
26   **crux, crucis** (*f.*), cross.
         cruce afficere, to afflict with the cross, crucify.
     quod supplicium: "a punishment that," *antecedent incorporated into the
     relative clause* (see the grammar note on page 30).
27   **minor, minārī** (1), **minātus sum**, to threaten.

30. Gaius Julius Caesar

C. Iūlius Caesar, nōbilissimā Iūliōrum familiā nātus, agēns annum sextum et decimum patrem āmīsit. Ā puerō vidētur populārem factiōnem in rē pūblicā secūtus esse, eō magis quod Marius Iūliam, Caesaris amitam, in mātrimōnium dūxisset. Ipse Cornēliam dūxit uxōrem, fīliam Cinnae, quī Sullae inimīcissimus erat. Cum Sulla victor Caesarem, sīcut multōs aliōs, iussisset uxōrem repudiāre, ille recūsāvit. Bonīs deinde spoliātus cum etiam ad necem quaererētur, mūtātā veste nocte urbe ēlapsus est. Quamquam tum quārtānae morbō labōrābat, prope per singulās noctēs labebrās commūtāre cōgēbātur, et dēnique ā Sullae lībertō comprehēnsus est. Eī vix, datā pecūniā, persuāsit ut sē dīmitteret. Postrēmō per propinquōs et affīnēs suōs veniam impetrāvit. Satis tamen cōnstat Sullam monuisse eōs quī adulēscentī veniam petēbant eum aliquandō nōbilium partibus exitiō futūrum esse; nam Caesarī multōs Mariōs inesse.

Stīpendia prīma in Asiā fēcit, ubi in expugnātiōne Mytilēnārum corōnā cīvicā dōnātus est. Mortuō Sullā, Rhodum sēcēdere statuit, ut per ōtium Apollōniō Molōnī, tum clārissimō dīcendī magistrō, operam daret. Hūc dum trānsit, ā praedōnibus captus est mānsitque apud eōs prope quadrāgintā diēs. Per omne autem illud spatium ita sē gessit ut praedōnibus pariter terrōrī venerātiōnīque esset. Redēmptus inde ab amīcīs classem contrāxit captōsque praedōnēs cruce affēcit, quod supplicium saepe inter iocum minātus erat.

1	100 B.C.
2	85 B.C.
3	
4	
5	84 B.C.
6	
7	82 B.C.
8	
9	
10	
11	
12	
13	
14	
15	
16	
17	
18	81 B.C.
19	78 B.C.
20	77 B.C.
21	
22	
23	
24	
25	
26	
27	

Caesar

28   Quaestōrī: "To (him as) quaestor."
     ulterior, ulterius, *gen.* ulteriōris, on the farther side, further.
     ulterior Hispānia: "Further Spain," a province occupying the western
       half of the Iberian peninsula.
29   *porticus, -ūs (*f.*), colonnade, portico.
30   apparātus, -a, -um, prepared, sumptuous.
31   M. Bibulus, -ī (*m.*), Marcus Bibulus (Caesar's colleague in his aedileship,
       praetorship, and consulship).
     sēparātim (*adv.*), apart, separately.
32   cōnflō (1), to bring about, cause, produce, run up (a debt).
33   opus (*indeclinable noun*) (*n.*), need.
     opus est, there is need to someone (*dat.*) for something (*abl.* or *gen.*),
       someone needs something.
     mīliēns (*adv.*), a thousand times.
     sēstertius, -ī, *gen. pl.* sēstertium (*m.*), sesterce (a Roman coin, worth one
       quarter of the denarius, which was the basic silver coin of Rome).
       mīliēns sēstertium: short for mīliēns centēna ("one hundred times")
       mīlia sēstertium = 100,000,000 sesterces.
34   Marcus Crassus, -ī (*m.*), Marcus Licinius Crassus (one of the richest men
       of Rome and a member of the first triumvirate, a political alliance of
       Caesar, Pompey, and Crassus formed in 60 B.C.).
35   displiceō (2) (+ *dat.*), to displease, be displeasing.
     ūllī: *dative.*
37   diurnus, -a, -um, daily.
     diurna ācta: "daily actions."
     perscrībō, perscrībere (3), perscrīpsī, perscrīptum, to write out, record,
       register.
38   lēgēs . . . pertulit: "he passed laws"; compare the standard idiom lēgem
       ferre, to propose or pass a law.
     *prō (*prep.* + *abl.*), on behalf of.
39   *praecipuē (*adv.*), especially, chiefly.
     effēcit ut . . . : for the *result clause as object of a verb of effort*, see the
       grammar note on pages 136–137.
40   obstō, obstāre (1), obstitī (+ *dat.*), to stand in the way, oppose, object to.
41   abditus, -a, -um, hidden, secluded.
     abstineō, abstinēre (2), abstinuī, abstentum (+ *abl.*), to keep away from.
42   signō (1), to seal.
43   Iūlius, -ī (*m.*), Julius (the second of Caesar's three names, Gaius Iūlius
       Caesar).

45   peragō, peragere (3), perēgī, perāctum, to complete.
     in potestātem redigere, to bring under the power of.
46   Germānī, -ōrum (*m. pl.*), the Germans.
48   *commentārius, -ī (*m.*), notebook, diary, notes.
     rēs gestae, rērum gestārum (*f. pl.*), exploits, achievements, deeds.
49   ūtī: *infinitive* of ūtor.
     *historia, -ae (*f.*), account, history.
50   Cicerō, Cicerōnis (*m.*), Marcus Tullius Cicero (106–43 B.C.; statesman and
       orator; see section 31).
     sānus, -a, -um, sound, rational, sensible.

Quaestōrī ulterior Hispānia obvēnit. Aedīlis praeter 28 69 B.C.
comitium ac forum etiam Capitōlium ōrnāvit porticibus. 29 65 B.C.
Vēnātiōnēs autem lūdōsque apparātissimōs et cum collēgā 30
M. Bibulō et sēparātim ēdidit. Hīs rēbus patrimōnium ef- 31
fūdit tantumque aes aliēnum cōnflāvit ut ipse dīceret sibi 32
opus esse mīliēns sēstertium, ut habēret nihil. Posteā soci- 33 60 B.C.
etātem cum Gnaeō Pompeiō et Marcō Crassō iūnxit, nē quid 34
agerētur in rē pūblicā, quod displicēret ūllī ex tribus. Cōn- 35 59 B.C.
sul deinde creātus cum M. Bibulō prīmus omnium cōnsu- 36
lum īnstituit ut diurna ācta et senātūs et populī perscrīber- 37
entur atque ēderentur. Aliquot lēgēs prō Pompeiō et Crassō 38
sociīs pertulit, praecipuēque effēcit ut ipse prōvinciam Gal- 39
liam obtinēret. Bibulus, cum frūstrā lēgibus obstitisset, per 40
reliquum annī tempus domī abditus cūriā abstinuit. 41
Nōnnūllī igitur, cum tabulās signārent, per iocum ad- 42
didērunt nōn Caesare et Bibulō, sed Iūliō et Caesare cōn- 43
sulibus. 44

Caesar, cōnsulātū perāctō, novem annīs Galliam in 45 58–
potestātem populī Rōmānī redēgit. Germānōs quoque ag- 46 49 B.C.
gressus est atque prīmus imperātōrum Rōmānōrum in Bri- 47
tanniam trānsiit. Ipse commentāriōs rērum gestārum cōn- 48
fēcit, quibus aliōs ūtī in scrībendā historiā voluit. Sed, ut 49
ait Cicerō, "Sānōs quidem hominēs ā scrībendō dēterruit; 50
nihil est enim in historiā pūrā et illūstrī brevitāte commen- 51
tāriōrum dulcius." 52

---

51 **pūrus, -a, -um**, pure, unadorned.
  *illūstris, -is, -e, bright, distinguished, illustrious; (*of writing*) clear, lucid.
  brevitās, brevitātis (*f.*), brevity, conciseness, terseness.
52 **dulcis, -is, -e**, pleasant, delightful.

52   **Parthī , -ōrum** (*m. pl.*), the Parthians (a semi-nomadic people living to the east of the Roman Empire in parts of what are now Jordan, Iraq, and Iran).

53   **Iūlia, -ae** (*f.*), Julia (daughter of Caesar).
    *gener, generī (*m.*), son-in-law.

54   **socer, socerī** (*m.*), father-in-law.
    aemulātiō, aemulātiōnis (*f.*), rivalry.
    ērumpō, ērumpere (3), **ērūpī, ēruptum**, to break out.

55   **Iam prīdem ... erant**: "... had long since been (and still was)."
    suspectus, -a, -um, regarded with mistrust, suspect.

56   **Pompeiānus, -a, -um**, Pompeian, of Pompey.

57   **ex lēge ante lātā**: in 52 B.C., Caesar (with Pompey's support) arranged for the tribunes to introduce a law allowing him to run for the consulship *in absentia*. The law passed, and it appears that Caesar intended to run in 50 for the consulship of 49 B.C. However, he needed to remain in Gaul for one additional year, so he actually sought to run in the elections of 49 for the consulship of 48.

58   **licēret**: for the use of this *impersonal verb*, see the grammar note on page 153.
    Pompeiō probante: Pompey had become more and more jealous of Caesar's achievements in Gaul and of his growing reputation; he also wanted to be accepted among the inner circle of aristocrats. For these reasons he gradually drew apart from Caesar. The final break came when Pompey joined the senatorial conservatives in opposing Caesar's plan to run for the consulship of 48 while still in Gaul.

61   **Rubicō, Rubicōnis** (*m.*), Rubicon (a small stream near modern Rimini in northern Italy, marking the boundary between Italy and Cisalpine Gaul; see note to 29:54).

62   **morātus**: "delaying"; note that the *perfect participle* of deponent verbs may often best be translated with a *present tense* in English.

63   **fert**: "says," "reports."
    quod sī: "but if."

65   **ālea, -ae** (*f.*), die.

66   **Brundisium, -ī** (*n.*), Brundisium (a port in southeast Italy on the Adriatic Sea).

67   **Pompeius ... profūgerat**: Pompey intended to fight Caesar in southern Italy, and he was raising troops in that area when he learned that Caesar had defeated a senatorial army under L. Domitius Ahenobarbus in central Italy. He realized that he had no hope of retaining control of Italy, so he and many of the senators decided to cross into Greece and to mobilize their forces there.

68   **prohibeō** (2), to hold back, prevent, prohibit someone (*acc.*) from doing something (*infinitive*).

69   **validus, -a, -um**, strong, powerful.

Cum intereā Crassus apud Parthōs interfectus esset, et   52   53 B.C.
mortua Iūlia, Caesaris fīlia, quae nūpta Pompeiō generī   53
socerīque concordiam tenēbat, statim aemulātiō ērūpit.   54
Iam prīdem Pompeiō suspectae Caesaris opēs erant, et   55
Caesarī Pompeiāna dignitās gravis. Dēnique Caesar, ut sē   56   52 B.C.
tuērētur, postulāvit ut ex lēge ante lātā sibi absentī al-   57
terum cōnsulātum petere licēret. Hoc inimīcī, Pompeiō   58
probante, negāvērunt atque iussērunt Caesarem ante cer-   59
tam diem exercitum prōvinciamque trādere.   60

Iniūriā incēnsus ad Rubicōnem flūmen, quī prōvinciae fī-   61   49 B.C.
nis erat, cum exercitū prōcessit. Ibi paulum morātus, ut   62
fāma fert, "Etiam nunc," inquit, "regredī possumus; quod sī 63
hoc flūmen trānsierimus, omnia armīs agenda erunt."   64
Postrēmō exclāmāvit: "Iacta est ālea." Tum, exercitū flū-   65
men trāductō bellōque cīvīlī inceptō, Brundisium profectus   66
est, quō Pompeius cum magnā parte senātūs profūgerat.   67
Pompeium trānsīre in Ēpīrum prohibēre frūstrā cōnātus   68
iter in Hispāniam fēcit, ubi validissimās Pompeiī cōpiās   69
vīcit.   70

Adverbs of Place

Latin has a number of adverbs of place, of which you have recently met
several in your reading (see above, lines 62, 67, and 69). Here is a
complete chart:

hīc, here, in this place
hūc, here, to this place
hinc, from here, from this place

illīc, there, in that place
illūc, there, to that place
illinc, from there, from that place

ibi, there, in that place
eō, there, to that place
inde, from that place

ubi? where? in what place?
quō? where? to what place?
unde? from where? from what place?

(continued on next page)

71 **Pharsālicus, -a, -um**, of *or* at Pharsalus (a town in Thessaly in northern Greece).

73 **quī Pompeium interficī iusserat**: see 29:57–59.

īnsidiae, -ārum (*f. pl.*), ambush, plot, trap.

īnsidiās Caesarī tendēbat: Caesar attempted to settle a quarrel between Ptolemy and his older sister Cleopatra, who had been named joint rulers in their father's will. Ptolemy turned against Caesar, besieged him in the palace at Alexandria, and was ultimately defeated by him.

74 **tendō, tendere** (3), **tetendī, tentum**, to stretch out, lay out.

Cleopātra, -ae (*f.*), Cleopatra VII (queen of Egypt).

75 ***minor, minus**, *gen.* **minōris**, smaller, younger.

Pharnacēs, Pharnacis (*m.*), Pharnaces II (son of Mithridates and king of Bosporus).

76 **occāsiō, occāsiōnis** (*f.*), occasion, opportunity.

rebellō (1), to rebel.

citō (*adv.*), quickly.

77 **fūdit**: at the battle of Zela in Pontus in 47 B.C.

78 **Scīpiō, Scīpiōnis** (*m.*), Quintus Caecilius Metellus Pius Scipio (an opponent of Caesar and the commander of the Roman forces in north Africa loyal to Pompey's cause).

Iuba, -ae (*m.*), Juba (a Numidian king who supported Pompey).

80 **dēvīcit**: at the battle of Thapsus in 46 B.C.

81 **superāvit**: at Munda in 45 B.C.

dubius, -a, -um, wavering, indecisive, precarious.

83 **increpō** (1), to scold, rebuke.

84 **servāsset**: = **servāvisset**, *subjunctive* in a ***quod*** *causal clause* (see the grammar note on page 78).

recēdō, recēdere (3), **recessī, recessum**, to withdraw, retreat.

85 **verēcundia, -ae** (*f.*), restraint, modesty, shame.

86 **quater** (*adv.*), four times.

Adverbs of Place (continued)

The first two sets are clearly connected to the demonstratives **hic, haec, hoc** and **ille, illa, illud**.

The words in the fourth set (**ubi, quō**, and **unde**) can introduce *direct questions* in main clauses, or they can introduce *indirect questions* in subordinate clauses, e.g.:

Quō Pompeius profūgit?
Where did Pompey flee?

Caesar scīvit **quō** Pompeius profūgisset.
Caesar knew where Pompey had fled.

These words can also serve as *relative adverbs*, introducing clauses that are similar in function to *relative clauses*, e.g.:

Brundisium profectus est, **quō** Pompeius . . . profūgerat. (30:66–67)
He set out for Brundisium, to which place/where Pompey had fled.

Deinde in Ēpīrum profectus Pompeium Pharsālicō   71   48 B.C.
proeliō superāvit et fugientem ad Aegyptum persecūtus est.   72
Ptolemaeum rēgem, quī Pompeium interficī iusserat īnsidi-   73
āsque Caesarī tendēbat, vīcit atque rēgnum Cleopātrae   74
frātrīque minōrī permīsit. Pharnacem, Mithridātis fīlium,   75
quī occāsiōne temporum ad rebellandum ūtēbātur, tam cito   76
fūdit ut celeritātem victōriae posteā tribus verbīs sig-   77   47 B.C.
nificāret, "Vēnī, vīdī, vīcī." Deinde Scīpiōnem et Iubam,   78
Numidiae rēgem, quī reliquiās Pompeiānārum partium in   79
Āfricā coēgerat, dēvīcit. Postrēmō Pompeiī fīliōs in His-   80   46 B.C.
pāniā superāvit; quod proelium tam ācre tamque dubium   81   45 B.C.
fuit ut Caesar equō dēscenderet cōnsistēnsque ante suōs   82
cēdentēs fortūnam increpāret, quod sē in eum exitum   83
servāsset, dēnūntiāretque mīlitibus vēstīgiō sē nōn re-   84
cessūrum. Verēcundiā magis quam virtūte aciēs restitūta   85
est. Rōmam inde rediit, ubi quater triumphāvit.   86

Impersonal Verbs and Verbs Used Impersonally

Caesar postulāvit ut sibi absentī alterum cōnsulātum petere **licēret**.
(based on 30:56–58)

*Caesar demanded that <u>to run for a second consulship</u> **be permitted** to him while absent.*

*Caesar demanded that **it be permitted** to him while absent <u>to run for a second consulship</u>.*

*Caesar demanded that he **be permitted** <u>to run for a second consulship</u> in absentia.*

The verb **licēret** is called an *impersonal verb*. Its subject is never a person, such as "I," "you," or "she." Instead, its subject is an infinitive or an infinitive clause. In the sentence above, **alterum cōnsulātum petere**, "to run for a second consulship," is the subject of **licēret**. The verb **licēret** is third person singular because the infinitive phrase "to run for a second consulship" in the equivalent of a neuter singular noun or the pronoun "it." Impersonal verbs are, in fact, usually defined in vocabulary lists with "it" as subject and are often so translated, e.g., as above, "that *it* be permitted to him . . . <u>to run for a second consulship</u>." In English we may translate personally: "that *he* be permitted to run. . . ."

Note the use of the dative case **sibi absentī**, "that it be permitted <u>to him while absent</u>," better English, "that he be permitted . . . in absentia." Compare the use of the dative case with the impersonal passive of special intransitive verbs (see the grammar note on pages 72–73).

(continued on page 155)

88 **fāstī, -ōrum** (*m. pl.*), days on which it is lawful (**fās**) to conduct business, a list of festival days, calendar.
corrigō, corrigere (3), **corrēxī, corrēctum**, to correct, improve, reform.
89 **accommodō** (1), to adapt to, adjust to.
suppleō, supplēre (2), **supplēvī, supplētum**, to fill up, bring to full strength.
comitia, -ōrum (*n. pl.*), assembly (of the Roman people to elect magistrates), election (taking place in the assembly).
90 **dīmidius, -a, -um**, half.
91 **candidātus, -ī** (*m.*), candidate for office.
This word reflects the Roman practice of wearing a specially whitened toga (**toga candida**) when seeking public office.
ambitus, -ūs (*m.*), illegal campaigning, bribery.
*****damnō** (1), to find guilty, condemn.
92 **admittō, admittere** (3), **admīsī, admissum**, to allow, admit.
93 **medicīna, -ae** (*f.*), medicine, medical science.
profiteor, profitērī (2), **professus sum**, to practice.
94 **doctor, doctōris** (*m.*), teacher.
cīvitāte dōnāvit: the doctors and teachers would have been Greek.
Iūs . . . dīxit: "He enforced the law."
labōriōsus, -a, -um, laborious, energetic.
95 **sevērus, -a, -um**, severe, strict.
repetundae, -ārum (*f. pl.*), extortion.
The word **repetundae** or the full phrase **pecūniae repetundae** refers to the legal process of seeking back (**repetere**) or recovering money acquired by extortion. Many Roman officials in the provinces, from governors on down, took advantage of their offices by amassing fortunes through bribery and extortion. Caesar wished to end this practice to provide a better life for people in the provinces as well as greater political stability.
96 **merx, mercis** (*f.*), merchandise.
portōrium, -ī (*n.*), port duty, tax.
97 **sūmptuārius, -a, -um**, relating to expenses, sumptuary, against extravagence.
dispōnō, dispōnere (3), **disposuī, dispositum**, to place here and there, distribute, station.
98 **macellum, -ī** (*n.*), butcher shop, meat market.
obsōnium, -ī (*n.*), shopping items, food.
vetō, vetāre (1), **vetuī, vetitum**, to forbid.

Bellīs cīvīlibus cōnfectīs conversus iam ad administran- 87 45 B.C.
dam rem pūblicam fāstōs corrēxit annumque ad cursum 88
sōlis accommodāvit. Senātum supplēvit, comitiīsque cum 89
populō dīvīsīs sibi sūmpsit iūs nōmindandae dīmidiae partis 90
candidātōrum. Eōs quī lēge Pompeiī dē ambitū damnātī 91
erant restituit atque admīsit ad honōrēs etiam prōscrīp- 92
tōrum līberōs. Omnēs medicīnam Rōmae professōs et 93
līberālium artium doctōrēs cīvitāte dōnāvit. Iūs labōriōsis- 94
simē ac sevērissimē dīxit. Dē repetundīs damnātōs etiam ē 95
senātū mōvit. Peregrīnārum mercium portōria īnstituit. 96
Lēgem praecipuē sūmptuāriam exercuit, dispositīs circā 97
macellum custōdibus quī obsōnia vetita retinērent. 98

Impersonal Verbs and Verbs Used Impersonally (*continued*)

Oportet "it is right/proper" is another impersonal verb, and the phrase
necesse est "it is necessary" is used impersonally. Some verbs such as
accidō, accidere, "to fall down," **cōnstō, cōnstāre,** "to be established," and
conveniō, convenīre, "to come together," which can be used *personally*,
are also used *impersonally*, e.g.:

accidit	it happens
cōnstat	it is apparent, it is consistent, it is agreed
convenit	it is agreed

You have seen these verbs used in the following passages, which you
may want to review now: 22:7, 22:15–17, 25:84–85, 26:45, 27:3–4, and
30:14.

In addition to the infinitive as subject, you will find other phrases
or clauses used as the subject of impersonal verbs, e.g.:

accusative and infinitive
ut + subjunctive
subjunctive without **ut**

(*Exercises on page 157*)

99 īnstruō, īnstruere (3), īnstrūxī, īnstrūctum, to build, construct.
100 exstruō, exstruere (3), exstrūxī, exstrūctum, to build, erect.
theātrum, -ī (n.), theater.
102 ad certum modum: "to a certain limit."
103 *quisque, quaeque, quidque, each.
optima quaeque: *neuter plural,* "each (of the) best things," "all the best
things."
104 bibliothēca, -ae (f.), library.
quās maximās posset: = quam maximās.
105 Pomptīnus, -a, -um, Pomptine (the name given to an area about thirty
miles southeast of Rome, lying between the Volscian mountains and
the sea; much of the area was marshy and filled with mosquitos,
which carried malaria).
ēmittere: "to drain."
106 Fūcīnus, -a, -um, Fucine (the name of a lake in Samnium).
mare Superum, maris Superī (n.), Adriatic Sea (literally, Upper Sea).
Āpennīnus, -ī (m.), Apennine Mountains.
107 dorsum, -ī (n.), back, ridge.
perfodiō, perfodere (3), perfōdī, perfossum, to dig through, pierce.
Isthmus Corinthius, -ī (m.), Isthmus of Corinth.
Dācī, -ōrum (m. pl.), the Dacians (a people living along the north bank
of the Danube River in what is now Rumania).
108 Thrācia, -ae (f.), Thrace (a region to the northeast of Greece).
coerceō (2), to enclose, confine.
109 bellum īnferre (+ dat.), to wage war against.

110 meditor, meditārī (1), meditātus sum, to think over, reflect on.
praeveniō, praevenīre (4), praevēnī, praeventum, to come before, pre-
cede, anticipate, forestall.
111 in perpetuum: "forever."
agere: "to act."
īnsolēns, īnsolentis, extravagant, insolent.
112 assurgō, assurgere (3), assurrēxī, assurēctum, to rise up, stand up (as a
mark of respect).
113 Antōnius, -ī (m.), Marcus Antonius (Marc Antony, 83–30 B.C.; colleague
with Caesar as consul in 44 B.C.).
115 *rōstra, -ōrum (n. pl.), rostra (speaker's platform in the Roman Forum,
so-called because it was decorated with the beaks of ships taken from
the battle of Antium in 338 B.C.).
117 offēnsus, -a, -um, offended, displeased.
*amplius (*comparative adv.*), more (than).
sexāgintā, sixty.
Cassius, -ī (m.), Gaius Cassius Longinus (one of the leading assassins of
Caesar).
118 Brūtus, -ī (m.), Marcus Junius Brutus (another of the leading assassins
of Caesar).
119 *Īdūs, -uum (f. pl.), Ides (fifteenth day of March, May, July, and October,
and the thirteenth day of the other months).
*Mārtius, -a, -um, of March.

Dē ōrnandā īnstruendāque urbe multa cōgitābat, im- 99
prīmīs ingēns Mārtis templum extruere theātrumque 100
summae magnitūdinis sub Tarpeiō monte. Habēbat in ani- 101
mō etiam haec: iūs cīvīle ad certum modum redigere atque 102
ex ingentī cōpiā lēgum optima quaeque in paucissimōs li- 103
brōs cōnferre; bibliothēcās Graecās Latīnāsque quās max- 104
imās posset īnstituere; siccāre Pomptīnās palūdēs; ēmittere 105
Fūcīnum lacum; viam mūnire ā marī Superō per Āpennīnī 106
dorsum ad Tiberim; perfodere Isthmum Corinthium; Dācōs, 107
quī sē in Pontum et Thrāciam effūderant, coercēre; mox 108
Parthīs īnferre bellum per Armeniam. 109

Eum tālia agentem et meditantem mors praevēnit. Dic- 110 44 B.C.
tātor enim in perpetuum creātus agere īnsolentius coepit; 111
senātum ad sē venientem sedēns excēpit et quendam ut as- 112
surgeret monentem īrātō vultū respexit. Cum Antōnius, 113
comes Caesaris in omnibus bellīs et tum cōnsulātūs collēga, 114
capitī eius in sellā aureā sedentis prō rōstrīs diadēma, īn- 115
signe rēgium, imposuisset, id ita ab eō est repulsum ut nōn 116
offēnsus vidērētur. Quā rē amplius sexāgintā virī, Cassiō et 117
Brūtō ducibus, in eum coniūrāvērunt atque cōnstituērunt 118
eum Īdibus Mārtiīs in senātū interficere. 119

Exercise 7
Read aloud and translate; identify the subject of each impersonal verb:

1. Cōnstat Caesarem maximam pecūniam effūdisse ad lūdōs magnificōs ēdendōs.
2. Oportuit Caesar societātem cum Pompeiō Crassōque faceret.
3. Necesse erat Caesarī prōvinciam habēre ubi pecūniam obtinēre
   posset.
4. Inter Caesarem et Pompeium convēnit Caesarem Galliam,
   Pompeium Hispāniam obtentūrum esse.
5. Accidit ut Caesar multās victōriās obtinēret in Galliā.
6. Novem post annīs, Caesar secundum cōnsultātum petere voluit
   sed nōn licēbat eī flūmen Rubicōnem trānsīre cum exercitū suō.

120   **dēterrēbant . . . monēbat:** "tried to. . ."

    harūspex, harūspicis (*m.*), soothsayer (a priest who foretold the future by inspecting the vital organs of animals or the flight of birds).

121   **Spūrinna, -ae** (*m.*), Spurinna.

    ultrā (*prep. + acc.*), beyond, past.

123   **irrīdeō, irrīdēre** (2), **irrīsī, irrīsum**, to laugh at, mock.

124   **noxa, -ae** (*f.*), harm, injury.

125   **assideō, assidēre** (2), **assēdī, assessum**, to sit down.

126   **coniūrātī, -ōrum** (*m. pl.*), conspirators.

    circumstō, circumstāre (1), **circumstetī**, to surround, stand around.

127   **propius** (*comparative adv.*), nearer.

    *****accēdō, accēdere** (3), **accessī, accessum**, to approach.

128   **renuō, renuere** (3), **renuī**, to nod refusal to, deny, refuse.

    humerus, -ī (*m.*), shoulder.

    apprehendō, apprehendere (3), **apprehendī, apprehēnsum**, to seize, take hold of.

129   **Casca, -ae** (*m.*), Publius Longus Casca (one of two brothers who took part in the conspiracy to assassinate Caesar).

    adversum: "turned toward (him)," "front on."

130   **īnfrā** (*prep. + acc.*), below, under.

    bracchium, -ī (*n.*), arm.

131   **graphium, -ī** (*n.*), stilus.

    trāiciō, trāicere (3), **trāiēcī, trāiectum**, to pierce.

    cōnātus: translate as *present*, as often with the *perfect participle of deponent verbs.*

    prōsiliō, prōsilīre (4), **prōsiluī**, to jump forward, jump to one's feet.

132   **tardō** (1), to slow down, hinder.

133   **obvolvō, obvolvere** (3), **obvolvī, obvolūtum**, to wrap up, cover up.

134   **plaga, -ae** (*f.*), blow, wound.

    *****cōnfodiō, cōnfodere** (3), **cōnfōdī, cōnfossum**, to stab.

Caesar crossing the Rubicon

Quamquam prōdigia eum dēterrēbant et harūspex 120
Spūrinna monēbat ut cavēret perīculum quod nōn ultrā 121
Mārtiās Īdūs prōferrētur, statuit tamen eō diē senātum 122
habēre. Dum cūriam intrat, Spūrinnam irrīsit, quod sine 123
ūllā suā noxā Īdūs Mārtiae adessent. "Vēnērunt quidem," 124
inquit Spūrinna, "sed nōn praeteriērunt." Caesarem assi- 125
dentem coniūrātī speciē officiī circumstetērunt; ūnus deinde 126
quasi aliquid rogātūrus propius accessit et, cum Caesar 127
renueret, ab utrōque humerō togam apprehendit. Dum 128
Caesar clāmat, "Ista quidem vīs est," Casca eum adversum 129
vulnerat paulum īnfrā iugulum. Caesar Cascae bracchium 130
arreptum graphiō trāiēcit cōnātusque prōsilīre aliō vulnere 131
tardātus est. Deinde ut animadvertit undique sē strictīs 132
pūgiōnibus petī, togā caput obvolvit et tribus et vīgintī 133
plāgīs cōnfossus est. Cum Marcum Brūtum, quem fīliī locō 134
habēbat, in sē irruentem vīdisset, dīxisse fertur: "Tū 135
quoque, mī fīlī!" 136

The assassination of Caesar, as depicted by a sculptor on the
outside of the Folger Shakespeare Library in Washington, D.C.

137   *percussor, percussōris (m.), assailant, assassin.
       triennium, -ī (n.), three-year period, three years.
       supervīvō, supervīvere (3), supervīxī, supervīctum, to remain alive.
138   *naufragium, -ī (n.), shipwreck.

141   prīncipibus: note that the word prīnceps can be used either as a noun,
       "leader," "chief," "leading citizen," or as an adjective, "leading,"
       "foremost."
       rārior, more unusual.
           Quō rārior . . . hōc laudanda magis: "The more unusual . . . the
           more . . ."
       moderātiō, moderātiōnis (f.), control, regulation, self-control.
142   clēmēns, clēmentis, gentle, mild, merciful, compassionate.
143   scrīnium, -ī (n.), letter case.
144   *dīversus, -a, -um, different, opposite.
145   *neuter, neutra, neutrum, neither.
       combūrō, combūrere (3), combussī, combustum, to burn up
146   in (prep. + acc.), (here) against.
       gravius (comparative adv.), more seriously, more harshly.
       locum: "opportunity," "opening."
           gravius cōnsulendī locum: "opportunity of planning/acting more
           harshly."
147   oblīvīscor, oblīvīscī (3), oblītus sum, to forget.

Percussōrum autem nēmō ferē trienniō amplius super- 137
vīxit.   Damnātī omnēs variīs cāsibus periērunt, pars 138
naufragiō, pars proeliō; nōnnūllī sēmet interfēcērunt eōdem 139
illō pūgiōne, quō Caesarem cōnfōderant. 140

Quō rārior in rēgibus et prīncipibus virīs moderātiō, hōc 141
laudanda magis est.   Caesar victōriā cīvīlī clēmentissimē 142
ūsus est; cum enim scrīnia dēprehendisset epistulārum ad 143
Pompeium missārum ab eīs quī vidēbantur aut in dīversīs 144
aut in neutrīs fuisse partibus, legere nōluit, sed combussit, 145
nē forte in multōs gravius cōnsulendī locum darent. Cicerō 146
hanc laudem eximiam Caesarī tribuit, quod nihil oblīvīscī 147
solēret nisi iniūriās. 148

1   **equestrī genere**: "(a man) of equestrian birth," *ablative of description* (see the grammar note on page 134).
     Arpīnum, -ī (*n.*), Arpinum (a town in Latium, birthplace of Marius and of Cicero).
4   **intersum, interesse** (*irreg.*), **interfuī** (+ *dat.*), to take part in, attend.
5   **honōrēs**: "political offices," a common meaning of this word.
     viam mūnīre, to pave the way.
6   ***ēloquentia, -ae** (*f.*), eloquence.
     incumbō, incumbere (3), **incubuī, incubitum**, to bend over, lie on, apply oneself to.
7   **versor, versārī** (1), **versātus sum**, to be involved in, engaged in.
8   ***causam dīcere**, to plead a case.
     ***studiōsus, -a, -um**, eager, enthusiastic.
     sector, sectārī (1), **sectātus sum**, to follow.
     prīvātim (*adv.*), privately.

10   **lībertātem**: "(commitment to) freedom (of speech)."
     Sullānī, -ōrum (*m. pl.*), partisans of Sulla.
11   **Rōscius, -ī** (*m.*), Sextus Roscius (Roscius' father was killed in 81 B.C., and relatives wanted to enter his name on the proscription lists and to confiscate his property; they were aided by Sulla's freedman Chrysogonus, who charged Sextus Roscius with murdering his father).
     ***parricīdium, -ī** (*n.*), parricide (murder of a parent or close relative).
12   **Chrȳsogonus, -ī** (*m.*), Chrysogonus (unprincipled freedman of Sulla's).
13   **adversārius, -ī** (*m.*), enemy.
16   **gratiā** (+ *preceding gen.*), for the sake of.
     Antiochus, -ī (*m.*), Antiochus of Ascalon (Greek philosopher; visited Rome and headed the Academy in Athens; frequently quoted by his pupil Cicero).
18   **rhētor, rhētoris** (*m.*), rhetorician, teacher of rhetoric.
     disertus, -a, -um, eloquent.
20   **fleō, flēre** (2), **flēvī, flētum**, to cry.
21   **laude**: "its reputation," *ablative of separation* with **prīvārētur** (see grammar note on page 55).

31. Marcus Tullius Cicero

Marcus Tullius Cicerō, equestrī genere, Arpīnī, quod est 1   106 B.C.
Volscōrum oppidum, nātus est. Nōndum adultus ā patre 2
Rōmam missus est, ut celeberrimōrum magistrōrum scholīs 3
interesset. Cum nūllā rē magis ad summōs in rē pūblicā 4
honōrēs viam mūnīrī posse intellegeret quam arte dīcendī 5
et ēloquentiā, tōtō animō in eius studium incubuit; in quō 6
quidem ita versātus est ut nōn sōlum eōs quī in forō et 7
iūdiciīs causās dīcerent studiōsē sectārētur, sed prīvātim 8
quoque dīligentissimē sē exercēret. 9

Prīmum ēloquentiam et lībertātem adversus Sullānōs 10   80 B.C.
ostendit. Erat enim Rōscius quīdam, dē parricīdiō accūsā- 11
tus, quem ob potentiam Chrȳsogonī, Sullae lībertī, quī in 12
eius adversāriīs erat, nēmō alius dēfendere audēbat; Cicerō 13
tamen tantā ēloquentiae vī eum dēfendit ut iam tum in arte 14
dīcendī nēmō eī pār esse vidērētur. Posteā Athēnās 15   79–
studiōrum grātiā petiit, ubi Antiochum philosophum 16
studiōsē audīvit. Inde ēloquentiae causā Rhodum sē con- 17   77 B.C.
tulit, ubi Molōnem, Graecum rhētorem tum disertissimum, 18
magistrum habuit. Quī cum Cicerōnem dīcentem audīvis- 19
set, flēvisse dīcitur, quod per hunc Graecia ēloquentiae 20
laude prīvārētur. 21

Cicero

22   **quaestor**: financial officer assigned to a province, responsible to the prae-
      tor or governor (see line 27).
23   **cum**: "since."
24   **annōna, -ae** (*f.*), year's crop, grain supply.
      Siculī, -ōrum (*m. pl.*), the Sicilians.
26   **iūstitia, -ae** (*f.*), justice, fairness.
28   **flōreō** (2), to be in one's prime, be prosperous, flourish.
29   ***patrōnus, -ī** (*m.*), patron, pleader, advocate.
      habērētur: "was held," "was considered."

30   **L. Sergius Catilīna, L. Sergiī Catilīnae** (*m.*), Lucius Sergius Catiline (an
      ambitious aristocrat, who, after failing to be elected consul, formed a
      conspiracy to seize power for himself and his followers).
      ***coniūrātiō, coniūrātiōnis** (*f.*), conspiracy, plot.
31   **cōnstantia, -ae** (*f.*), steadiness, constancy, steadfastness.
      ēgregiā virtūte, cōnstantiā, cūrā: "with . . . ," *ablatives of manner.*
      comprimō, comprimere (3), **compressī, compressum**, to curb, restrain,
      suppress.
32   **familiāris, -is, -e**, familiar, intimate; (*here*) belonging to the family.
      reī familiāris: "his family's wealth."
      profundō, profundere (3), **profūdī, profūsum**, to pour out, spend freely,
      waste.
      inopia, -ae (*f.*), lack.
      dominor, dominārī (1), **dominātus sum**, to be master, domineer.
33   **petītiō, petītiōnis** (*f.*), candidacy, campaign for (+ *gen.*).
      repulsa, -ae (*f.*), defeat at the polls, rejection.
36   **praesēns, praesentis**, present.
37   **ōrātiōnem habēre**, to deliver a speech.
38   **patefaciō, patefacere** (3), **patefēcī, patefactum**, to reveal.
      restinguō, restinguere (3), **restīnxī, restīnctum**, to quench, extinguish,
      put out.
39   **minitor, minitārī** (1), **minitātus sum**, to make threats, threaten.
      incendium . . . restīnctūrum esse minitāns: this refers to the method of
      fighting fires by destroying buildings adjacent to the ones on fire so
      that the fire cannot spread. Catiline is threatening, in a half-veiled
      way, to defend himself (put out "his fire") by causing harm to others.
40   **signa īnferre** (+ *dat.*), to bring military standards against, attack.
41   **remaneō, remanēre** (2), **remānsī**, to stay behind, remain.

Adjectives with Special Genitive and Dative Singular Forms

In the passage on the opposite page, you will notice that **nūllīus** (22) is
genitive case and **ūllī** (27) dative. These are two of a small group of adjectives that are declined for the most part like 1st and 2nd declension
nouns and adjectives but that have special endings (-**īus** and -**ī**) in the
genitive and dative singular. The group includes:

alter, altera, alterum   the other (of two), a second
neuter, neutra, neutrum   neither (of two)

Rōmam reversus quaestor Siciliam habuit. Nūllīus vērō   22   75 B.C.
quaestūra aut grātior aut clārior fuit; cum enim magna tum   23
esset annōnae difficultās, initiō molestus fuit Siculīs, quōs   24
cōgeret frūmenta in urbem mittere; posteā vērō, dīligentiam   25
et iūstitiam et cōmitātem eius expertī, honōrēs quaestōrī   26
suō maiōrēs quam ūllī umquam praetōrī dētulērunt. Ē Si-   27
ciliā reversus Rōmam in causīs dīcendīs ita flōruit ut inter   28
omnēs causārum patrōnōs et esset et habērētur prīnceps.   29

Among other famous cases, Cicero represented the Sicilians, whom he had come to know during his quaestorship (75 B.C.), when they brought suit against Verres, a former governor of Sicily, for extortion and other crimes he had committed while in office. Cicero argued his case so brilliantly in 70 B.C. that he needed to deliver only the first of five speeches he had prepared, since Verres fled from Rome after the first day of the trial. We next see Cicero as consul (63 B.C.).

Cōnsul deinde factus L. Sergiī Catilīnae coniūrātiōnem   30   63 B.C.
ēgregiā virtūte, cōnstantiā, cūrā compressit. Catilīna reī   31
familiāris, quam profūderat, inopiā et dominandī cupiditāte   32
incēnsus erat indignātusque quod in petītiōne cōnsulātūs   33
repulsam passus esset; coniūrātiōne igitur factā senātum   34
interimere, cōnsulēs trucīdāre, urbem incendere, dīripere   35
aerārium cōnstituerat. Cicerō autem in senātū, praesente   36
Catilīnā, vehementem ōrātiōnem habuit et cōnsilia eius   37
patefēcit; tum ille, incendium suum ruīnā sē restīnctūrum   38
esse minitāns, Rōmā profūgit et ad exercitum, quem   39
parāverat, profectus est signa illātūrus urbī. Sed sociī eius,   40
quī in urbe remānserant, comprehēnsī in carcere necātī   41
sunt.   42

Adjectives with Special Genitive and Dative Singular Forms
(*continued*)

nūllus, -a, -um	no, none
sōlus, -a, -um	alone, only
tōtus, -a, -um	all, the whole, entire
ūllus, -a, -um	any
ūnus, -a, -um	one
uter, utra, utrum	which (of two)
uterque, utraque, utrumque	each (of two), both

The irregular genitive and dative singular endings are the same for masculine, feminine, and neuter. Compare the genitives and datives of **ille, illa, illud** and of **ipse, ipsa, ipsum** given on pages 183 and 184.

43   eō magis: "the more for that (reason)," "any the more."
      inceptum, -ī (n.), thing begun, project, undertaking.
      dēsistō, dēsistere (3), dēstitī, dēstitum, to stop, cease.
      īnfestīs signīs: "ready to attack," "on the offensive" (literally, "with hostile
        standards"). This refers to the **signa**, standards mounted on poles, car-
        ried by each unit of a Roman army. If the **signa** were **īnfesta**, "hostile,"
        "on the attack," then the army was on the offensive.
44   Antōnius, -ī (m.), Gaius Antonius Hybrida (Cicero's colleague in the
        consulship in 63 B.C. and uncle of the famous Marc Antony).
45   opprimitur: the battle took place near Pistoria, early in January of 62 B.C.
      ātrōciter (adv.), horribly, fiercely.
      dīmicātum sit: impersonal passive (see the grammar note on pages 76–
        77).
          Quam atrōciter dīmicātum sit: "How fiercely . . ."; this indirect ques-
          tion is the object of **docuit**. Note that the perfect tense (**docuit**) is
          here regarded as a primary tense, since the reference is clearly to
          present time ("has taught" not "taught"). It therefore establishes
          primary sequence, and the perfect subjunctive is used in the indi-
          rect question. For the basic rules for sequence of tenses, see the
          chart on page 64.
46   quem locum quisque . . . cēperat, . . . tegēbat: "whatever place each man
        took, . . . he covered," past general structure with pluperfect indicative
        in the subordinate clause and imperfect indicative in the main clause.
        In English the generality of the statement is expressed by translating
        quem locum as "whatever place," and the pluperfect verb in the subor-
        dinate clause is translated simply "took," and not "had taken."
48   cadāver, cadāveris (n.), corpse.
      pulcherrima: "most glorious."
49   sī . . . cecidisset: a past contrary to fact conditional clause (see the gram-
        mar note on page 105). The main clause is expressed by the exclama-
        tion **pulcherrima mors!**

51   inimīcitiae, -ārum (f. pl.), feuds.
      tempestāte: note that **tempestās** can mean simply "time" (= **tempus**), as
        well as "storm."
52   compōnō, compōnere (3), composuī, compositum, to settle.
53   ēnītor, ēnītī (3), ēnīsus sum, to struggle, strive, take pains.
55   ad pācem ineundam: "to enter upon/undertake peace."
57   Octāviānus, -ī (m.), Gaius Octavius (Octavian, adopted posthumously by
        Julius Caesar under the terms of his will and thereby named Gaius
        Julius Caesar Octavianus; the future emperor Augustus).
58   adversor, adversārī (1), adversātus sum (+ dat.), to oppose, resist.

Neque eō magis ab inceptō Catilīna dēstitit, sed īnfestīs   43   62 B.C.
signīs Rōmam petēns exercitū Antōniī, Cicerōnis collēgae,   44
opprimitur. Quam ātrōciter dīmicātum sit exitus docuit;   45
nēmō hostium bellō superfuit; nam quem locum quisque in   46
pugnandō cēperat, eum mortuus tegēbat. Catilīna longē ā   47
suīs inter hostium cadāvera repertus est—pulcherrima   48
mors, sī prō patriā sīc concidisset! Senātus populusque   49
Rōmānus Cicerōnem patrem patriae appellāvit.   50

Later on, Cicero was driven into exile by his enemy Clodius on a charge of having put Roman citizens (the conspirators whom he had executed) to death without proper trial. He was recalled not long after, however, only to become embroiled in the rivalry between Caesar and Pompey.

Gravissimae inimīcitiae illā tempestāte inter Caesarem   51   60 B.C.
et Pompeium ortae sunt, ut rēs nisi bellō compōnī nōn posse   52
vidērētur. Cicerō quidem summō studiō ēnītēbātur ut eōs   53
inter sē reconciliāret et ā bellī cīvīlis calamitātibus dēter-   54
rēret; sed cum neutrum ad pācem ineundam movēre posset,   55   49 B.C.
Pompeium secūtus est. Tamen ā Caesare victōre veniam   56   48 B.C.
accēpit. Cum Caesar occīsus esset, Octāviānō, Caesaris   57   44 B.C.
hērēdī, fāvit Antōniōque adversātus est, atque effēcit ut ille   58   44–
ā senātū hostis iūdicārētur.   59   43 B.C.

A member of the family of the Lentuli. The praetor P. Cornelius Lentulus Sura was an important member of Catiline's conspiracy.

61 **prōscrībō, prōscrībere** (3), **prōscrīpsī, prōscrīptum**, to proscribe, outlaw.
62 **trānsversus, -a, -um**, lying crosswise; (*of roads*) directed slantwise across the main route.
   trānsversīs itineribus: "by back roads."
63 **cōnscendō, cōnscendere** (3), **cōnscendī, cōnscēnsum**, to board, embark on.
   Macedonia, -ae (*f.*), Macedonia (a region to the north of Greece).
64 **aliquotiēns** (*adv.*), several times.
   altum, -ī (*n.*), deep sea.
   prōvehō, prōvehere (3), **prōvexī, prōvectum**, to transport, convey, carry forth.
   adversus, -a, -um, turned toward, opposite, unfavorable.
65 **iactātiō, iactātiōnis** (*f.*), tossing to and fro, swaying.
66 **taedium, -ī** (*n.*), weariness.
   fuga, -ae (*f.*), flight.
   aliquandō (*adv.*), sometime, someday, at last.
67 **moriar**: *future indicative* or *present subjunctive* expressing a *wish*.
68 **adventō** (1, *frequentative*), to approach.
70 **prōmineō** (2), to jut out, lean out.
   Prōminentī . . . praebentī: "For him as he was . . . ," *dative of reference*.
71 **immōtus, -a, -um**, motionless, still.
   cervīx, cervīcis (*f.*), neck.
   praebentī: "exposing . . . (to danger)."

76 **cōgitātiō, cōgitātiōnis** (*f.*), reflection, meditation, plan, design.
   cōnferō, cōnferre (*irreg.*), **contulī, collātum**, to bring together, collect, direct, devote.
78 **angor, angōris** (*m.*), anguish.
79 **indignus, -a, -um** (+ *abl.*), unworthy.
   doctus, -a, -um, learned.
80 **rūs, rūris** (*n.*) (*often pl. with sing. meaning*), the country.
   peragrō (1), to travel through.
   abdō, abdere (3), **abdidī, abditum**, to hide, withdraw.
82 **philosophia, -ae** (*f.*), philosophy.
83 **honestus, -a, -um**, honorable, respectable.
   molestia, -ae (*f.*), annoyance, worry, trouble.
86 **ēvertō, ēvertere** (3), **ēvertī, ēversum**, to overturn, overthrow.

Sed Antōnius, initā cum Octāviānō societāte, Cicerōnem 60 43 B.C.
iam diū sibi inimīcum prōscrīpsit. Quā rē audītā, Cicerō 61
trānsversīs itineribus in vīllam, quae ā marī nōn longē 62
aberat, fugit indeque nāvem cōnscendit, in Macedoniam 63
trānsitūrus. Cum aliquotiēns in altum prōvectus ventīs ad- 64
versīs relātus esset, neque iactātiōnem maris patī posset, 65
taedium tandem et fugae et vītae eum cēpit; aliquandō re- 66
gressus ad vīllam, "Moriar," inquit, "in patriā saepe ser- 67
vātā." Adventantibus percussōribus, servī parātī ad dīmi- 68
candum erant; sed ipse eōs dēpōnere lectīcam et quiētōs 69
patī quod sors inīqua cōgeret iussit. Prōminentī ex lectīcā 70
et immōtam cervīcem praebentī caput praecīsum est. 71
Manūs quoque praecīsae sunt; caput relātum est ad 72
Antōnium iussūque eius inter duās manūs in rōstrīs posi- 73
tum. 74

Quamdiū rēs pūblica lībera stābat, Cicerō in eam cūrās 75
cōgitātiōnēsque ferē omnēs suās cōnferēbat et plūs operae 76
pōnēbat in agendō quam in scrībendō. Cum autem omnia 77
potestāte ūnīus C. Iūliī Caesaris tenērentur, nōn sē an- 78
gōribus dēdidit nec indignīs homine doctō voluptātibus. 79
Vītāns cōnspectum forī urbisque rūra peragrābat abdē- 80
batque sē, quantum licēbat, et sōlus erat. Cum animus 81
autem nihil agere nōn poterat, sē ad philosophiam referre 82
cōnstituit atque ita honestissimē molestiās dēpōnere. Huic 83
studiō Cicerō adulēscēns multum temporis tribuerat, et iam 84
senex omnem cūram ad scrībendum convertit. Eō modō 85
plūra brevī tempore ēversā rē pūblicā scrīpsit, quam multīs 86
annīs eā stante scrīpserat. 87

The **societās** in line 60 was an alliance among Octavian, Marc
Antony, and Lepidus. Under this arrangement, known as the Second
Triumvirate, the three agreed to share in ruling the Roman empire.
Lepidus, however, was soon pushed aside, and for ten years Octavian
ruled the western half of the empire and Antony the eastern. Relations
between the two became strained (particularly after Antony divorced
Octavian's sister in order to marry Cleopatra, queen of Egypt). In 31
B.C. Octavian defeated Antony and Cleopatra in a naval battle at
Actium in Greece, and became sole ruler of the Roman world.

Octavian believed that rule by one man was the only way to avoid
further civil strife. He therefore took steps to legalize his rule while
preserving the appearance of Republican government. He became the
first emperor and was granted the title Augustus by the Senate. The
form of government he created endured for 500 years.

Time Line

N.B. Dates shown with a question mark are not absolutely reliable.

B.C. ? 1184   Fall of Troy
? 753   Foundation of Rome
753–510   Rule by kings
509   Expulsion of Etruscan kings
    Republic established
494   Secession of plebs; first tribunes elected
390   Gauls sack Rome
281–275   War with Tarentum and Pyrrhus
264–241   First Punic War
227   Sicily, Sardinia, and Corsica organized as provinces
218–201   Second Punic War
218   Hannibal crosses Alps to invade Italy
210   P. Cornelius Scipio commander in Spain
203–202   Hannibal returns to Africa; battle of Zama
149–146   Third Punic War; Carthage destroyed
133   Tribunate of Tiberius Gracchus
123–122   Tribunates of Gaius Gracchus
107–100   Consulships of Marius
91–87   Social or Italian War
86   Seventh consulship of Marius
82–79   Dictatorship of Sulla
67   Pompey suppresses the pirates
63   Consulship of Cicero; conspiracy of Catiline
60   First Triumvirate (Caesar, Pompey, Crassus)
58–49   Caesar governor of Gaul
49–45   Civil war between Caesar and Pompey and his supporters
44   Assassination of Caesar
43   Second Triumvirate (Octavian, Antony, Lepidus)
43   Murder of Cicero on Antony's orders

Grammatical Index

The grammatical notes included in this book are listed here. Entries in boldface refer to the boxed grammatical notes and are identified by section and page number. Entries in italics refer to grammatical notes in the running vocabularies and are identified by section and line number as well as by page number. In each grammatical category, the boxed grammar notes are listed first, followed by the notes in the running vocabularies.

Forms

I. Nouns

Number Case	1st Declension Fem.	2nd Declension Masc.	Masc.	Neut.	3rd Declension Masc.	Fem.	Neut.
Singular							
Nom.	puélla	sérvus	púer	báculum	páter	vōx	nómen
Gen.	puéllae	sérvī	púerī	báculī	pátris	vócis	nóminis
Dat.	puéllae	sérvō	púerō	báculō	pátrī	vócī	nóminī
Acc.	puéllam	sérvum	púerum	báculum	pátrem	vócem	nómen
Abl.	puéllā	sérvō	púerō	báculō	pátre	vóce	nómine
Plural							
Nom.	puéllae	sérvī	púerī	bácula	pátrēs	vócēs	nómina
Gen.	puellárum	servórum	puerórum	baculórum	pátrum	vócum	nóminum
Dat.	puéllīs	sérvīs	púerīs	báculīs	pátribus	vócibus	nōmínibus
Acc.	puéllās	sérvōs	púerōs	bácula	pátrēs	vócēs	nómina
Abl.	puéllīs	sérvīs	púerīs	báculīs	pátribus	vócibus	nōmínibus

4th Declension Fem.	Neut.	5th Declension Masc.
mánus	génū	díēs
mánūs	génūs	diéī
mánuī	génū	diéī
mánum	génū	díem
mánū	génū	díē
mánūs	génua	díēs
mánuum	génuum	diérum
mánibus	génibus	diébus
mánūs	génua	díēs
mánibus	génibus	diébus

178

II. Adjectives

Number Case	1st and 2nd Declension			3rd Declension		
	Masc.	*Fem.*	*Neut.*	*Masc.*	*Fem.*	*Neut.*
Singular						
Nominative	mágnus	mágna	mágnum	ómnis	ómnis	ómne
Genitive	mágnī	mágnae	mágnī	ómnis	ómnis	ómnis
Accusative	mágnum	mágnam	mágnum	ómnem	ómnem	ómne
Ablative	mágnō	mágnā	mágnō	ómnī	ómnī	ómnī
Plural						
Nominative	mágnī	mágnae	mágna	ómnēs	ómnēs	ómnia
Genitive	magnórum	magnárum	magnórum	ómnium	ómnium	ómnium
Accusative	mágnōs	mágnās	mágna	ómnēs	ómnēs	ómnia
Ablative	mágnīs	mágnīs	mágnīs	ómnibus	ómnibus	ómnibus

Case	*Masc.*	*Fem.*	*Neut.*	*Masc.*	*Fem.*	*Neut.*	*Masc.*	*Fem.*	*Neut.*
Nominative	únus	úna	únum	dúo	dúae	dúo	trēs	trēs	tría
Genitive	ūníus	ūníus	ūníus	duórum	duárum	duórum	tríum	tríum	tríum
Accusative	únum	únam	únum	dúōs	dúās	dúo	trēs	trēs	tría
Ablative	únō	únā	únō	duóbus	duábus	duóbus	tríbus	tríbus	tríbus

III. Numerical Adjectives or Numbers

Cardinal

I	ūnus, -a, -um, one
II	duo, -ae, -o, two
III	trēs, trēs, tria, three
IV	quattuor, four
V	quīnque, five
VI	sex, six
VII	septem, seven
VIII	octō, eight
IX	novem, nine
X	decem, ten
XI	ūndecim, eleven
XII	duodecim, twelve
XX	vīgintī, twenty
L	quīnquāgintā, fifty
C	centum, a hundred
D	quīngentī, -ae, -a, five hundred
M	mīlle, a thousand

Ordinal

prīmus, -a, -um, first
secundus, -a, -um, second
tertius, -a, -um, third
quārtus, -a, -um
quīntus, -a, -um
sextus, -a, -um
septimus, -a, -um
octāvus, -a, -um
nōnus, -a, -um
decimus, -a, -um
ūndecimus, -a, -um
duodecimus, -a, -um
vīcēsimus, -a, -um
quīnquāgēsimus, -a, -um
centēsimus, -a, -um
quīngentēsimus, -a, -um
mīllēsimus, -a, -um

N.B. The cardinal numbers from **quattuor** to **centum** do not change their form to indicate case and gender.

IV. Comparative Adjectives

Number Case	Masculine	Feminine	Neuter
Singular			
Nom.	púlchrior	púlchrior	púlchrius
Gen.	pulchrióris	pulchrióris	pulchrióris
Dat.	pulchriórī	pulchriórī	pulchriórī
Acc.	pulchriórem	pulchriórem	púlchrius
Abl.	pulchrióre	pulchrióre	pulchrióre
Plural			
Nom.	pulchriórēs	pulchriórēs	pulchrióra
Gen.	pulchriórum	pulchriórum	pulchriórum
Dat.	pulchrióribus	pulchrióribus	pulchrióribus
Acc.	pulchriórēs	pulchriórēs	pulchrióra
Abl.	pulchrióribus	pulchrióribus	pulchrióribus

Adjectives have *positive, comparative,* and *superlative* forms. You can recognize the comparative by the letters *-ior/-ius/-iōr-* and the superlative by the letters *-issimus, -errimus,* or *-illimus,* e.g.:

ignavus, *lazy*	ignāvior	ignāvissimus, -a, -um
pulcher, *beautiful*	pulchrior	pulcherrimus, -a, -um
facilis, *easy*	facilior	facillimus, -a, -um

Some adjectives are irregular in the comparative and superlative, e.g.:

bonus, *good*	melior, *better*	optimus, *best*
malus, *bad*	peior, *worse*	pessimus, *worst*
magnus, *big*	maior, *bigger*	maximus, *biggest*
parvus, *small*	minor, *smaller*	minimus, *smallest*
multus, *much*	plūs, *more*	plūrimus, *most, very much*
multī, *many*	plūrēs, *more*	plūrimī, *most, very many*

Note that comparative adjectives are declined like 3rd declension nouns and not like 3rd declension adjectives; that is, they are not i-stems.

V.   Present Active Participles

Number Case	Masculine	Feminine	Neuter
Singular			
Nom.	párāns	párāns	párāns
Gen.	parántis	parántis	parántis
Dat.	parántī	parántī	parántī
Acc.	parántem	parántem	párāns
Abl.	paránte	paránte	paránte
Plural			
Nom.	parántēs	parántēs	parántia
Gen.	parántium	parántium	parántium
Dat.	parántibus	parántibus	parántibus
Acc.	parántēs	parántēs	parántia
Abl.	parántibus	parántibus	parántibus

Present active participles are i-stems, but they may have either *-e* (as above) or *-ī* in the ablative singular.

Summary:

> 3rd declension adjectives (i-stems):
> > ablative singular: *-ī*
> > genitive plural: *-ium*
> > neuter nominative/accusative plural: *-ia*
>
> Comparative adjectives (not i-stems):
> > ablative singular: *-e*
> > genitive plural: *-um*
> > neuter nominative/accusative plural: *-a*
>
> Present active participles (i-stems)
> > ablative singular: *-e* or *-ī*
> > genitive plural: *-ium*
> > neuter nominative/accusative plural: *-ia*

VI. Demonstrative Adjectives and Pronouns

Number Case	Masc.	Fem.	Neut.	Masc.	Fem.	Neut.
Singular						
Nom.	is	éa	id	ídem	éadem	ídem
Gen.	éius	éius	éius	eiúsdem	eiúsdem	eiúsdem
Dat.	éī	éī	éī	eídem	eídem	eídem
Acc.	éum	éam	id	eúndem	eándem	ídem
Abl.	éō	éā	éō	eódem	eádem	eódem
Plural						
Nom.	éī	éae	éa	eídem	eaédem	éadem
Gen.	eórum	eárum	eórum	eōrúndem	eārúndem	eōrúndem
Dat.	éīs	éīs	éīs	eísdem	eísdem	eísdem
Acc.	éōs	éās	éa	eósdem	eásdem	éadem
Abl.	éīs	éīs	éīs	eísdem	eísdem	eísdem

Number Case	Masc.	Fem.	Neut.	Masc.	Fem.	Neut.
Singular						
Nom.	hic	haec	hoc	ílle	ílla	íllud
Gen.	húius	húius	húius	illíus	illíus	illíus
Dat.	húic	húic	húic	íllī	íllī	íllī
Acc.	hunc	hanc	hoc	íllum	íllam	íllud
Abl.	hōc	hāc	hōc	íllō	íllā	íllō
Plural						
Nom.	hī	hae	haec	íllī	íllae	ílla
Gen.	hórum	hárum	hórum	illórum	illárum	illórum
Dat.	hīs	hīs	hīs	íllīs	íllīs	íllīs
Acc.	hōs	hās	haec	íllōs	íllās	ílla
Abl.	hīs	hīs	hīs	íllīs	íllīs	íllīs

The intensive adjective **ipse, ipsa, ipsum** has the same endings as **ille, illa, illud** except for **ipsum** in the neuter nominative and accusative singular.

The demonstrative **iste, ista, istud** has the same endings as **ille, illa, illud**.

VII. Intensive Adjective

Number Case	Masc.	Fem.	Neut.
Singular			
Nom.	ípse	ípsa	ípsum
Gen.	ipsíus	ipsíus	ipsíus
Dat.	ípsī	ípsī	ípsī
Acc.	ípsum	ípsam	ípsum
Abl.	ípsō	ípsā	ípsō
Plural			
Nom.	ípsī	ípsae	ípsa
Gen.	ipsórum	ipsárum	ipsórum
Dat.	ípsīs	ípsīs	ípsīs
Acc.	ípsōs	ípsās	ípsa
Abl.	ípsīs	ípsīs	ípsīs

The demonstrative adjectives and pronouns and the intensive adjective are irregular, but many endings are those of the 1st and 2nd declensions, and the genitive and dative singulars show similarities:

hic, haec, hoc:	huius	huic
ille, illa, illud:	illīus	illī
is, ea, id:	eius	eī
ipse, ipsa, ipsum:	ipsīus	ipsī

VIII. Relative and Interrogative Pronouns and Adjectives

	Singular			Plural		
	Masc.	**Fem.**	**Neut.**	**Masc.**	**Fem.**	**Neut.**
Nom.	quī	quae	quod	quī	quae	quae
Gen.	cúius	cúius	cúius	quórum	quárum	quórum
Dat.	cúi	cúi	cúi	quíbus	quíbus	quíbus
Acc.	quem	quam	quod	quōs	quās	quae
Abl.	quō	quā	quō	quíbus	quíbus	quíbus

The interrogative pronoun **quis, quid,** "who?" "what?" has the same forms as the relative pronoun, except for the nominative masculine/feminine singular **quis** and the nominative and accusative neuter singular **quid**. In the singular, the feminine has the same forms as the masculine. In the plural, all forms are the same as those of the relative pronoun. The interrogative adjective **quī, quae, quod,** "which?" "what?" has the same forms as the relative pronoun.

IX. Indefinite Adjectives and Pronouns

Number Case	Masc.	Fem.	Neut.	Masc.	Fem.	Neut.
Singular						
Nom.	quídam	quaédam	quóddam	áliquī	áliqua	áliquod
Gen.	cuiúsdam	cuiúsdam	cuiúsdam	álicuius	álicuius	álicuius
Dat.	cuídam	cuídam	cuídam	álicui	álicui	álicui
Acc.	quéndam	quándam	quóddam	áliquem	áliquam	áliquod
Abl.	quódam	quádam	quódam	áliquō	áliquā	áliquō
Plural						
Nom.	quídam	quaédam	quaédam	áliquī	áliquae	áliqua
Gen.	quōrúndam	quārúndam	quōrúndam	aliquórum	aliquárum	aliquórum
Dat.	quibúsdam	quibúsdam	quibúsdam	alíquibus	alíquibus	alíquibus
Acc.	quósdam	quásdam	quaédam	áliquōs	áliquās	áliqua
Abl.	quibúsdam	quibúsdam	quibúsdam	alíquibus	alíquibus	alíquibus

The indefinite pronoun **quīdam, quaedam, quiddam**, "a certain one," "a certain thing," has the same forms as the indefinite adjective given above ("a certain," "certain"), except for **quiddam** in the neuter nominative and accusative singular. The indefinite pronoun **aliquis, aliquid**, "someone," "anyone," "something," "anything," has the forms of the interrogative pronoun **quis, quid**, "who?" "what?" as do the pronouns **quisque, quidque**, "each," and **quisquam, quidquam (quicquam)**, "anyone," "anything."

X. Personal and Demonstrative Pronouns

Case	Singular					Plural				
	1st	2nd	3rd			1st	2nd	3rd		
			Masc.	Fem.	Neut.			Masc.	Fem.	Neut.
Nom.	égo	tū	is	éa	id	nōs	vōs	éī	éae	éa
Gen.	méī	túī	éius	éius	éius	nóstrī	véstrī	eórum	eárum	eórum
Dat.	míhi	tíbi	éī	éī	éī	nóbīs	vóbīs	éīs	éīs	éīs
Acc.	mē	tē	éum	éam	id	nōs	vōs	éōs	éās	éa
Abl.	mē	tē	éō	éā	éō	nóbīs	vóbīs	éīs	éīs	éīs

XI. Reflexive Pronoun

Case	Singular	Plural
Nom.	—	—
Gen.	súī	súī
Dat.	síbi	síbi
Acc.	sē	sē
Abl.	sē	sē

The reflexive pronoun given above is that of the third person, "of himself/herself," "of themselves," etc. For the first and second persons, the personal pronouns may be used as reflexives, e.g., **meī**, **mihi**.

XII. Adverbs

Latin adverbs may be formed from adjectives of the 1st and 2nd declensions by adding *-ē* to the base of the adjective, e.g., **strēnuē**, "strenuously," from **strēnuus, -a, -um**. To form an adverb from a 3rd declension adjective, add *-iter* to the base of the adjective or *-ter* to bases ending in **-nt-**, e.g., **breviter**, "briefly," from **brevis, -is, -e**, and **prūenter**, "wisely," from **prūdēns, prūdentis**.

The comparative ends in *-ius*.

The superlative ends in *-issimē*, *-errimē*, or *-illimē*, e.g.:

lentē, *slowly*	lentius	lentissimē
fēlīciter, *luckily*	fēlīcius	fēlīcissimē
dīligenter, *carefully*	dīligentius	dīligentissimē
celeriter, *quickly*	celerius	celerrimē
facile, *easily*	facilius	facillimē

Some adverbs are irregular:

bene, *well*	melius, *better*	optimē, *best*
male, *badly*	peius, *worse*	pessimē, *worst*
magnopere, *greatly*	magis, *more*	maximē, *most*
paulum, *little*	minus, *less*	minimē, *least*
multum, *much*	plūs, *more*	plūrimum, *most*

Some adverbs are not formed from adjectives:

diū, *for a long time*	diūtius	diūtissimē
saepe, *often*	saepius	saepissimē
sērō, *late*	sērius	sērissimē

XIII. Regular Verbs Active: Infinitive, Imperative, Indicative

			1st Conjugation	2nd Conjugation	3rd Conjugation		4th Conjugation
Present Infinitive			paráre	habére	míttere	iácere (-iō)	audíre
Imperative			párā	hábē	mítte	iáce	aúdī
			paráte	habéte	míttite	iácite	audíte
Present	Singular	1	párō	hábeō	míttō	iáciō	aúdiō
		2	párās	hábēs	míttis	iácis	aúdīs
		3	párat	hábet	míttit	iácit	aúdit
	Plural	1	parámus	habémus	míttimus	iácimus	audímus
		2	parátis	habétis	míttitis	iácitis	audítis
		3	párant	hábent	míttunt	iáciunt	aúdiunt
Imperfect	Singular	1	parábam	habébam	mittébam	iaciébam	audiébam
		2	parábās	habébās	mittébās	iaciébās	audiébās
		3	parábat	habébat	mittébat	iaciébat	audiébat
	Plural	1	parabámus	habēbámus	mittēbámus	iaciēbámus	audiēbámus
		2	parabátis	habēbátis	mittēbátis	iaciēbátis	audiēbátis
		3	parábant	habébant	mittébant	iaciébant	audiébant
Future	Singular	1	parábō	habébō	míttam	iáciam	aúdiam
		2	parábis	habébis	míttēs	iáciēs	aúdiēs
		3	parábit	habébit	míttet	iáciet	aúdiet
	Plural	1	parábimus	habébimus	mittémus	iaciémus	audiémus
		2	parábitis	habébitis	mittétis	iaciétis	audiétis
		3	parábunt	habébunt	míttent	iácient	aúdient

XIV. Regular Verbs Active: Indicative, Infinitive (continued)

Perfect Infinitive			parāvísse	habuísse	mīsísse	iēcísse	audīvísse
Perfect	*Singular*	1	parā́vī	hábuī	mī́sī	iḗcī	audī́vī
		2	parāvístī	habuístī	mīsístī	iēcístī	audīvístī
		3	parā́vit	hábuit	mī́sit	iḗcit	audī́vit
	Plural	1	parā́vimus	habúimus	mī́simus	iḗcimus	audī́vimus
		2	parāvístis	habuístis	mīsístis	iēcístis	audīvístis
		3	parāvḗrunt	habuḗrunt	mīsḗrunt	iēcḗrunt	audīvḗrunt
Pluperfect	*Singular*	1	parā́veram	habúeram	mī́seram	iḗceram	audī́veram
		2	parā́verās	habúerās	mī́serās	iḗcerās	audī́verās
		3	parā́verat	habúerat	mī́serat	iḗcerat	audī́verat
	Plural	1	parāverā́mus	habuerā́mus	mīserā́mus	iēcerā́mus	audīverā́mus
		2	parāverā́tis	habuerā́tis	mīserā́tis	iēcerā́tis	audīverā́tis
		3	parā́verant	habúerant	mī́serant	iḗcerant	audī́verant
Future Perfect	*Singular*	1	parā́verō	habúerō	mī́serō	iḗcerō	audī́verō
		2	parā́veris	habúeris	mī́seris	iḗceris	audī́veris
		3	parā́verit	habúerit	mī́serit	iḗcerit	audī́verit
	Plural	1	parāvérimus	habuérimus	mīsérimus	iēcérimus	audīvérimus
		2	parāvéritis	habuéritis	mīséritis	iēcéritis	audīvéritis
		3	parā́verint	habúerint	mī́serint	iḗcerint	audī́verint

XV. Regular Verbs Passive: Indicative

			1st Conjugation	2nd Conjugation	3rd Conjugation		4th Conjugation
Present	*Singular*	1	pórtor	móveor	míttor	iácior	aúdior
		2	portáris	movéris	mítteris	iáceris	audíris
		3	portátur	movétur	míttitur	iácitur	audítur
	Plural	1	portámur	movémur	míttimur	iácimur	audímur
		2	portáminī	movéminī	mittíminī	iacíminī	audíminī
		3	portántur	movéntur	mittúntur	iaciúntur	audiúntur
Imperfect	*Singular*	1	portábar	movébar	mittébar	iaciébar	audiébar
		2	portābáris	movēbáris	mittēbáris	iaciēbáris	audiēbáris
		3	portābátur	movēbátur	mittēbátur	iaciēbátur	audiēbátur
	Plural	1	portābámur	movēbámur	mittēbámur	iaciēbámur	audiēbámur
		2	portābáminī	movēbáminī	mittēbáminī	iaciēbáminī	audiēbáminī
		3	portābántur	movēbántur	mittēbántur	iaciēbántur	audiēbántur
Future	*Singular*	1	portábor	movébor	míttar	iáciar	aúdiar
		2	portáberis	movéberis	mittéris	iaciéris	audiéris
		3	portábitur	movébitur	mittétur	iaciétur	audiétur
	Plural	1	portábimur	movébimur	mittémur	iaciémur	audiémur
		2	portābíminī	movēbíminī	mittéminī	iaciéminī	audiéminī
		3	portābúntur	movēbúntur	mitténtur	iaciéntur	audiéntur

		PERFECT PASSIVE		PLUPERFECT PASSIVE		FUTURE PERFECT PASSIVE	
Singular	1	portátus, -a	sum	portátus, -a	éram	portátus, -a	érō
	2	portátus, -a	es	portátus, -a	érās	portátus, -a	éris
	3	portátus, -a, -um	est	portátus, -a, -um	érat	portátus, -a, -um	érit
Plural	1	portátī, -ae	súmus	portátī, -ae	erámus	portátī, -ae	érimus
	2	portátī, -ae	éstis	portátī, -ae	erátis	portátī, -ae	éritis
	3	portátī, -ae, -a	sunt	portátī, -ae, -a	érant	portátī, -ae, -a	érunt

XVI. Regular Verbs Active: Subjunctive

			1st Conjugation	2nd Conjugation	3rd Conjugation		4th Conjugation
Present	Singular	1	párem	hábeam	míttam	iáciam	aúdiam
		2	párēs	hábeās	míttās	iáciās	aúdiās
		3	páret	hábeat	míttat	iáciat	aúdiat
	Plural	1	parḗmus	habeámus	mittámus	iaciámus	audiámus
		2	parḗtis	habeátis	mittátis	iaciátis	audiátis
		3	párent	hábeant	míttant	iáciant	aúdiant
Imperfect	Singular	1	parárem	habérem	mítterem	iácerem	audírem
		2	parárēs	habérēs	mítterēs	iácerēs	audírēs
		3	paráret	habéret	mítteret	iáceret	audíret
	Plural	1	parārḗmus	habērḗmus	mitterḗmus	iacerḗmus	audīrḗmus
		2	parārḗtis	habērḗtis	mitterḗtis	iacerḗtis	audīrḗtis
		3	parárent	habérent	mítterent	iácerent	audírent

			1st Conjugation	2nd Conjugation	3rd Conjugation		4th Conjugation
Perfect	Singular	1	paráverim	habúerim	míserim	iécerim	audíverim
		2	paráveris	habúeris	míseris	iéceris	audíveris
		3	paráverit	habúerit	míserit	iécerit	audíverit
	Plural	1	parāvérimus	habuérimus	mīsérimus	iēcérimus	audīvérimus
		2	parāvéritis	habuéritis	mīséritis	iēcéritis	audīvéritis
		3	paráverint	habúerint	míserint	iécerint	audíverint
Pluperfect	Singular	1	parāvíssem	habuíssem	mīsíssem	iēcíssem	audīvíssem
		2	parāvíssēs	habuíssēs	mīsíssēs	iēcíssēs	audīvíssēs
		3	parāvísset	habuísset	mīsísset	iēcísset	audīvísset
	Plural	1	parāvissḗmus	habuissḗmus	mīsissḗmus	iēcissḗmus	audīvissḗmus
		2	parāvissḗtis	habuissḗtis	mīsissḗtis	iēcissḗtis	audīvissḗtis
		3	parāvíssent	habuíssent	mīsíssent	iēcíssent	audīvíssent

XVII. Regular Verbs Passive: Subjunctive

			1st Conjugation	2nd Conjugation	3rd Conjugation		4th Conjugation
Present	Singular	1	párer	hábear	míttar	iáciar	aúdiar
		2	paréris	habeáris	mittáris	iaciáris	audiáris
		3	parétur	habeátur	mittátur	iaciátur	audiátur
	Plural	1	parémur	habeámur	mittámur	iaciámur	audiámur
		2	parémini	habeámini	mittámini	iaciámini	audiámini
		3	paréntur	habeántur	mittántur	iaciántur	audiántur
Imperfect	Singular	1	parárer	habérer	mítterer	iácerer	audírer
		2	pararéris	habéréris	mitteréris	iaceréris	audíréris
		3	pararétur	habérétur	mitterétur	iacerétur	audírétur
	Plural	1	pararémur	habérémur	mitterémur	iacerémur	audírémur
		2	pararémini	habérémini	mitterémini	iacerémini	audírémini
		3	pararéntur	habéréntur	mitteréntur	iaceréntur	audíréntur

The perfect passive subjunctive consists of the perfect passive participle plus the present subjunctive of the verb **esse** (see p. 195), e.g., **parátus sim**. The pluperfect passive subjunctive consists of the perfect passive participle plus the imperfect subjunctive of the verb **esse** (see page 195), e.g., **parátus essem**.

XVIII. Irregular Verbs:
Infinitive, Imperative, Indicative

			ésse	pósse	vélle	nolle
Infinitive			ésse	pósse	vélle	nolle
Imperative			es	—	—	nólī
			éste	—	—	nōlíte
Present	*Singular*	1	sum	póssum	vólō	nólō
		2	es	pótes	vīs	nōn vīs
		3	est	pótest	vult	nōn vult
	Plural	1	súmus	póssumus	vólumus	nólumus
		2	éstis	potéstis	vúltis	nōn vúltis
		3	sunt	póssunt	vólunt	nólunt
Imperfect	*Singular*	1	éram	póteram	volébam	nōlébam
		2	érās	póterās	volébās	nōlébās
		3	érat	póterat	volébat	nōlébat
	Plural	1	erámus	poterámus	volēbámus	nōlēbámus
		2	erátis	poterátis	volēbátis	nōlēbátis
		3	érant	póterant	volébant	nōlébant
Future	*Singular*	1	érō	póterō	vólam	nólam
		2	éris	póteris	vólēs	nólēs
		3	érit	póterit	vólet	nólet
	Plural	1	érimus	potérimus	volémus	nōlémus
		2	éritis	potéritis	volétis	nōlétis
		3	érunt	póterunt	vólent	nólent

XIX. Irregular Verbs:
Infinitive, Imperative, Indicative
(continued)

Infinitive			málle	íre	férre	férrī	fíerī
Imperative			—	ī	fer	férre	—
			—	íte	férte	feríminī	—
Present	Singular	1	málō	éō	férō	féror	fíō
		2	mávīs	īs	fers	férris	fīs
		3	mávult	it	fert	fértur	fit
	Plural	1	málumus	ímus	férimus	férimur	fímus
		2	māvúltis	ítis	fértis	feríminī	fítis
		3	málunt	éunt	férunt	ferúntur	fíunt
Imperfect	Singular	1	mālébam	íbam	ferébam	ferébar	fiébam
		2	mālébās	íbās	ferēbās	ferēbáris	fiébās
		3	mālébat	íbat	ferébat	ferēbátur	fiébat
	Plural	1	mālēbámus	ībámus	ferēbámus	ferēbámur	fiēbámus
		2	mālēbátis	ībátis	ferēbátis	ferēbáminī	fiēbátis
		3	mālébant	íbant	ferébant	ferēbántur	fiébant
Future	Singular	1	málam	íbō	féram	férar	fíam
		2	máles	íbis	féres	feréris	fíes
		3	málet	íbit	féret	ferétur	fiet
	Plural	1	mālémus	íbimus	ferémus	ferémur	fiémus
		2	mālétis	íbitis	ferétis	feréminī	fiétis
		3	málent	íbunt	férent	feréntur	fient

Note: perfect, pluperfect, and future perfect tenses are formed regularly from the perfect stem plus the regular endings for each tense. These tenses of **fīō** are made up of the participle **factus, -a, -um** plus **sum**, **eram**, and **erō** respectively.

XX. Irregular Verbs: Subjunctive

Present	*Singular*	1	sim	póssim	vélim	nólim
		2	sīs	póssīs	vélīs	nólīs
		3	sit	póssit	vélit	nólit
	Plural	1	sīmus	possímus	velímus	nōlímus
		2	sītis	possítis	velítis	nōlítis
		3	sint	póssint	vélint	nólint
Imperfect	*Singular*	1	éssem	póssem	véllem	nóllem
		2	éssēs	póssēs	véllēs	nóllēs
		3	ésset	pósset	véllet	nóllet
	Plural	1	essémus	possémus	vellémus	nōllémus
		2	essétis	possétis	vellétis	nōllétis
		3	éssent	póssent	véllent	nóllent
Perfect	*Singular*	1	fúerim	potúerim	volúerim	nōlúerim
		2	fúeris	potúeris	volúeris	nōlúeris
		3	fúerit	potúerit	volúerit	nōlúerit
	Plural	1	fuérimus	potuérimus	voluérimus	nōluérimus
		2	fuéritis	potuéritis	voluéritis	nōluéritis
		3	fúerint	potúerint	volúerint	nōlúerint
Pluperfect	*Singular*	1	fuíssem	potuíssem	voluíssem	nōluíssem
		2	fuíssēs	potuíssēs	voluíssēs	nōluíssēs
		3	fuísset	potuísset	voluísset	nōluísset
	Plural	1	fuissémus	potuissémus	voluissémus	nōluissémus
		2	fuissétis	potuissétis	voluissétis	nōluissétis
		3	fuíssent	potuíssent	voluíssent	nōluíssent

XXI. Irregular Verbs: Subjunctive (continued)

Present	*Singular*	1	málim	éam	féram	férar	fíam
		2	málīs	éās	férās	feráris	fíās
		3	málit	éat	férat	ferátur	fíat
	Plural	1	mālímus	eámus	ferámus	ferámur	fiámus
		2	mālítis	eátis	ferátis	feráminī	fiátis
		3	málint	éant	férant	ferántur	fíant
Imperfect	*Singular*	1	mállem	írem	férrem	férrer	fíerem
		2	mállēs	írēs	férrēs	ferréris	fíerēs
		3	mállet	íret	férret	ferrétur	fíeret
	Plural	1	māllémus	īrémus	ferrémus	ferrémur	fierémus
		2	māllétis	īrétis	ferrétis	ferréminī	fierétis
		3	mállent	írent	férrent	ferréntur	fíerent
Perfect	*Singular*	1	mālúerim	íverim	túlerim	látus sim	fáctus sim
		2	mālúeris	íveris	túleris	látus sīs	fáctus sīs
		3	mālúerit	íverit	túlerit	látus sit	fáctus sit
	Plural	1	māluérimus	īvérimus	tulérimus	látī símus	fáctī símus
		2	māluéritis	īvéritis	tuléritis	látī sítis	fáctī sítis
		3	mālúerint	íverint	túlerint	látī sint	fáctī sint
Pluperfect	*Singular*	1	māluíssem	īvíssem	tulíssem	látus éssem	fáctus éssem
		2	māluíssēs	īvíssēs	tulíssēs	látus éssēs	fáctus éssēs
		3	māluísset	īvísset	tulísset	látus ésset	fáctus ésset
	Plural	1	māluissémus	īvissémus	tulissémus	látī essémus	fáctī essémus
		2	māluissétis	īvissétis	tulissétis	látī essétis	fáctī essétis
		3	māluíssent	īvíssent	tulíssent	látī éssent	fáctī éssent

Note: the perfect active infinitive of **eō, īre, īvī** or **iī, itum** is often syncopated or shortened to **īsse**. The pluperfect subjunctive of this verb and its compounds may also present this shortened form, e.g., **redīsset, perīsset**, and **adīsset**.

XXII. Infinitives

Present		Perfect	
Active	Passive	Active	Passive
1 paráre	parárī	parāvísse	parátus, -a, -um ésse
2 habére	habérī	habuísse	hábitus, -a, -um ésse
3 míttere	míttī	mīsísse	míssus, -a, -um ésse
4 audíre	audírī	audīvísse	audítus, -a, -um ésse
Future			
Active			
1 parātúrus, -a, -um ésse			
2 habitúrus, -a, -um ésse			
3 missúrus, -a, -um ésse			
4 audītúrus, -a, -um ésse			

XXIII. Participles

Present		Perfect	
Active	Passive	Active	Passive
1 párāns, parántis			parátus, -a, -um
2 hábēns, habéntis			hábitus, -a, -um
3 míttēns, mitténtis			míssus, -a, -um
4 aúdiēns, audiéntis			audítus, -a, -um
Future			
Active			
1 parātúrus, -a, -um			
2 habitúrus, -a, -um			
3 missúrus, -a, -um			
4 audītúrus, -a, -um			

Vocabulary

This vocabulary includes all basic words that do not appear in the running vocabularies. It also includes all words that appear in the running vocabularies with asterisks, since these words are usually not repeated in the running vocabularies when they reappear in the stories. The numbers in parentheses refer to the section and line number where words that have an asterisk appear for the first time. Most names of people and places are listed in separate indexes following this vocabulary list, with designation of the section and line number where they appear for the first time and with designation of page numbers for maps on which the places may be located.

A

ā, ab (*prep.* + *abl.*), from; (*with passive verbs*) by

abdūcō, abdūcere (3), **abdūxī, abductum,** to lead away, take away (7:40)

abeō, abīre (*irreg.*), **abiī, abitum,** to go away

absēns, absentis, absent (24:13)

absum, abesse (*irreg.*), **āfuī,** to be away, be absent, be distant

abundō (1), to overflow, be in flood (2:2)

ac (*conj.*), and, than, as

accēdō, accēdere (3), **accessī, accessum,** to agree with, enter upon, approach, be added to (26:4, 30:127)

accidit, accidere (3), **accidit,** to happen

accipiō, accipere (3), **accēpī, acceptum,** to receive, get, accept, welcome

accumbō, accumbere (3), **accubuī, accubitum,** to recline (at table)

accūsō (1), to accuse, reproach

ācer, ācris, ācre, sharp, pointed, fierce (20:61)

aciēs, -ēī (*f.*), line of battle, battle formation, battle (1:25)

ācriter (*adv.*), fiercely

ad (*prep.* + *acc.*), to, toward, at, near, in accordance with, for

addō, addere (3), **addidī, additum,** to add, apply

adeō (*adv.*), so much, to such an extent

adeō, adīre (*irreg.*), **adiī, aditum,** to come to, approach

adiciō, adicere (3), **adiēcī, adiectum,** to add

adipīscor, adipīscī (3), **adeptus sum,** to reach, obtain, win (24:14)

adiuvō, adiuvāre (1), **adiūvī, adiūtum,** to help

administrō (1), to manage, direct, administer (9:48)

admīrātiō, admīrātiōnis (*f.*), amazement, admiration

admīror, admīrārī (1), **admīrātus sum,** to wonder (at), admire, be surprised, amazed

admittō, admittere (3), **admīsī, admissum,** to allow, admit

admodum (*adv.*), very, quite

adolēscō, adolēscere (3), **adolēvī, adultum,** to mature, grow up (2:2)

adsum, adesse (*irreg.*), adfuī, to be
present, be near

adulēscēns, adulēscentis (*m.*), young
man, youth

adultus, -ī (*m*), grown, mature, adult
(9:1)

adveniō, advenīre (4), advēnī, adventum, to come to, reach, arrive at

adventus, -ūs (*m.*), arrival, approach
(1:16)

adversus (*prep. + acc.*), contrary to,
opposite, against (1:24)

adversus, -a, -um, turned toward,
opposite, unfavorable (27:50,
31:64)

aedificium, -ī (*n.*), building

aedificō (1), to build

aedīlis, aedīlis (*m.*), aedile (25:7)

aeger, aegra, aegrum, ill, sick
aegrē (*adv.*), with difficulty
aegrē ferre, to take badly, resent

aequālis, aequālis (*m.*), companion of
the same age, comrade

aequō (1), to make equal

aequus, -a, -um, calm, level

aerārium, -ī (*n.*), treasury

aes, aeris (*n.*), bronze, money
aes aliēnum, aeris aliēnī (*n.*),
debt

aetās, aetātis (*f.*), age, time of life
(3:23)

Āfer, Āfra, Āfrum, African (25:33)

afferō, afferre (*irreg.*), attulī, allā-
tum, to bring, bring to, bring in

afficiō, afficere (3), affēcī, affectum,
to affect, afflict, strike (7:51)

Āfricānus, -a, -um, African; (*as a
cognōmen*) Africanus (25:95)

ager, agrī (*m.*), field, territory, land

aggredior, aggredī (3), aggressus
sum, to attack (1:17)

agnōscō, agnōscere (3), agnōvī, agni-
tum, to recognize

agō, agere (3), ēgī, āctum, to do,
drive, act, spend, pass (time),
lead (life), negotiate
triumphum agere, to celebrate
a triumph

ait, (he, she) says, said

Albānus, -a, -um, Alban (2:4)

aliēnus, -a, -um, belonging to another, alien, foreign (9:38)

aliquandō (*adv.*), sometime, someday, at last (9:20, 31:66)

aliquī, aliqua, aliquod, some (or
other)

aliquis, aliquid, someone, something

aliquot (*indeclinable adj.*), several,
some, a few (9:49)

aliter (*adv.*), otherwise, differently
(22:36)

alius, alia, aliud, another, other, different
aliī . . . aliī, some . . . others

Alliēnsis, -is, -e, Allian (an adjective
formed from the name of the
river Allia) (20:12)

alloquor, alloquī (3), allocūtus sum,
to speak to (5:41)

Alpēs, Alpium (*f. pl.*), the Alps

alter, altera, alterum, the other (of
two), a second

altus, -a, -um, tall, high, deep

alveus, -ī (*m.*), basket (3:7)

ambō, ambae, ambō, both

amīcitia, -ae (*f.*), friendship (8:21)

amīcus, -ī (*m.*), friend

āmittō, āmittere (3), āmīsī, āmissum, to lose (1:19)

amor, amōris (*m.*), love, affection

amphitheātrum, -ī (*n*), amphitheater

amplius (*comparative adv.*), more
(than) (30:117)

ancilla, -ae (*f.*), slave-woman

animadvertō, animadvertere (3), animadvertī, animadversum, to notice, punish, inflict capital punishment upon (+ in + *acc.*)
(27:43)

animus, -ī (*m.*), mind, spirit, zeal,
courage, character
in animō habēre, to intend

annus, -ī (*m.*), year

ante (*prep. + acc.*), before, in front of;
(*adv.*) before

anteā (*adv.*), previously, before

antequam (*conj.*), before

antīquus, -a, -um, old, ancient

anxius, -a, -um, nervous, anxious
(7:21)

aperiō, aperīre (4), aperuī, apertum,
to open, reveal

apertus, -a, -um, open

appāritor, appāritōris (m.), attendant, servant (9:29)

appellō (1), to call, name (1:1)

appropinquō (1) (+ dat.), to approach, draw near to

apud (prep. + acc.), at the house of,
with, near, in front of, before

aqua, -ae (f.), water

ara, -ae (f.), altar

arcessō, arcessere (3), arcessīvī,
arcessītum, to summon, send for,
induce (of sleep)

arcus, -ūs (m.), arch

ārdeō, ārdēre (2), ārsī, to burn,
blaze, be on fire

ārea, -ae (f.), open space, threshing-
floor

argenteus, -a, um, made of silver, silver

arma, -ōrum, (n. pl.), weapons, arms

armātus, -a, -um, armed, under
arms

    armātī, -ōrum (m. pl.), armed
    men

arripiō, arripere (3), arripuī, arreptum, to grab hold of, snatch, seize

ars, artis (f.), skill, art, pursuit

arx, arcis (f.), citadel, fortress; (in
Rome) the Citadel (one of the two
peaks on the Capitoline Hill; the
other is called the Capitōlium or
Capitol) (5:25, 20:15)

assurgō, assurgere (3), assurrēxī, as-
surrēctum, to rise up, stand up

at (conj.), but

Athēnae, -ārum (f. pl.), Athens

atque (conj.), and

auctor, auctōris (m.), originator, pro-
poser, author, person responsible
(12:23)

auctōritās, auctōritātis (f.), prestige,
influence, authority (19:9)

audācia, -ae (f.), boldness, audacity
(10:34)

audāx, audācis, bold

audeō, audēre (2, semi-deponent),
ausus sum, to dare

audiō, audīre (4), audīvī, audītum, to
hear, listen to

auferō, auferre (irreg.), abstulī, ablā-

tum, to carry away, take away

augeō, augēre (2), auxī, auctum, to
increase, enlarge

augurium, -ī (n.), a sign of divine
will, augury (the science of interpreting the will of the gods from
the flight of birds and other
events in nature) (4:3)

aureus, -a, -um, golden

aurīga, -ae (m.), charioteer

aurum, -ī (n.), gold (20:45)

aut (conj.), or

    aut . . . aut, either . . . or

autem (particle), however, but,
moreover

auxilium, -ī (n.), help

āvertō, āvertere (3), āvertī, āversum,
to turn away, divert

avis, avis (m. or f.), bird

avunculus, -ī (m.), uncle

B

baculum, -ī (n.), stick, staff

barbarus, -ī (m.), barbarian, foreigner (25:26)

bellum, -ī (n.), war

    bellum gerere, to wage war
    (22:16)

    bellum īnferre (+ dat.), to wage
    war against (30:109)

bene (adv.), well

benignitās, benignitātis (f.), kindness, good deeds (9:3)

benignus, -a, -um, kind (5:5)

bonus, -a, -um, good

    bona, -ōrum (n. pl.), goods, pos-
    sessions (11:6)

    bonī, -ōrum (m. pl.), good men,
    patriotic men (26:40)

brevis, -is, -e, short, brief

Britannicus, -a, -um, British

C

cadō, cadere (3), cecidī, cāsum, to
fall, fall in battle

caedēs, caedis (f.), slaughter, murder
(10:23)

caedō, caedere (3), cecīdī, caesum, to
strike, cut down, kill (7:37)

caelum, -ī (n.), sky, heaven

caerimōnia, -ae (f.), ceremony (6:21)

calamitās, calamitātis (f.), disaster, calamity (7:51)

calidus, -a, -um, warm

calor, calōris (m.), heat

campus, -ī (m.), plain, field

canis, canis (m. or f.), dog

cantō (1), to sing

capiō, capere (3), cēpī, captum, to capture, seize, take
>   arma capere, to take up arms
>   cōnsilium capere, to form a plan

Capitōlīnus, -a, -um, Capitoline (4:16)

captīvus, -ī (m.) or captīva, -ae (f.), prisoner

caput, capitis (n.), head, capital

carcer, carceris (m), cell, jail (8:6)

carpentum, -ī (n.), two-wheeled carriage (10:40)

cārus, -a, -um (+ dat.), dear, dear to, beloved

castra, -ōrum (n. pl.), (military) camp (13:4)

cāsus, -ūs (m.), misfortune, calamity (22:37)

causa, -ae (f.), reason, cause, lawsuit, case
>   causā (+ preceding gen.), for the sake of
>   causam dīcere, to plead a case (31:8)

caveō, cavēre (2), cāvī, cautum, to watch out, be careful

cēdō, cēdere (3), cessī, cessum, to come, go, withdraw, retreat, yield something (acc.) to someone (dat.) (19:7)

celeber, celebris, celebre, famous

celebrō (1), to frequent, celebrate

celeritās, celeritātis (f.), speed

celeriter (adv.), quickly

cēnō (1), to dine, eat dinner

cēnsus, -ūs (m.), census (register of citizens according to wealth) (10:1)

centum, a hundred

centuriō, centuriōnis (m.), centurion, (commander of an infantry company) (20:62)

certāmen, certāminis (n.), contest, struggle, strife (6:1)

certō (1), to contend, compete, fight, struggle (10:11)

certus, -a, -um, certain, determined, fixed
>   certiōrem facere, to make more certain, inform

cessō (1), to be idle, do nothing, delay

cēterī, -ae, -a, the rest, the others, other

cēterum (adv.), for the rest, yet

cibus, -ī (m.), food

cingō, cingere (3), cīnxī, cīnctum, to surround

circā (prep. + acc.), around, near (9:11); (adv.) around, nearby (3:9)

circēnsis, -is, -e, in the circus

circum (prep. + acc.), around

circumeō, circumīre (irreg.), circumiī, circumitum, to go around

circumsistō, circumsistere (3), to surround

circumveniō, circumvenīre (4), circumvēnī, circumventum, to surround

circus, -ī (m.), circle, racetrack, circus (stadium for chariot racing)

cīvīlis, -is, -e, civil, civilian (27:27)

cīvis, cīvis (m.), citizen

cīvitās, cīvitātis (f.), citizenship, state (5:1)

clādēs, clādis (f.), loss, defeat, disaster

clāmō (1), to shout, exclaim

clāmor, clāmōris (m.), shout, shouting, noise

clārus, -a, -um, clear, distinguished, famous (1:4)

classis, classis (f.), class, division, fleet (10:1)

claudō, claudere (3), clausī, clausum, to shut, close

clausus, -a, -um, shut, closed

cloāca, -ae (f.), sewer, drain (9:12)

Clūsīnus, -a, -um, of Clusium (the most important Etruscan city) (14:2)

coepī, coepisse, coeptum (only

perfect normally used), I began

cōgitō (1), to think, consider

cognōmen, cognōminis (*n.*), surname of a family or individual (usually derived from some personal characteristic or achievement)

cognōscō, cognōscere (3), **cognōvī, cognitum**, to find out, learn, hear of

cōgō, cōgere (3), **coēgī, coāctum**, to compel, force, collect, drive

cohors, cohortis (*f.*), military cohort (20:63)

collēga, -ae (*m.*), colleague, companion (22:18)

collis, collis (*m.*), hill

colloquium, -ī (*n.*), conversation, conference, parley (1:11)

colloquor, colloquī (3), **collocūtus sum**, to converse, speak together

colō, colere (3), **coluī, cultum**, to cultivate

columna, -ae (*f.*), column, pillar

comes, comitis (*m.* or *f.*), companion

cōmitās, cōmitātis (*f.*), kindness, friendliness, courtesy (25:26)

comitium, -ī (*n.*), comitium (an open area in the Forum, in front of the Senate House, used for assemblies) (14:24)

comitor, comitārī (1), **comitātus sum**, to accompany

commentārius, -ī (*m.*), notebook, diary, notes (30:48)

committō, committere (3), **commīsī, commissum**, to bring together, entrust, commit

    pugnam *or* **proelium committere**, to join battle

commoveō, commovēre (2), **commōvī, commōtum**, to move, upset, stir up

    commōtus, -a, -um, moved, excited

commūnis, -is, -e, universal, common

commūtō (1), to change, exchange (22:33)

comparō (1), to buy, obtain, get ready

comparō (1), to compare, couple, match (3:20)

compleō, complēre (2), **complēvī, complētum**, to fill, complete

complexus, -ūs (*m.*), embrace

comprehendō, comprehendere (3), **comprehendī, comprehēnsum**, to catch, seize, arrest (9:34)

concidō, concidere (3), **concidī**, to fall down, fall in battle

conciliō (1), to bring together, win over, bring about, acquire (6:16)

concitō (1), to stir up, rouse (5:23)

concordia, -ae (*f.*), harmony, agreement (16:19)

concurrō, concurrere (3), **concurrī, concursum**, to run together, rush up

condemnō (1), to condemn

condiciō, condiciōnis (*f.*), agreement, terms, condition (25:84)

condō, condere (3), **condidī, conditum**, to found, establish

cōnferō, cōnferre (*irreg.*), **contulī, collātum**, to bring together, collect, direct, devote (20:15, 31:76)

    sē cōnferre, to bring oneself, go (20:15)

cōnficiō, cōnficere (3), **cōnfēcī, cōnfectum**, to make, accomplish, finish, finish off, kill, wear out, exhaust, chew

cōnfodiō, cōnfodere (3), **cōnfōdī, cōnfossum**, to stab (30:134)

cōnfugiō, cōnfugere (3), **cōnfūgī**, to flee for refuge

congredior, congredī (3), **congressus sum**, to come together

congressus, -ūs (*m.*), meeting (6:17)

coniciō, conicere (3), **coniēcī, coniectum**, to throw

coniungō, coniungere (3), **coniūnxī, coniūnctum** (+ *dat.*), to join together

coniūnx, coniugis (*m.* or *f.*), spouse, husband, wife (5:12)

coniūrātiō, coniūrātiōnis (*f.*), conspiracy, plot (31:30)

coniūrō (1), to take an oath together, plot (12:28)

cōnor, cōnārī (1), **cōnātus sum**, to try, attempt

cōnscendō, cōnscendere (3), **cōn-**

scendī, cōnscēnsum, to board, embark on

cōnsecrō (1), to dedicate

cōnsēnsus, -ūs (m.), agreement, common purpose

cōnsequor, cōnsequī (3), cōnsecūtus sum, to follow, catch up to, overtake

cōnsīdō cōnsīdere (3), cōnsēdī, to sit down

cōnsilium, -ī (n.), plan, scheme, intention, idea, consultation, advice, intelligence, good sense
    cōnsilium capere, to form a plan

cōnsistō, cōnsistere (3), cōnstitī, to halt, stop, stand, be firm, remain

cōnsōbrīnus, -ī (m.), first cousin

cōnspectus, -ūs (m.), sight, view (9:15)

cōnspiciō, cōnspicere (3), cōnspexī, cōnspectum, to catch sight of, see

cōnstituō, cōnstituere (3), cōnstituī, cōnstitūtum, to decide

cōnstō, cōnstāre (1), cōnstitī, cōnstātum, to be established, cost, be composed, consist (21:30)
    cōnstat, it is consistent, it is agreed (26:45, 30:14)

cōnsul, cōnsulis (m.), consul (one of two chief officials in Roman government)

cōnsulāris, -is, -e, consular, belonging to a consul, having the status of an ex-consul (19:1)

cōnsulātus, -ūs (m.), consulship (27:31)

cōnsulō, cōnsulere (3), cōnsuluī, cōnsultum, to consult; (+ dat.) to give thought to, pay attention to

cōnsultum, -ī (n.), decree

contemnō, contemnere (3), contempsī, contemptum, to scorn

contendō, contendere (3), contendī, contentum, to contend, fight, advance, go quickly (22:2, 29:6)

contineō, continēre (2), continuī, contentum, to confine, hold, contain

continuō (1), to extend, continue, renew (19:5)

continuus, -a, -um, continuous, suc-

cessive (10:23)

contiō, contiōnis (f.), public meeting (25:19)

contrā (prep. + acc.), against, in violation of (19:5)

contrahō, contrahere (3), contrāxī, contractum, to draw together (10:22)

cōnūbium, -ī (n.), marriage, right of marriage (5:3)

conveniō, convenīre (4), convēnī, conventum, to come together, meet, assemble; (+ dat.) to agree, be consistent with
    convenit (impersonal), it is agreed, agreement is reached

convertō, convertere (3), convertī, conversum, to turn (around)

convīvium, -ī (n.), feast, banquet, dinner

convocō (1), to call together, summon

coorior, coorīrī (4), coortus sum, to rise up, arise

cōpia, -ae (f.), supply, abundance; (pl.) troops (1:25)

Corinthius, -a, -um, Corinthian, from Corinth (a city in Greece) (8:11)

corpus, corporis (n.), body

corripiō, corripere (3), corripuī, correptum, to seize, grab

corrumpō, corrumpere (3), corrūpī, corruptum, to break, corrupt, seduce (12:12)

crēdō, crēdere (3), crēdidī, crēditum (+ dat.), to trust, believe

creō (1), to appoint, choose, elect, create

crēscō, crēscere (3), crēvī, crētum, to grow, prosper, thrive (1:21)

crīnēs, crīnium (m. pl.), hair

crūdēlis, -is, -e, cruel
    crūdēliter (adv.), cruelly

crūdēlitās, crūdēlitātis (f.), cruelty

crux, crucis (f.), cross

cubiculum, -ī (n.), room, bedroom

culpa, -ae (f.), fault, blame

cultus, -ūs (m.), cultivation, worship, training, education (6:15)

cum (prep. + abl.), with

cum (conj.), since, because, when, after, although
   cum prīmum, as soon as
cūnctī, -ae, -a, all
cupiditās, cupiditātis (f.), desire, passion, ambition (21:33)
cupidus, -a, -um (+ gen.), desirous of, eager for (10:20)
cupiō, cupere (3), cupīvī, cupītum, to desire, want
cūr (adv.), why
cūra, -ae (f.), care, anxiety
cūria, -ae (f.), curia (a political unit), meeting-place of a cūria, Senate House (5:34)
currō, currere (3), cucurrī, cursum, to run
cursus, -ūs (m.), running, course, path (3:10)
custōdia, -ae (f.), watch, custody, prison, military guard post, guards (3:4)
custōs, custōdis (m.), guard

D
damnō (1), to find guilty, condemn (30:91)
dē (prep. + abl.), down from, concerning, about
dea, -ae (f.), goddess
dēbeō (2), to owe; (one) ought, should, must
dēcēdō, dēcēdere (3), dēcessī, dēcessum, to withdraw, die
decem, ten
December, Decembris, Decembre, December
dēcernō, dēcernere (3), dēcrēvī, dēcrētum, to determine, decide, settle, decree, assign (4:2, 25:57)
decet (+ acc.), (someone) should
decimus, -a, -um, tenth
dēcurrō, dēcurrere (3), dēcurrī, dēcursum, to run down, perform military drills (4:11, 25:62)
dēdō, dēdere (3), dēdidī, dēditum, to hand over, surrender, give up (3:19)
dēdūcō, dēdūcere (3), dēdūxī, dēductum, to show into, bring, escort
dēfendō, dēfendere (3), dēfendī,

dēfēnsum, to defend
dēferō, dēferre (irreg.), dētulī, dēlātum, to carry, bring, grant, award (6:9)
dēfessus, -a, -um, tired
dēficiō, dēficere (3), dēfēcī, dēfectum, to run short, be lacking, defect (25:70)
dēiciō, dēicere (3), dēiēcī, dēiectum, to throw down, bring down (9:32)
deinde (adv.), then, next
dēleō, dēlēre (2), dēlēvī, dēlētum, to destroy
dēliciae, -ārum (f. pl.), delight
dēligō, dēligere, (3) dēlēgī, dēlēctum, to choose, pick out (7:19)
dēmum (adv.), finally
dēnique (adv.), finally (14:22)
dēnūntiō (1), to declare, order, warn someone (dat.) to do something (ut + subjunctive)
dēpōnō, dēpōnere (3), dēposuī, dēpositum, to lay down, put aside, set down, resign
dēprehendō, dēprehendere (3), dēprehendī, dēprehēnsum, to get hold of, surprise, catch in the act (12:9)
dēscendō, dēscendere (3), dēscendī, dēscēnsum, to come or go down, climb down
dēserō, dēserere (3), dēseruī, dēsertum, to abandon
dēsiliō, dēsilīre (4), dēsiluī, to leap down
dēspērō (1), to give up hope, despair of (16:16)
dēspondeō, dēspondēre (2), dēspondī, dēspōnsum, to betroth, promise in marriage
dēsum, dēesse (irreg.), dēfuī, dēfutūrus (+ dat.), to be lacking, be missing (21:34)
dēterreō (2), to frighten away, discourage, deter (29:17)
deus, -ī (m.), god
dēvincō, dēvincere (3), dēvīcī, dēvictum, to conquer, subdue (23:41)
dextra or dextera, -ae (f.), right hand
diadēma, diadēmatis (n.), diadem, crown (26:24)

dīcō, dīcere (3), dīxī, dictum, to say,
speak, tell, name
    causam dīcere, to plead a case
    (31:8)
    dictus est, was named (19:16)
dictātor, dictātōris (m.), dictator
(chosen to lead the state for six
months during a crisis) (7:7)
dictātūra, -ae (f.), dictatorship
(19:26)
diēs, diēī (m. or f. when designating
a specific day), day
    in diēs, every day, day by day
    diem dē or ex diē, from day to
    day
difficilis, -is, -e, difficult
difficultās, difficultātis (f.), difficulty
dignitās, dignitātis (f.), dignity, authority, prestige (28:48)
dīligēns, dīligentis, diligent,
painstaking, thorough
    dīligenter (adv.), carefully
dīligentia, -ae (f.), diligence, faithful-
ness (26:4)
dīligō, dīligere (3), dīlēxī, dīlectum,
to love, have special regard for
dīmicō (1), to fight, struggle (28:33)
dīmittō, dīmittere (3), dīmīsī, dīmis-
sum, to send away, let go, dis-
band
dīripiō, dīripere (3), dīripuī, dīrep-
tum, to tear apart, pillage, ravage, plunder (20:17)
discēdō, discēdere (3), discessī,
discessum, to depart, leave, go
away
discrībō, discrībere (3), discrīpsī, discrīptum, to divide (6:19)
discrīmen, discrīminis (n.), crisis
(1:22)
dispār, disparis, unequal, different
(7:18)
dissēnsiō, dissēnsiōnis (f.), disagreement, strife (16:1)
diū (adv.), for a long time
dīversus, -a, -um, different, opposite
(13:9, 30:144)
dīvidō, dīvidere (3), dīvīsī, dīvīsum,
to force apart, divide, distribute
(3:14)
dīvus, -a, -um, divine, deified

dīvus, -ī (m.), god
dō, dare (1), dedī, datum, to give
doceō, docēre (2), docuī, doctum, to
teach
doleō (2), to be sorry, be sad, hurt
dolus, -ī (m.), trick (5:26)
domesticus, -a, -um, of one's own
household, individual, private
domina, -ae (f.), mistress, lady of the
house
dominus, -ī (m.), master
domus, -ūs (f.), house, home
    domī, at home
    domō, from home
    domum, to home, home
dōnō (1), to give, present, present or
honor someone or something
(acc.) with something (abl.)
(15:15)
dōnum, -ī (n.), gift
dormiō, dormīre (4), dormīvī, dormī-
tum, to sleep
dōs, dōtis (f.), dowry (21:37)
ducentī, -ae, -a, two hundred (13:17)
dūcō, dūcere (3), dūxī, ductum, to
lead, take, bring, draw out, prolong
    in mātrimōnium dūcere, to
    marry
dum (conj.), while, as long as
duo, duae, duo, two
duodecim, twelve
duodecimus, -a, -um, twelfth
dūrō (1), to last, endure (13:17)
dux, ducis (m.), leader, general
(1:12)

E

ē, ex (prep. + abl.), from, out of, out
from, according to
ēdō, ēdere (3), ēdidī, ēditum, to put
forth, publish, show, display, put
on (25:63)
ēducō (1), to bring up, educate (3:11)
ēdūcō, ēdūcere (3), ēdūxī, ēductum,
to lead out
efferō, efferre (irreg.), extulī, ēlātum,
to carry out, bring out, lift, raise
efficiō, efficere (3), effēcī, effectum, to
bring about (28:10)
effugiō, effugere (3), effūgī, to run

away, escape, flee

effundō, effundere (3), **effūdī, effū-sum**, to pour out, squander (25:93)

ego, meī, I, me

ēgredior, ēgredī (3), **ēgressus sum**, to go out, leave, disembark

ēgregius, -a, -um, distinguished, exceptional (20:39)

ēlābor, ēlābī (3), **ēlāpsus sum**, to slip down, slide down, escape

ēloquentia, -ae (f.), eloquence (31:6)

ēmittō, ēmittere (3), **ēmīsī, ēmissum**, to send out, utter, drain

enim (*postpositive particle*), for

ēniteō (2), to shine forth, be distinguished

eō (*adv.*), there, to that place

eō, īre (*irreg.*), **īvī, ītum**, to go

epistula, -ae (f.), letter

eques, equitis (m.), horseman, cavalryman (16:7)

equester, equestris, equestre, equestrian, belonging to the equestrian order (15:15, 26:29)

equus, -ī (m.), horse

ērēctus, -a, -um, attentive, alert (7:21)

ergā (*prep.* + *acc.*), toward

ēripiō, ēripere (3), **ēripuī, ēreptum**, to snatch from, rescue

ērūdītus, -a, -um, learned, scholarly

ērumpō, ērumpere (3), **ērūpī, ēruptum**, to break out

et (*conj.*), and

    et . . . et . . ., both . . . and . . .

etiam (*conj. and adv.*), also, even

etsī (*conj.*), although (9:24)

ēvadō, ēvadere (3), **ēvāsī, ēvāsum**, to escape, climb (to the top)

ēvertō, ēvertere (3), **ēvertī, ēversum**, to overturn, overthrow

ēvocō (1), to call out, summon

ex: see **ē**

excēdō, excēdere (3), **excessī, excessum**, to go out, leave

excipiō, excipere (3), **excēpī, exceptum**, to take out, pick up, catch, welcome, receive, sustain, withstand

excitō (1), to stir up, excite, rouse,

wake (someone) up

    excitātus, -a, -um, wakened, aroused

exclāmō (1), to exclaim, shout out

excūsō (1), to excuse, justify

execror, execrārī (1), **execrātus sum**, to curse

exemplum, -ī (n.), example, precedent (12:27)

exerceō, exercēre (2), **exercuī, exercitum**, to practice, train, put into effect, make, enforce (the law)

exercitus, -ūs (m.), army (5:36)

exigō, exigere (3), **exēgī, exāctum**, to pass, spend (time) (21:36)

exilium, -ī (n.), exile (11:5)

eximius, -a, -um, outstanding

exitium, -ī (n.), destruction

exitus, -ūs (m.), end, close, end of one's life

expellō, expellere (3), **expulī, expulsum**, to drive out, expel

experior, experīrī (4), **expertus sum**, to test, try, experience

expōnō, expōnere (3), **exposuī, expositum**, to set out, expose, explain (3:20)

expugnō (1), to assault, storm, conquer (12:14)

exspectō (1), to look out for, wait for

exstinguō, exstinguere (3), **exstinxī, exstinctum**, to extinguish, put out, kill

exstō, exstāre (1), **exstitī**, to stand out, be visible, exist (8:6)

exstruō, exstruere (3), **exstrūxī, exstrūctum**, to build, erect

extrahō, extrahere (3), **extrāxī, extractum**, to pull out, drag out

exul, exulis (m.), an exile (8:13)

F

facilis, -is, -e, easy

    facile (*adv.*), easily

    facilius (*comparative adv.*), more easily

facinus, facinoris (n.), deed, act, crime, evil deed (9:28)

faciō, facere (3), **fēcī, factum**, to make, do

factiō, factiōnis (f.), doing, (political)

faction (6:1)

factiō populāris, factiōnis populāris (*f.*), the faction of the **populārēs**, those who supported popular political causes

factum, -ī (*n.*), deed (11:1)

facultās, facultātis (*f.*), opportunity

fallō, fallere (3), **fefellī, falsum,** to deceive, trick, escape the notice of (20:37)

fāma, -ae (*f.*), fame, reputation, story (1:20)

famēs, famis (*f.*), hunger (17:6)

familia, -ae (*f.*), family, household, household slaves

familiārēs, familiārium (*m. pl.*), close friends

fānum, -ī (*n.*), shrine, temple (10:5)

faveō, favēre (2), **fāvī, fautum** (+ *dat.*), to favor, support

favor, favōris (*m.*), favor, support (25:8)

fēlīx, fēlīcis, lucky, happy, fortunate

fēmina, -ae (*f.*), woman

ferē (*adv.*), almost, approximately

ferō, ferre (*irreg.*), **tulī, lātum,** to carry, bring, bear, endure, say, report, call

    aegrē ferre, to take badly, resent

    fertur, is said, is reported (17:1)

    lēgem ferre, to propose or pass a law

ferōx, ferōcis, fierce, savage, ferocious

    ferōciter (*adv.*), fiercely, savagely

festīnō (1), to hurry

fidēs, fideī (*f.*), reliability, loyalty, good faith, trust, pledge

fīlia, -ae (*f.*), daughter

fīlius, -ī (*m.*), son

fīniō (4), to finish, limit

fīnis, fīnis (*m.*), end, boundary; (*pl.*) borders, territory (18:12)

fīnitimus, -a, -um, neighboring (4:16)

fīō, fierī (*irreg.*), **factus sum,** to become, be made, be done, happen

firmō (1), to strengthen, consolidate (6:11)

firmus, -a, -um, firm, stable (5:1)

flamma, -ae (*f.*), flame, fire

flectō, flectere (3), **flexī, flexum,** to turn, go, change (3:10)

flōreō (2), to be in one's prime, be prosperous, flourish

flūmen, flūminis (*n.*), river (14:11)

foedus, foederis (*n.*), treaty (6:14)

fore: future infinitive of **sum**

foris, foris (*f.*), door; (*pl.*) double doors

forte (*adv.*), by chance

fortis, -is, -e, brave, strong

fortitūdō, fortitūdinis (*f.*), strength, courage

fortūna, -ae (*f.*), fate, luck (18:27, 20:23)

forum, -ī (*n.*), forum, marketplace

frangō, frangere (3), **frēgī, frāctum,** to break, overcome, crush (7:51)

frāter, frātris (*m.*), brother

fraus, fraudis (*f.*), deception, trickery (11:17)

frīgidus, -a, -um, cold

frōns, frontis (*f.*), forehead

frūmentum, -ī (*n.*), grain (20:22)

frūstrā (*adv.*), in vain

frūstror, frūstrārī (1), **frūstrātus sum,** to deceive, trick (15:2)

fugiō, fugere (3), **fūgī, fugitum,** to flee, run away

fugō (1), to put to flight, drive away

fundō, fundere (3), **fūdī, fūsum,** to pour out, rout, defeat (28:14)

fundus, -ī (*m.*), farm (28:36)

fūnus, fūneris (*n.*), funeral

furor, furōris (*m.*), frenzy

fustis, fustis (*m.*), club, cudgel

futūrus, -a, -um: future participle of **sum**

G

Gabīnus, -a, -um, relating to Gabiī (a town to the south of Rome in Latium) (20:56)

Gallicus, -a, -um, of Gaul, Gallic (20:2)

Gallus, -a, -um, of Gaul, Gallic; (*m. pl.*) the Gauls (20:3)

gaudium, -ī (n.), joy
geminus, -a, -um, twin, double
(3:23)
    geminī, -ōrum (m. pl.), twins
gemō, gemere (3), gemuī, gemitum,
to groan
gener, generī (m.), son-in-law
(30:53)
gēns, gentis (f.), family, clan, tribe,
people
genus, generis (n.), kind, race, family, birth
gerō, gerere (3), gessī, gestum, to
wear, do, accomplish, carry on,
conduct, manage, govern
    bellum gerere, to wage war
    (22:16)
    imperium gerere, to hold
    power
    sē gerere, to carry oneself, be-
    have
gladius, -ī (m.), sword
glōria, -ae (f.), fame, glory
glōriōsus, -a, -um, glorious (21:36)
Graecia, -ae (f.), Greece
Graecus, -a, -um, Greek; (m. pl.) the
Greeks
grātiās agere (+ dat.), to thank
grātus, -a, -um, pleasing, dear (to),
loved (by), thankful
gravis, -is, -e, heavy, serious, oppres-
sive
    graviter (adv.), seriously, im-
    pressively

H
habeō (2), to have, hold, consider
    in animō habēre, to intend
habitō (1), to live, dwell, inhabit
haud (adv.), not
hērēs, hērēdis (m.), heir (10:37)
hīc (adv.), here
hic, haec, hoc, this
Hispāniēnsis, -is, -e, Spanish (23:72)
historia, -ae (f.), account, history
(30:49)
hodiē (adv.), today
homō, hominis (m.), man, person
honor, honōris (m.), honor, respect,
esteem, high political office
hōra, -ae (f.), hour

hortor, hortārī (1), hortātus sum, to
encourage, urge
hortus, -ī (m.), garden
hospes, hospitis (m.), friend, host,
guest
hospita, -ae (f.), hostess, female
guest (26:8)
hospitium, -ī (n.), hospitality, rules
of hospitality, banquet (5:15)
hostis, hostis (m.), enemy
hūc (adv.), here, to here
    hūc illūc, here and there, this
    way and that
hūmānus, -a, -um, human
humerus, -ī (m.), shoulder
humī, on the ground
humilis, -is, -e, humble, low (9:19)

I
iaceō (2), to lie, be lying down
iaciō, iacere (3), iēcī, iactum, to
throw, lay (foundations)
iam (adv.), now, already
iānua, -ae (f.), door
ibi (adv.), there
īdem, eadem, idem, same
Īdūs, -uum (f. pl.), Ides (fifteenth day
of March, May, July, and
October, and the thirteenth day
of the other months) (30:119)
igitur (conj.), therefore
ignōrō (1), to be ignorant, not to
know
ignōscō, ignōscere (3), ignōvī, ignō-
tum (+ dat.), to forgive
ille, illa, illud, that; he, she, it
illīc (adv.), there
illūdō, illūdere (3), illūsī, illūsum, to
make fun of, mock
illūstris, -is, -e, bright, distinguished, illustrious; (of writing)
clear, lucid (29:48, 30:51)
imāgō, imāginis (f.), likeness, mask
imitor, imitārī (1), imitātus sum, to
imitate (6:24)
immemor, immemoris, forgetful
impediō (4), to hinder, prevent
imperātor, imperātōris (m.), general,
commander (20:24)
imperium, -ī (n.), power, empire, dominion, rule, command (2:5)

imperō (1) (+ *dat.*), to order, rule, command

impetrō (1), to obtain, succeed in one's request, obtain one's request

impetus, -ūs (*m.*), attack

impleō, implēre (2), **implēvī, implētum,** to fill (1:20)

impōnō, impōnere (3), **imposuī, impositum,** to place on, put

imprīmīs (*adv.*), especially (27:2)

in (*prep.* + *acc.*), into, onto, against; (+ *abl.*) in, on

incēdō, incēdere (3), **incessī,** to march, go

incendium, -ī (*n.*), fire

incendō, incendere (3), **incendī, incēnsum,** to burn, set on fire
    incēnsus, -a, -um, blazing, burning

incidō, incidere (3), **incidī, incāsum,** to fall into, fall onto

incipiō, incipere (3), **incēpī, inceptum,** to begin

incitō (1), to spur on, urge on, drive, rouse

incolumis, -is, -e, unhurt, safe and sound

incūsō (1), to reproach, accuse, complain (3:18)

inde (*adv.*), from there, then, next

indignātiō, indignātiōnis (*f.*), anger, indignation, sense of injury (5:16)

indignitās, indignitātis (*f.*), insult, disgrace (8:13)

indignor, indignārī (1), **indignātus sum,** to be unhappy, complain, be indignant (17:2)

ineō, inīre (*irreg.*), **iniī, initum,** to go in, enter, undertake, enter upon, be engaged in (19:3)

īnferior, īnferius, *gen.* **īnferiōris,** lower, inferior, less

īnferō, īnferre (*irreg,*), **intulī, illātum,** to bring in, carry in (5:29)
    bellum īnferre (+ *dat.*), to wage war against
    signa īnferre (+ *dat.*), to attack
    sē īnferre, to rush in

īnfestus, -a, -um, dangerous, hostile (14:3)

ingenium, -ī (*n.*), intelligence, ingenuity, natural endowments, character

ingēns, ingentis, huge, big

ingredior, ingredī (3), **ingressus sum,** to go in, enter

inimīcitiae, -ārum (*f. pl.*), feuds

inimīcus, -ī (*m.*), (personal or political) enemy (25:58)

inīquus, -a, -um, unfair, unfavorable, too great (20:48)

initium, -ī (*n.*), beginning
    initiō, in the beginning, at first

iniūria, -ae (*f.*), wrongdoing, injustice, insult, injury (5:22)

iniussū (*indeclinable abl.* + *gen.* or *possessive adjective*), without an order (from) (9:51)

iniūstus, -a, -um, unjust

inops, inopis, poor, needy, destitute

inquit, (he, she) says, said

īnsequor, īnsequī (3), **īnsecūtus sum,** to follow, succeed (22:25)

īnsidiae, -ārum (*f. pl.*), ambush, plot, trap

īnsigne, īnsignis (*n.*), insignia, mark, token (4:13)

īnstituō, īnstituere (3), **īnstituī, īnstitūtum,** to establish, appoint, teach, train (26:6)

īnsula, -ae (*f.*), island

īnsum, inesse (*irreg.*), **īnfuī** (+ *dat.*), to be in

integer, integra, integrum, unharmed, complete, whole (7:24)

intellegō, intellegere (3), **intellēxī, intellēctum,** to understand, realize

intendō, intendere (3), **intendī, intentum,** to stretch out, aim at

intentus, -a, -um, intent, eager

inter (*prep.* + *acc.*), between, among

intercipiō, intercipere (3), **intercēpī, interceptum,** to intercept, cut off

intereā (*adv.*), meanwhile

interficiō, interficere (3), **interfēcī, interfectum,** to kill (1:3)

interim (*adv.*), meanwhile (9:47)

interimō, interimere (3), **interēmī, interēmptum,** to do away with, abolish, destroy, kill (26:19)

interrēgnum, -ī (*n.*), interregnum (period between one king's death and the election of his successor) (6:3)

interrogō (1), to ask

intrā (+ *acc.*), inside, within

intrō (1), to enter

intueor, intuērī (2), **intuitus sum**, to look at, watch (24:5)

invehō, invehere (3), **invexī, invectum**, to carry into; (*passive*) to be carried into, ride into, sail into (10:40)

inveniō, invenīre (4), **invēnī, inventum**, to come upon, find

invideō, invidēre (2), **invīdī, invīsum** (+ *dat.*), to envy, begrudge

invītō (1), to invite

iocus, -ī (*m.*), joke, joking **per iocum**, as a joke

ipse, ipsa, ipsum, -self, very

īra, -ae (*f.*), anger

īrācundia, -ae (*f.*), irritability, bad temper

īrātus, -a, -um, angry

irrumpō, irrumpere (3), **irrūpī, irruptum**, to burst in

irruō, irruere (3), **irruī**, to rush on, attack (26:29)

is, ea, id, this, that; he, she, it

iste, ista, istud, that of yours, that, that very (22:15)

ita (*adv.*), thus, so, in this way, as follows, in such a way

Italia, -ae (*f.*), Italy

Italicus, -a, -um, Italian (26:39)

itaque (*adv.*), and so, therefore

item (*adv.*), likewise, in the same way (10:20)

iter, itineris (*n.*), journey, road, route **iter facere**, to travel

iterum (*adv.*), again, a second time

iubeō, iubēre (2), **iussī, iussum**, to order, bid

iūcundus, -a, -um, pleasant, delightful

iūdicium, -ī (*n.*), judgment, decision, trial (7:46)

iūdicō (1), to judge, proclaim, declare, think (12:11)

iugulum, -ī (*n.*), throat (26:56)

iugum, -ī (*n.*), yoke (19:25)

iungō, iungere (3), **iūnxī, iūnctum**, to join

iūnior, iūnius, *gen.* **iūniōris**, younger

iūrō (1), to swear (13:2)

iūs, iūris (*n.*), law, right, privilege, jurisdiction, authority, justice (1:23)

iussū (*indeclinable abl. + gen.*), by the order (of) (3:20)

iūstus, -a, -um, just, fair (6:8)

iuvenis, iuvenis (*m.*), young man

L

labor, labōris (*m.*), work, toil, labor, effort, suffering

labōrō (1), to work, suffer

lacrima, -ae (*f.*), tear

lacus, -ūs (*m.*), lake (23:36)

laedō, laedere (3), **laesī, laesum**, to harm

laetus, -a, -um, happy

lapis, lapidis (*m.*), stone

largītiō, largītiōnis (*f.*), distribution of gifts, land, or doles, largess, bribery (26:16)

lateō (2), to lie in hiding, hide

Latīnus, -a, -um, Latin

latrō, latrōnis (*m.*), robber (3:12)

laudō (1), to praise

laus, laudis (*f.*), praise, reputation (18:25)

lavō, lavāre (1), **lāvī, lāvātum** *or* **lōtum**, to wash

lectīca, -ae (*f.*), litter

lectus, -ī (*m.*), bed, couch

lēgātus, -ī (*m.*), envoy, ambassador, legate (high-ranking officer)

legiō, legiōnis (*f.*), legion, army (18:24)

legō, legere (3), **lēgī, lēctum**, to read, gather, choose (2:10)

levis, -is, -e, light, slight, minor (24:5)

lēx, lēgis (*f.*), law (6:10) **lēgem ferre**, to propose or pass a law

liber, librī (*m.*), book

līber, lībera, līberum, free, outspoken, unrestricted, unrestrained

(12:7)

līberālis, -is, -e, worthy of a free man, liberal (9:21)

līberālitās, līberālitātis (*f.*), courtesy, generosity

līberī, -ōrum (*m. pl.*), children

līberō (1) (+ *abl.*), to set free, free from

lībertās, lībertātis (*f.*), freedom (23:37)

lībertus, -ī (*m.*), freedman

licentia, -ae (*f.*), license, liberty (25:60)

licet, licēre (2, *impersonal*), **licuit**, it is allowed, permitted, one may

līctor, līctōris (*m.*), lictor (an official who attended Roman magistrates and carried the **fascēs**, symbols of official power)

līmen, līminis (*n.*), threshold, doorway

litterae, -ārum (*f. pl.*), letter, epistle, literature

lītus, lītoris (*n.*), shore

locus, -ī (*m.*; *n.* in *pl.*), place, rank, birth

longus, -a, -um, long
    longē (*adv.*), far, by far

loquor, loquī (3), **locūtus sum**, to speak, talk

lūctor, lūctārī (1), **lūctātus sum**, to wrestle

lūdibrium, -ī (*n.*), derision, laughing-stock, object of scorn, plaything

lūdus, -ī (*m.*), game, school; (*pl.*) games (as in the Circus)

lūmen, lūminis (*n.*), light, torch

lūna, -ae (*f.*), moon (6:18)

lūxus, -ūs (*m.*), luxury, luxurious living, extravagance (12:9)

M

magis (*comparative adv.*), more, rather

magister, magistrī (*m.*), master, captain
    magister equitum, magistrī equitum (*m.*), master of the horse (second in command to the dictator) (24:3)

magistrātus, -ūs (*m.*), office, official, magistrate

magnificus, -a, -um, magnificent

magnitūdō, magnitūdinis (*f.*), greatness, large number, size (28:34)

magnus, -a, -um, big, great, large

maiestās, maiestātis (*f.*), majesty, dignity

maior, maius, *gen.* **maiōris**, greater, larger
    maiōrēs, maiōrum (*m. pl.*), ancestors

mālō, mālle (*irreg.*), **māluī**, to prefer

malus, -a, -um, bad, evil

mandātum, -ī (*n.*), order, instruction

mandō (1), to order, command, commit, entrust (8:3)

maneō, manēre (2), **mānsī, mānsum**, to remain, stay, wait, wait for, await

manus, -ūs (*f.*), hand, band (of men), group

mare, maris (*n.*), sea, ocean

Mārtius, -a, -um, of March (30:119)

māter, mātris (*f.*), mother

mātrimōnium, -ī (*n.*), marriage
    in mātrimōnium dare, to give in marriage
    in mātrimōnium dūcere, to marry

mātrōna, -ae (*f.*), married woman, matron

maximus, -a, -um, very great, greatest, very large
    maximē (*superlative adv.*), very much, especially

medicus, -ī (*m.*), doctor

medium, -ī (*n.*), middle

medius, -a, -um, mid-, middle of

melior, melius, *gen.* **meliōris**, better

memorō (1), to remind, mention, bring up (9:2)

mēns, mentis (*f.*), mind (12:23)

mēnsis, mēnsis (*m.*), month

meritō (*adv.*), deservedly, rightly

metuō, metuere (3), **metuī**, to fear, be afraid of (1:20)

metus, -ūs (*m.*), fear

meus, mea, meum, my, mine

migrō (1), to move, migrate (1:6)

mīles, mīlitis (*m.*), soldier

mīlia, mīlium (*n. pl.*), thousand, thousands

mīlle (*indeclinable noun and adjective*), a thousand

minimus, -a, -um, very small, least
minimē (*adv.*), very little, not at all, not in the least, hardly

ministerium, -ī (*n.*), service, work (17:3)

minor, minus, *gen.* **minōris**, smaller, younger (30:75)
minus (*comparative adv.*), less

minuō, minuere (3), **minuī, minūtum**, to lessen, reduce, decrease

mīrābilis, -is, -e, wonderful, amazing

mīrus, -a, -um, wonderful, marvelous, strange, surprising, amazing

miser, misera, miserum, unhappy, miserable, wretched

Mithridāticus, -a, -um, Mithridatic (27:32)

mītis, -is, -e, gentle, mild

mittō, mittere (3), **mīsī, missum**, to send

moderātiō, moderātiōnis (*f.*), control, regulation, self-control

modus, -ī (*m.*), way, method, means, measure
modo (*adv.*), only, just now, recently (28:46)

moenia, moenium (*n. pl.*), walls, fortifications (1:25)

molestus, -a, -um, troublesome, annoying

moneō (2), to advise, warn

mōns, montis (*m.*), mountain, hill

mōnstrō (1), to show

monumentum, -ī (*n.*), monument, tomb

mora, -ae (*f.*), delay (6:6)

morbus, -ī (*m.*), illness

morior, morī (3), **mortuus sum**, to die

moror, morārī (1), **morātus sum**, to delay, remain, stay

mors, mortis (*f.*), death

mortuus, -a, -um, dead

mōs, mōris (*m.*), custom; (*pl.*) habits, character (6:15)

moveō, movēre (2), **mōvī, mōtum**, to move

mox (*adv.*), soon, presently

muliebris, -is, -e, of a woman, womanly (10:31)

mulier, mulieris (*f.*), woman

multitūdō, multitūdinis (*f.*), crowd, large number, group of people

multus, -a, -um, much; (*pl.*) many
multō (*adv.*), much
multum (*adv.*), much, long

mūniō (4), to build, fortify, protect (4:12)

mūrus, -ī (*m.*), wall

mūtō (1), to change

mutuus, -a, -um, mutual, common, of each other

N

nam (*particle*), for, because

nārrō (1), to tell (a story)

nāscor, nāscī (3), **nātus sum**, to be born

nātūra, -ae (*f.*), nature

nātus, -ī (*m.*), son

naufragium, -ī (*n.*), shipwreck (30:138)

nāvālis, -is, -e, naval (22:3)

nāvis, nāvis (*f.*), ship

nē (+ *subjunctive*), in case, to prevent, not to

nē . . . quidem, not even (20:14)

nec (*conj.*), and . . . not, nor
nec . . . nec . . . , neither . . . nor . . .

necō (1), to kill, put to death

negō (1), to refuse, deny, say no (20:8)

negōtium, -ī (*n.*), business, task (8:3)

nēmō, nēminis (*m.*), no one

nepōs, nepōtis (*m.*), grandson (3:24)

neque (*conj.*), and . . . not, but . . . not, nor
neque . . . neque, neither . . . nor

neuter, neutra, neutrum, neither (of two) (30:145)

nex, necis (*f.*), killing, murder, death (12:29)

nihil (*indecl. noun*), nothing

nihilum, -ī (*n.*), nothing

nisi (*conj.*), unless, if . . . not, except

nōbilis, -is, -e, noble, famous
nōbilēs, nōbilium (*m. pl.*), aristocrats, nobles, patricians

(27:31)

nōbilitās, nōbilitātis (*f.*), aristocracy, nobility

noctūrnus, -a, -um, happening during the night

nōlō, nōlle (*irreg.*), **nōluī**, to be unwilling, not wish, refuse

nōmen, nōminis (*n.*), name

nōminō (1), to name, call by name

nōn (*adv.*), not, no

    nōn modo . . . sed etiam, not only . . . but also

    nōn sōlum . . . sed etiam, not only . . . but also

nōndum (*adv.*), not yet

nōnnūllī, -ae, -a, some

nōs, nostrum, we, us

noster, nostra, nostrum, our

novem, nine

novus, -a, -um, new

nox, noctis (*f.*), night

nūbō, nūbere (3), **nūpsī, nūptum** (+ *dat.*), to marry

nūllus, -a, -um, no, none

numerus, -ī (*m.*), number

numquam (*adv.*), never

nunc (*adv.*), now

nūntiō (1), to announce, report (5:41)

nurus, -ūs (*f.*), daughter-in-law (12:8)

nusquam (*adv.*), nowhere

O

ō: used with a noun in the vocative case

ob (*prep. + acc.*), on account of, because of (3:15)

obsecrō (1), to beseech, beg, pray

observō (1), to watch, pay attention to

obses, obsidis (*m.*), hostage (15:1)

obsideō, obsidēre (2), **obsessī, obsessum**, to besiege

obsidiō, obsidiōnis (*f.*), siege, blockade (20:20)

obtineō, obtinēre (2), **obtinuī, obtentum**, to get hold of, be in charge of (27:40)

obveniō, obvenīre (4), **obvēnī, obventum** (+ *dat.*), to fall to the lot of,

be assigned to (28:4)

occāsiō, occāsiōnis (*f.*), occasion, opportunity

occīdō, occīdere (3), **occīdī, occīsum**, to kill

occupō (1), to seize

occurrō, occurrere (3), **occurrī, occursum** (+ *dat.*), to meet

octāvus, -a, -um, eighth

octō, eight

oculus, -ī (*m.*), eye

offerō, offerre (*irreg.*), **obtulī, oblātum**, to offer (21:5)

officium, -ī (*n.*), favor, courtesy, service, duty, obligation (9:3)

ōlim (*adv.*), once, once upon a time, formerly

omnis, -is, -e, all, the whole, every, each

    omnīnō (*adv.*), at all, altogether, entirely

onus, oneris (*n.*), load, burden

opera, -ae (*f.*), effort

    operam dare (+ *dat.*), to give attention to, devote oneself to

operiō, operīre (4), **operuī, opertum**, to hide, cover

oppidum, -ī (*n.*), town

opprimō, opprimere (3), **oppressī, oppressum**, to overwhelm, crush, conquer

oppugnō (1), to attack (18:15)

ops, opis (*f.*), wealth; (*pl.*) resources, power (1:21)

optimus, -a, -um, best, very good, excellent

    optimē (*superlative adv.*), best, very well, excellently

optō (1), to wish

opus, operis (*n.*), work, deed; (*pl.*) public works (9:9)

ōrāculum, -ī (*n.*), oracle (a prediction of future events given by a god; the place where such predictions are given) (11:32)

ōrātiō, ōrātiōnis (*f.*), speech

ōrātor, ōrātōris (*m.*), orator, speaker, herald

orbis, orbis (*m.*), circle, globe (5:42)

    orbis terrārum, the world, universe (5:42)

ōrdō, ōrdinis (*m.*), row, rank, class

orīgō, orīginis (*f.*), origin

orior, orīrī (4), ortus sum, to arise, begin

ōrnāmentum, -ī (*n.*), equipment, distinction, pride and joy; (*pl.*) jewelry, jewels (26:6)

ōrnō (1), to decorate, equip, beautify

ōrō (1), to ask (for), beg (for), pray (for)

ōs, ōris (*n.*), mouth, face

ōsculor, ōsculārī (1), ōsculātus sum, to kiss (11:46)

ostendō, ostendere (3), ostendī, ostentum, to show

ōtium, -ī (*n.*), leisure, free time, peace (7:3)

P

pacīscor, pascīscī (3), pactus sum, to make an arrangement, arrange (20:46)

paene (*adv.*), almost

palam (*adv.*), openly (9:2)

palūs, palūdis (*f.*), swamp, marsh (27:36)

pār, paris, equal (5:1)

parcō, parcere (3), pepercī (+ *dat.*), to spare

parēns, parentis (*m.* or *f.*), parent, relative

pāreō (2) (+ *dat.*), to obey

parō (1), to prepare, get ready

parricīdium, -ī (*n.*), parricide (murder of a parent or close relative) (31:11)

pars, partis (*f.*), part, direction; (*pl.*) duty, function, political faction (21:38, 28:40)

Parthus, -ī (*m.*), Parthian (30:52)

parvus, -a, -um, small

passim (*adv.*), here and there, everywhere (28:26)

passus, -ūs (*m.*), step, pace (16:18) mīlle passūs, *pl.* mīlia passuum, a mile (16:18)

pāstor, pāstōris (*m.*), shepherd (3:10)

pateō, patēre (2), patuī, to be open, be available, be attainable (9:26)

pater, patris (*m.*), father; (*pl.*) sena-

tors

patior, patī (3), passus sum, to suffer, endure, allow (11:37)

patria, -ae (*f.*), native land, fatherland, country (18:16)

patrimōnium, -ī (*n.*), patrimony, inheritance, estate, property (26:50)

patrōnus, -ī (*m.*), patron, pleader, advocate

patruus, -ī (*m.*), uncle

paucī, -ae, -a, few

paulātim (*adv.*), gradually, little by little

paulīsper (*adv.*), for a short time

paulō post (*adv.*), a little later

paulum (*adv.*), a little

pauper, pauperis, poor

pāx, pācis (*f.*), peace

pectus, pectoris (*n.*), chest, breast, heart

pecūnia, -ae (*f.*), money

pellō, pellere (3), pepulī, pulsum, to drive, drive out, repulse, defeat (2:8)

per (*prep.* + *acc.*), through, along, over

peragō, peragere (3), perēgī, perāctum, to complete

percussor, percussōris (*m.*), assailant, assassin (30:137)

percutiō, percutere (3), percussī, percussum, to strike

perdō, perdere (3), perdidī, perditum, to destroy

peregrīnus, -a, -um, foreign (6:3) peregrīnus, -ī (*m.*), foreigner

pereō, perīre (*irreg.*), periī, peritum, to perish, die (4:9)

perferō, perferre (irreg.), pertulī, perlātum, to carry through, pass (a law), announce, report

perfugiō, perfugere (3), perfūgī, perfugitum, to flee to (20:13)

perīculum, -ī (*n.*), danger

perītus, -a, -um (+ *gen.*), skilled in, experienced, expert (6:8)

permittō, permittere (3), permīsī, permissum (+ *dat.*), to let go, permit, entrust (11:47)

persequor, persequī (3), persecūtus

sum, to pursue, chase, hunt down

persuādeō, persuādēre (2), **persuāsī, persuāsum** (+ *dat.*), to persuade

perturbō (1), to disturb, upset, confuse (9:40)

    perturbātus, -a, -um, disturbed, upset, confused

perveniō, pervenīre (4), **pervēnī, perventum**, to arrive at, reach

pessimus, -a, -um (*superlative of* **malus**), worst, very bad

pestilentia, -ae (*f.*), disease, plague (7:50)

petō, petere (3), **petīvī** or **petiī, petītum**, to seek, look for, ask for, aim at, attack, run for (office)

philosophus, -ī (*m.*), philosopher (21:24)

placeō (2), to please

    placet (*impersonal*), it pleases, it seems good

    placuit, it was decided

plēbeius, -a, -um, plebeian (16:21)

plēbs, plēbis (*f.*), common people, plebeians, plebs (6:4)

plērusque, plēraque, plērumque, very great, very many

plumbum, -ī (*n.*), lead

plūrēs, plūra, *gen.* **plūrium**, more

plūrimus, -a, -um, most, very much; (*pl.*) very many

plūs (*comparative adv.*), more

plūs, plūris (*n.*), more

poena, -ae (*f.*), punishment, penalty

Poenus, -a, -um, Carthaginian; (*m. pl.*) the Carthaginians (22:10)

polliceor, pollicērī (2), **pollicitus sum**, to promise

Pompeiānus, -a, -um, Pompeian, of Pompey (30:56)

pondus, ponderis (*n.*), burden, weight (20:47)

pōnō, pōnere (3), **posuī, positum**, to put, place, station

pōns, pontis (*m.*), bridge

Ponticus, -a, -um, of Pontus (28:9)

populāris, -is, -e, popular, pleasing to the people, of or belonging to the political faction of the **populārēs** (10:32, 27:29)

    populārēs, populārium (*m.*

pl.), populares (members of the faction that supported reform and popular political causes, as opposed to the **bonī**, who supported the conservative political causes of the nobles or **optimātēs**, optimates) (27:29)

populus, -ī (*m.*), people, nation

porta, -ae (*f.*), gate

portendō, portendere (3), **portendī, portentum**, to predict, portend, foretell (9:19)

porticus, -ūs (*f.*), colonnade, portico (30:29)

portus, -ūs (*m.*), port, harbor (25:40)

poscō, poscere (3), **poposcī**, to ask for, demand

possum, posse (*irreg.*), **potuī**, to be able, can

post (*prep.* + *acc.*), after, behind; (*adv.*) after, later

posteā (*adv.*), afterwards, later on

posterus, -a, -um, next, following

postquam (*conj.*), after, when

postrēmus, -a, -um, last

    postrēmō (*adv.*), finally

postrīdiē (*adv.*), on the following day

postulō (1), to demand (4:5)

potentia, -ae (*f.*), power (8:17)

potestās, potestātis (*f.*), power (26:18)

potior, potīrī (4), **potītus sum** (+ *abl.*), to get control of, get possession of

potius (*adv.*), rather (7:11)

praebeō (2), to put forward, expose (to danger), display, show, provide

praecīdō, praecīdere (3), **praecīdī, praecīsum**, to lop off, cut off (29:61)

praecipuē (*adv.*), especially (30:39)

praeda, -ae (*f.*), booty, loot, cattle (taken in foraging raids) (1:9)

praedō, praedōnis (*m.*), robber, pirate (29:23)

praeferō, praeferre (*irreg.*), **praetulī, praelātum**, to carry in front

praeficiō, praeficere (3), **praefēcī, praefectum**, to put X (*acc.*) in charge of Y (*dat.*) (23:14)

praemittō, praemittere (3), praemīsī, praemissum, to send out ahead, send in advance (20:35)

praesēns, praesentis, present

praesidium, -ī (n.), protection, defense, assistance, help (9:20)

praesum, praeesse (irreg.), praefuī (+ dat.), to be in charge of, be in command of (25:2)

praeter (prep. + acc.), except, beyond, in addition to

praetereā (adv.), besides, too, moreover

praetereō, praeterīre (irreg.), praeteriī, praeteritum, to go past

praetextus, -a, -um, purple-bordered

praetor, praetōris (m.), praetor (in Rome, a magistrate concerned with the administration of justice; in a province, the chief administrative officer, the governor) (27:40)

premō, premere (3), pressī, pressum, to push on, crush, oppress (16:3)

pretium, -ī (n.), price, ransom

prīmus, -a, -um, first, early
cum prīmum (adv.), as soon as
prīmō (adv.), first, at first
prīmum (adv.), first, at first

prīnceps, prīncipis (m.), emperor, leader, chief, leading citizen; (as adj.) leading, foremost, first (23:27, 30:141)

prior, prius, gen. priōris, first (of two), previous
prius (adv.), previously, first

priusquam (conj.), before (7:32)

prīvātus, -a, -um, private, personal (9:3)
prīvātim (adv.), privately

prīvō (1) (+ abl.), to deprive of (14:3)

prō (prep. + abl.), in front of, before, for, in place of, on behalf of, in return for, instead of, as (6:5, 30:38)

probō (1), to approve, voice approval (7:15)

prōcēdō, prōcēdere (3), prōcessī, prōcessum, to step forward, advance, go forward

procul (adv.), in the distance, far off, far from (+ abl.)

prōdigium, -ī (n.), miraculous event, sign, portent (8:18)

prōdūcō, prōdūcere (3), prōdūxī, prōductum, to lead out, lead forth

proelium, -ī (n.), battle (7:14)

prōferō, prōferre (irreg.), prōtulī, prōlātum, to carry forward, continue, extend

proficīscor, proficīscī (3), profectus sum, to set out, leave

profugiō, profugere (3), profūgī, to flee, flee to; (+ ad + acc.) to flee to for help (4:16)

profugus, -ī (m.), refugee (1:5)

prōgredior, prōgredī (3), prōgressus sum, to go forward, advance

prōiciō, prōicere (3), prōiēcī, prōiectum, to throw forth (26:32)

proinde (adv.), consequently, accordingly, therefore (5:42)

prōmptus, -a, -um, quick to respond, eager

prope (prep. + acc.), near; (adv.), near, nearly, almost

properō (1), to hurry (7:31)

propinquus, -ī (m.), relative

propior, propius, gen. propiōris, nearer

prōpōnō, prōpōnere (3), prōposuī, prōpositum, to put forth, offer (21:16)

propter (prep. + acc.), on account of, because of

prorumpō, prorumpere (3), prorūpī, proruptum, to burst forth, burst out

proscrībō, proscrībere (3), proscrīpsī, proscrīptum, to proscribe, outlaw
proscrīptī, -ōrum (m. pl.), proscribed (28:35)

prōvincia, -ae (f.), province (25:57)

proximus, -a, -um, nearest, closest (5:38)

pūblicus, -a, -um, public

pudor, pudōris (m.), sense of honor, sense of shame (14:17)

puella, -ae (f.), girl

puer, puerī (m.), boy, slave

pūgiō, pūgiōnis (m.), dagger

pugna, -ae (f.), fight, battle

pugnō (1), to fight
pulcher, pulchra, pulchrum, beautiful, handsome, distinguished
Pūnicus, -a, um, Punic, Carthaginian (22:1)
pūniō (4), to punish
putō (1), to think, consider

Q

quadrāgintā, forty
quaerō, quaerere (3), **quaesīvī, quaesītum**, to seek, look for, ask (for)
quaestor, quaestōris (*m.*), quaestor (financial officer) (27:14)
quaestūra, -ae (*f.*), quaestorship (28:2)
quālis, -is, -e, what sort of, in what state or condition
quam (*in comparisons*), than; (*in exclamations or questions*) how; (+ *superlative*) as . . . as possible
quamdiū (*adv.*), as long as (21:33)
quam prīmum (*adv.*), as soon as possible
quamquam (*conj.*), although
quantus, -a, -um, how big, how much, as much as
    quantum (*adv.*), how much, as much as
quā rē, because of which thing, therefore
quārtus, -a, -um, fourth
quasi (*conj.* or *adv.*), as if
quattuor, four
-que, and
queror, querī (3), **questus sum**, to complain (10:12)
quī, quae, quod (*relative pronoun*), who, which, that; (*interrogative adjective*) what
quia (*conj.*), because (7:52)
quīdam, quaedam, quoddam, a certain; (*pl.*) some
quidem (*particle*), indeed
quiēs, quiētis (*f.*), rest, sleep
quiēscō, quiēscere (3), **quiēvī, quiētum**, to rest
quiētus, -a, -um, quiet, at rest, idle, inactive, uninvolved (9:10)
quīn (*adv.* or *conj.*), in fact, as a mat-

ter of fact; (+ *subj.*) that
quīnquāgēsimus, -a, -um, fiftieth
quīnque, five
quīntus, -a, -um, fifth
quis, quid, anyone, anything
quisquam, quicquam (quidquam), anyone, anything (13:3)
quisque, quaeque, quidque, each (30:103)
quō (*adv.*), where, to what place, to which place
quō (*conj. replacing* **ut** *when the clause contains a comparative*), in order that, so that (21:27)
quoad (*adv.*), as long as, until (2:1)
quod (*conj.*), because
quoniam (*conj.*), since
quoque (*adv.*), and, also

R

rapiō, rapere (3), **rapuī, raptum**, to snatch, seize
recēdō, recēdere (3), **recessī, recessum**, to withdraw, retreat
recipiō, recipere (3), **recēpī, receptum**, to receive, accept, take back, recapture, seize (11:19)
reconcilō (1), to reconcile, restore (17:12)
rēctē (*adv.*), rightly, properly
recūsō (1), to object, protest, refuse, reject (6:3)
reddō, reddere (3), **reddidī, redditum**, to give back, return, make
redeō, redīre (*irreg.*), **rediī, reditum**, to return, go back, come back
redigō, redigere (3), **redēgī, redāctum**, to drive back, reduce, raise (money by selling something) (24:10)
redimō, redimere (3), **redēmī, redēmptum**, to buy back, rescue, ransom (21:2)
referō, referre (*irreg.*), **retulī, relātum**, to bring back, refer, return
rēgia, -ae (*f.*), royal palace (9:13)
rēgīna, -ae (*f.*), queen
rēgius, -a, -um, royal, king's (3:3)
rēgnō (1), to reign, rule (2:1)
rēgnum, -ī (*n.*), kingdom, royal

power, kingship

regō, regere (3), **rēxī, rēctum**, to rule

regredior, regredī (3), **regressus sum**, to go back, return

relinquō, relinquere (3), **relīquī, relictum**, to leave, abandon

reliquiae, -ārum (*f. pl.*), remains (29:5)

reliquus, -a, -um, left, remaining, other (16:19)

remaneō, remanēre (2), **remānsī**, to stay behind, remain

remittō, remittere (3), **remīsī, remissum**, to send back, return (21:18)

removeō, removēre (2), **remōvī, remōtum**, to remove, move aside

renūntiō (1), to report, bring back word (25:85)

repellō, repellere (3), **reppulī, repulsum**, to drive off, drive back, beat back, turn aside, reject

reperiō, reperīre (4), **repperī, repertum**, to find (1:27)

repōnō, repōnere (3), **reposuī, repositum**, to replace, put back (8:16)

reprehendō, reprehendere (3), **reprehendī, reprehēnsum**, to blame, scold, rebuke

repudiō (1), to reject, divorce (30:7)

rēs, reī (*f.*), thing, property, matter, affair, situation, circumstance

    rēs mīlitāris, reī mīlitāris (*f.*), the art of war, military science (5:42)

    rēs pūblica, reī pūblicae (*f.*), state, government, politics (9:48)

    rē vērā, really, actually, in fact

rescindō, rescindere (3), **rescidī, rescissum**, to cut down (14:13)

resistō, resistere (3), **restitī** (+ *dat.*), to stop, fix oneself in a position, resist

respiciō, respicere (3), **respexī, respectum**, to look back (at), look around (at)

respondeō, respondēre (2), **respondī, respōnsum**, to reply, answer

respōnsum, -ī (*n.*), reply

restituō, restituere (3), **restituī,**

restitūtum, to bring back, restore (3:27)

retineō (2), to hold back, restrain, keep

revertō, revertere (3), **revertī, reversum**, to return (25:32)

revertor, revertī (3), **reversus sum**, to return

revocō (1), to recall, call back

rēx, rēgis (*m.*), king

Rhodus, -ī (*f.*), Rhodes (an island off the coast of Asia Minor)

rīte (*adv.*), properly, correctly

rixa, -ae (*f.*), quarrel, argument

rogō (1), to ask

Rōma, -ae (*f.*), Rome

Rōmānus, -a, -um, Roman; (*m. pl.*) the Romans

rōstra, -ōrum (*n. pl.*), rostra (speaker's platform in the Roman Forum, so-called because it was decorated with the beaks of ships taken from the battle of Antium in 338 B.C.) (30:115)

ruīna, -ae (*f.*), ruin, collapse

rūrsus (*adv.*), again, a second time

S

sacer, sacra, sacrum, sacred

    sacrum, -ī (*n.*), sacred rite, religious observance, ceremony, rite

sacerdōs, sacerdōtis (*m.* or *f.*), priest *or* priestess (2:10)

saepe (*adv.*), often

saeviō, saevīre (4), **saeviī, saevītum**, to be fierce, be savage, be brutal (28:33)

saltus, -ūs (*m.*), leaping, jumping

salūs, salūtis (*f.*), greetings, welfare, safety, survival (25:71)

salūtō (1), to greet

salvē, hail, hello

salvus, -a, -um, undamaged, all right, safe

sānctus, -a, -um, holy, sacred

sanguis, sanguinis (*m.*), blood

sapiēns, sapientis, wise, sensible (26:7)

satis (*adv.*), enough, sufficiently (26:16)

saxum, -ī (*n.*), rock
scelerātus, -a, -um, wicked
scelus, sceleris (*n.*), crime
schola, -ae (*f.*), school (26:10)
scīlicet (*particle*), as is apparent, evidently
sciō, scīre (4), scīvī, scītum, to know
scrībō, scrībere (3), scrīpsī, scrīptum, to write
sē, himself, herself, oneself, itself, themselves
sēcēdō, sēcēdere (3), sēcessī, sēcessum, to withdraw, go away (16:17)
sēcrētō (*adv.*), secretly
secundus, -a, -um, second, favorable
sed (*conj.*), but
sēdecim, sixteen
sedeō, sedēre (2), sēdī, sessum, to sit
sēdēs, sēdis (*f.*), seat, home (5:32)
sella, -ae (*f.*), sedan chair, seat, chair
sēmet: emphatic form of sē (26:57)
semper (*adv.*), always
senātus, -ūs (*m.*), senate
senectūs, senectūtis (*f.*), old age (18:9)
senex, senis (*m.*), old man
sentiō, sentīre (4), sēnsī, sēnsum, to feel, notice, realize
sepeliō, sepelīre (4), sepelīvī, sepultum, to bury
septem, seven
septimus, -a, -um, seventh
sequor, sequī (3), secūtus sum, to follow
sermō, sermonis (*m.*), conversation, talk
servitūs, servitūtis (*f.*), slavery (18:19)
servō (1), to save, keep, protect
servus, -ī (*m.*), slave
sex, six
sextus, -a, -um, sixth
sextus et decimus, sixteenth
sī (*conj.*), if
sīc (*adv.*), in this way, so
siccō (1), to dry out, drain (9:12)
Sicilia, -ae (*f.*), Sicily
sīcut (*conj.*), as, just as, like (29:50)
significō (1), to indicate, mean, signify (29:19)

signum, -ī (*n.*), signal, sign, military standard
  signa īnferre (+ *dat.*), to attack
silentium, -ī (*n.*), silence
silva, -ae (*f.*), woods
similis, -is, -e (+ *dat.*), like, similar (to)
simul (*adv.*), together, at the same time
simulō (1), to pretend
sīn (*conj.*), if however, if on the other hand, but if
sine (*prep.* + *abl.*), without
singulī, -ae, -a, one at a time, one each, each (7:33)
sinō, sinere (3), sīvī, sītum, to allow, permit
societās, societātis (*f.*), alliance (5:4)
socius, -ī (*m.*), ally, partner (23:32)
sōl, sōlis (*m.*), sun
soleō, solēre (2), solitus sum, to be accustomed, be in the habit of
solitūdō, solitūdinis (*f.*), loneliness, solitude
sollemnis, -is, -e, annual, religious, solemn
sōlus, sōla, sōlum, alone, only
  sōlum (*adv.*), only
  nōn sōlum . . . sed etiam, not only . . . but also
solvō, solvere (3), solvī, solūtum, to release, untie, loosen, free (7:42)
somnus, -ī (*m.*), sleep
soror, sorōris (*f.*), sister
sors, sortis (*f.*), fate, chance, lot (11:47)
spatium, -ī (*n.*), space, time, period (30:23)
speciēs, -ēī (*f.*), appearance, pretext (2:9)
spectāculum, -ī (*n.*), sight, spectacle, show
spectō (1), to watch, look at
spernō, spernere (3), sprēvī, sprētum, to scorn, reject (5:6)
spēs, speī (*f.*), hope (5:16)
spoliō (1), to strip, rob, deprive someone (*acc.*) of something (*abl.*) (7:37, 11:6)
spōnsus, -ī (*m.*), betrothed man, fi-

ancé, bridegroom
statim (*adv.*), immediately
statiō, statiōnis (*f.*), station, military
  guard post, sentry post
statua, -ae (*f.*), statue
statuō, statuere (3), **statuī,**
  statūtum, to set up, determine,
  decide (5:8)
stīpendium, -ī (*n.*), military service
  (27:1)
stō, stāre (1), **stetī, stātum,** to stand
strepitus, -ūs (*m.*), noise, din, clat-
  tering
stringō, stringere (3), **strīnxī, stric-
  tum,** to draw (a sword)
studiōsus, -a, -um, eager, enthusias-
  tic (31:8)
studium, -ī (*n.*), enthusiasm, study
stupeō (2), to be amazed, gape
suādeō, suādēre (2), **suāsī, suāsum,**
  to suggest, propose, recommend
  (21:6)
sub (*prep.* + *acc.*), under, beneath; (+
  abl.) under, beneath, at the foot
  of
subigō, subigere (3), **subēgī, subāc-
  tum,** to subdue
subitus, -a, -um, sudden
  subitō (*adv.*), suddenly
sublicius, -a, -um, resting on piles
  (8:6)
subsidium, -ī (*n.*), aid, support, help
successor, successōris (*m.*), successor
  (23:12)
sum, esse (*irreg.*), **fuī, futūrus,** to be
summoveō, summovēre (2), **sum-
  mōvī, summōtum,** to remove, expel, banish
summus, -a, -um, very greatest,
  greatest, highest (part of)
sūmō, sūmere (3), **sūmpsī, sūmptum,**
  to take, take up, pick out
super (*prep.* + *acc.*), above, upon
superbia, -ae (*f.*), pride, arrogance
  (5:19)
superior, superius, *gen.* **superiōris,**
  higher, previous, superior (7:34)
superō (1), to overcome, defeat
supersum, superesse (*irreg.*), **super-
  fuī** (+ *dat.*), to survive, be left over
  (7:33)

supplicium, -ī (*n.*), punishment
  (3:18)
suprā (*prep.* + *acc.*), above
sustineō, sustinēre (2), **sustinuī, sustentum,** to hold up, sustain, withstand, endure (7:36)
suus, sua, suum, his, her, its, their
  (own)

T

taberna, -ae (*f.*), shop
tabulae, -ārum (*f. pl.*), tablets,
  records
taceō (2), to be quiet
tālis, -is, -e, such, of this kind
  tālia (*n. pl.*), such things
tam (*adv.*), so
tamen (*adv.*), however, nevertheless
tamquam (*conj.*), as, as if, just as,
  like (11:41)
tandem (*adv.*), finally
tantus, -a, -um, so great, so much,
  such a big
  tantum (*adv.*), only
Tarpeius, -a, -um, Tarpeian (11:20)
tēctum, -ī (*n.*), roof, house
tegō, tegere (3), **tēxī, tēctum,** to
  cover, hide (12:28)
tēlum, -ī (*n.*), weapon, spear
tempestās, tempestātis (*f.*), storm,
  time
templum, -ī (*n.*), temple
temptō (1), to try
tempus, temporis (*n.*), time
teneō, tenēre (2), **tenuī, tentum,** to
  hold, occupy
tergum, -ī (*n.*), back, rear
ternī, -ae, -a, three each, three at
  once
terra, -ae (*f.*), earth, ground, land
terribilis, -is, -e, frightening
terror, terrōris (*m.*), terror, fear,
  dread
tertius, -a, -um, third
testāmentum, -ī (*n.*), will
thermae, -ārum (*f. pl.*), public baths
timeō, timēre (2), **timuī,** to fear, be
  afraid (of)
toga, -ae (*f.*), toga, (the garment
  worn by Roman males)
togātus, -a, -um, clad in a toga

tollō, tollere (3), **sustulī, sublātum**, to lift, raise up

tot (*indeclinable adj.*), so many

totidem (*indeclinable adj.*), just so many, just as many (27:52)

tōtus, -a, -um, all, the whole, entire

trādō, trādere (3), **trādidī, trāditum**, to hand over, hand down, relate

trādūcō, trādūcere (3), **trādūxī, trāductum**, to bring across, transfer (11:24)

trahō, trahere (3), **trāxī, tractum**, to drag, pull, prolong, keep (a person) waiting, delay (26:9)

trānō (1), to swim across (14:23)

trāns (*prep. + acc.*), across

trānseō, trānsīre (*irreg.*), **trānsiī, trānsitum**, to go across, cross over (1:28)

trānsiliō, trānsilīre (4), **trānsiluī**, to jump over (4:7)

trēs, tria, three

tribūnus, -ī (*m.*), tribune (17:13)

tribuō, tribuere (3), **tribuī, tribūtum**, to assign, distribute, devote, apply (10:3, 31:84)

trigeminus, -a, -um, threefold, triple, triplet (7:17)

trīgintā, thirty (5:34)

trīstis, -is, -e, sad

triumphō (1), to celebrate a triumph (19:25)

triumphus, -ī (*m.*), victory parade, triumph (25:94)

    triumphum agere, to celebrate a triumph

Troia, -ae (*f.*), Troy

Troiānus, -a, -um, Trojan; (*m. pl.*) the Trojans

trucīdō (1), to slay, slaughter, massacre (20:25)

tū, tuī, you (singular)

tueor, tuērī (2), **tūtus sum**, to see, look after, defend, protect (26:13)

tum (*adv.*), then

tumultus, -ūs (*m*), uproar, din, commotion

turba, -ae (*f.*), crowd

turbō (1), to disturb, upset, throw into confusion (14:15)

turpis, -is, -e, disgraceful (18:17)

tūtor, tūtōris (*m.*), guardian (8:22)

tūtus, -a, -um, safe (14:8)

tuus, -a, -um, your, yours

U

ubi (*adv.*), where, when

ūllus, -a, -um, any (12:26)

ultimus, -a, -um, last

ultrā (*prep. + acc.*), beyond, past

umbra, -ae (*f.*), shadow

umquam (*adv.*), ever

unde (*adv.*), from where, from which (21:37)

undique (*adv.*), on all sides, from all sides

unguentum, -ī (*n.*), ointment, perfume, oil

ūnus, -a, -um, one

urbānus, -a, -um, of *or* in the city

urbs, urbis (*f.*), city

urgeō, urgēre (2), **ursī**, to press, insist

usque ad (+ *acc.*), as far as, up to, all the way to (8:7)

ūsus, -ūs (*m*), use, practice, occasion

ut (*conj. + indicative*), as, when; (+ *subjunctive*), so that, in order that, that, to

uterque, utraque, utrumque, each (of two), both

ūtilis, -is, -e, useful

utinam (+ *subjunctive*): used to introduce a wish

ūtor, ūtī (3), **ūsus sum** (+ *abl.*), to use, practice (4:3)

utrum . . . an (*particle*), whether . . . or

uxor, uxōris (*f.*), wife

V

vacuus, -a, -um, empty

vae (*interj.*), woe, woe to (+ *dat.*) (20:50)

valeō (2), to be strong, be well, be valid

validus, -a, -um, strong, powerful

varius, -a, -um, different, various, varied

vāstō (1), to lay waste, ravage, destroy (22:23)

vehemēns, vehementis, violent,

forceful, powerful
vehementer (*adv.*), very much, violently, furiously, insistently
vel (*particle*), or, even
vel . . . vel, either . . . or
vēnātiō, vēnātiōnis (*f.*), hunting, animal hunt
vēndō, vēndere (3), **vēndidī, vēnditum**, to sell
venēnum, -ī (*n.*), poison (21:17)
venerātiō, venerātiōnis (*f.*), veneration, reverence, respect
venia, -ae (*f.*), kindness, favor, forgiveness (30:13)
veniō, venīre (4), **vēnī, ventum**, to come
venter, ventris (*m.*), stomach (17:3)
ventus, -ī (*m.*), wind
verbum, -ī (*n.*), word
vertō, vertere (3), **vertī, versum**, to turn (6:25)
vērus, -a, -um, true, real
    rē vērā, really, actually
    vērē (*adv.*), really, truly
    vērius (*comparative adv.*), more truly
    vērō (*adv.*), truly, really, actually
    vērum (*adv.*), but
vestibulum, -ī (*n.*), entrance passage, anteroom
vēstīgium, -ī (*n.*), track, footprint, trace
vestis, vestis (*f.*), clothing, garment
vetus, veteris, old
via, viae (*f.*), road, street, way
vīcēsimus, -a, -um, twentieth
vīcīnus, -a, -um, neighboring
victor, victōris (*m.*), conqueror, victor, winner; (*as adj.*) victorious
victōria, -ae (*f.*), victory

videō, vidēre (2), **vīdī, vīsum**, to see; (*in passive*) to seem
vīgintī, twenty
vīlla, -ae (*f.*), farmhouse, country estate
vincō, vincere (3), **vīcī, victum**, to win, conquer, overcome
vindicō (1), to get revenge, avenge (12:29)
violō (1), to do harm to, violate
vir, -ī (*m.*), man, husband
virga, -ae (*f.*), stick
virgō, virginis (*f.*), virgin, maiden
virītim (*adv.*), separately, to individuals (10:14)
virtūs, virtūtis (*f.*), courage, virtue (7:48)
vīs, vim (*acc.*), **vī** (*abl.*), *pl.* **vīrēs** (*f.*), violence, power, force; (*pl.*) strength
vīta, -ae (*f.*), life
vitium, -ī (*n.*), fault, vice
vītō (1), to avoid
vīvō, vīvere (3), **vīxī, vīctum**, to live
vīvus, -a, -um, alive, living (10:35)
vix (*adv.*), scarcely, with difficulty, only just
vocō (1), to call, invite, summon
volō, velle (*irreg.*), **voluī**, to wish, want, be willing
voluntās, voluntātis (*f.*), wish, desire, goodwill (9:51)
voluptās, voluptātis (*f.*), enjoyment, pleasure (17:4)
vōs, vestrum, you (*pl.*)
vōx, vōcis (*f.*), voice, word, saying, utterance
vulnerō (1), to wound
vulnus, vulneris (*n.*), wound
vultus, -ūs (*f.*), face, expression

Index of People

This index includes the names of all the people mentioned in the Latin stories. The numbers in parentheses such as (1:10) refer to the section and the line number where the name appears for the first time; the letter *n* after a line number means that the name appears in a note on that line. Names are usually given in their Latin forms, without macrons.

A

Aeneas (1:4)
Allucius (25:28)
Amulius (2:7)
Ancus: see Marcius
Antiochus of Ascalon (31:16)
Antonius Hybrida, Gaius (31:44)
Antonius, Marcus (Marc Antony) (30:113)
Apollo (11:40)
Apollonius Molo (30:20)
Ascanius (2:1)
Augustus (31:57n)

B

Bibulus, Marcus (30:31)
Bocchus (27:12)
Brennus (20:49)
Brutus, Lucius Iunius (11:33)
Brutus, Marcus Iunius (30:118)

C

Caesar, Gaius Iulius (29:52)
Camillus, Marcus Furius (20:23)

Casca, Publius Longus (30:129)
Cassius Longinus, Gaius (30:117)
Catilina, Lucius Sergius (31:30)
Chrysogonus (31:12)
Cicero, Marcus Tullius (30:50)
Cincinnatus, Lucius Quinctius (19:2)
Cinea (21:23)
Cinna, Lucius Cornelius (27:48)
Cleopatra VII (30:74)
Cloelia (15:1)
Cluilius (7:6)
Cominius, Pontius (20:31)
Coriolanus (18:4)
Cornelia, mother of the Gracchi (26:4)
Cornelia, wife of Caesar (30:5)
Crassus, Marcus Licinius (30:34)
Curiatii (7:18)

D

Demaratus (8:10)
Diana (10:5)
Domitius Ahenobarbus,

Lucius (30:67n)

E

Egeria (6:17)
Epicurus (21:24n)

F

Fabius Maximus Verrucosus Cunctator, Quintus (24:2)
Fabius, Quintus (24:9)
Fabricius Luscinus, Gaius (21:3)
Fausta (28:42)
Faustulus (3:10)
Faustus (28:42)
Fufidius (28:27)

G

Gracchus, Gaius Sempronius (26:1)
Gracchus, Tiberius Sempronius (26:1)

H

Hamilcar Barca (23:3)
Hannibal (23:6)
Hanno (22:4)
Hasdrubal (1) (23:12)
Hasdrubal (2) (25:41)
Herminius, Titus (14:17)

Index of Peoples, Places, and Maps

Use this index to find out quickly which map shows the place you are looking for. The numbers in boldface give the page numbers for the appropriate maps. The numbers in parentheses such as (1:10) refer to the section and the line number where the place name appears for the first time; the letter *n* after a line number means that the name appears in a note on that line. Names on a map are sometimes in a different form from that given in the text; e.g., the **Parthī** live in the area identified as **Parthia**. This is indicated by a cross-reference, e.g., Parthi (= Parthia). Names are usually given in their Latin forms, without macrons.

Credits

The authors and publisher wish to thank the following for permission to reproduce photographs and visuals:

Page viii: Alinari/Art Resource, New York. Page 1: William Francis Warden Fund; Courtesy, Museum of Fine Arts, Boston. Page 17: Map by David Perry. Page 40: H. L. Pierce Fund; Courtesy, Museum of Fine Arts, Boston. Page 51: Gilbert Lawall. Page 61: Kavaler/Art Resource, New York. Pages 63 and 85: From *The Living Language: A Latin Book for Beginners* by Wilbert Lester Carr and George Depue Hadzsits, copyright 1933 by W. L. Carr and G. D. Hadzsits, published by D. C. Heath and Company. Page 81: From *Latin for Today: First-Year Course* by Mason D. Gray and Thornton Jenkins, copyright 1928 by Mason D. Gray and Thornton Jenkins, published by Ginn and Company. Used by permission of Silver Burdett Ginn. Page 84: From *Latin for Today: Second-Year Course* by Mason D. Gray and Thornton Jenkins, copyright 1928 by Mason D. Gray and Thornton Jenkins, published by Ginn and Company. Used by permission of Silver Burdett Ginn. Pages 135 and 143: Courtesy of the American Numismatic Society, New York. Page 159: Used by permission of the Folger Shakespeare Library, Washington, D.C.

The authors wish to thank Marjorie Dearworth Keeley for help with preparing the facing and end vocabularies and to thank Professor Richard A. LaFleur of the University of Georgia and Lee T. Pearcy of the Episcopal Academy, Merion, PA, for reading this book in its penultimate version and making a number of useful suggestions.